shake

TEMPEST IN THE
CARIBBEAN

TEMPEST IN THE CARIBBEAN

JONATHAN GOLDBERG

University of Minnesota Press
Minneapolis
London

Frontispiece: "Art and Nation: Things You Must Learn from Day One," by Christopher Cozier. From *Work in Progress,* The Art Foundry, Barbados, 1998. Reproduced courtesy of the artist.

Lines from "Nametracks," by Edward Kamau Brathwaite, are reprinted from *Mother Poem* (New York: Oxford University Press, 1977). Lines from "X/Self's Xth Letter," by Edward Kamau Brathwaite, are reprinted from *X/Self* (New York: Oxford University Press, 1987). Lines from "Caliban," by Edward Kamau Brathwaite, are reprinted from *The Arrivants* (New York: Oxford University Press, 1967). Reprinted with permission from Oxford University Press.

Lines from "The Dream Sycorax Letter," by Edward Kamau Brathwaite, are reprinted with permission from *Black Renaissance / Renaissance Noire* 1, no. 1 (1996): 120–36.

Lines from "hard against the soul," by Dionne Brand, from *No Language Is Neutral* (Toronto: Coach House Press, 1990). Reprinted with permission from McClelland & Stewart Ltd., The Canadian Publishers.

Lines from *Notebook of a Return to the Native Land,* by Aimé Césaire, are reprinted from *The Collected Poetry,* translated by Clayton Eshleman and Annette Smith (Berkeley and Los Angeles: University of California Press, 1983). Reprinted with permission from the University of California Press.

Every effort has been made to obtain permission to reprint previously published material in this book. If any proper acknowledgment has not been made, we encourage copyright holders to notify us.

Published by the University of Minnesota Press
111 Third Avenue South, Suite 290
Minneapolis, MN 55401-2520
http://www.upress.umn.edu

Library of Congress Cataloging-in-Publication Data

Goldberg, Jonathan.
    Tempest in the Caribbean / Jonathan Goldberg.
       p.   cm.
    Includes bibliographical references (p.) and index.
    ISBN 0-8166-4260-5 (HC : alk. paper) — ISBN 0-8166-4261-3 (PB : alk. paper)
    1. Shakespeare, William, 1564–1616. Tempest.   2. Shakespeare, William, 1564–1616—
  Adaptations—History and criticism.   3. Shakespeare, William, 1564–1616—Appreciation—
  Caribbean Area.   4. Shakespeare, William, 1564–1616—Knowledge—Caribbean Area.
    5. Caribbean literature—20th century—History and criticism.   6. Caribbean Area—Intellectual
  life—20th century.   7. Postcolonialism—Caribbean Area.   8. Caribbean Area—In literature.
    9. Castaways in literature.   10. Islands in literature.   I. Title.
    PR2833 .G65 2003
    822.3'3—dc22

                                                                          2003015324

Printed in the United States of America on acid-free paper

The University of Minnesota is an equal-opportunity educator and employer.

12 11 10 09 08 07 06 05 04   10 9 8 7 6 5 4 3 2 1

Yes, Shakespeare, he used to write books, Moses, plays and poetry. He made the English language reach up to the heavens, touch the stars. He spanned the entire length and breadth of human emotions, like Columbus, discovered new continents, populated them with living creatures of flesh and blood and poetry. At a time when the rest of his countrymen waited like jackals to rob the Spaniards who returned with their blood-stained plunder from the New World, he created men of grandeur, big villains, towering heroes, new world men.

—Sylvia Wynter, *The Hills of Hebron*

To establish his own identity, Caliban, after three centuries, must himself pioneer into regions Caesar never knew.

—C. L. R. James, *Beyond a Boundary*

The morning was uneventful enough: a girl spilled ink from her inkwell all over her uniform; a girl broke her pen nib and then made a big to-do about replacing it; girls twisted and turned in their seats and pinched each other's bottoms; girls passed notes to each other. All this Miss Nelson must have seen and heard, but she didn't say anything—only kept reading her book: an elaborately illustrated edition of *The Tempest,* as later, passing by her desk, I saw.

—Jamaica Kincaid, *Annie John*

CONTENTS

PREFACE

THE SCENE: AN UNINHABITED ISLAND.

Tempest in the Caribbean is an essay in cultural theory and literary analysis situated at the crossing of Caribbean and early modern studies marked by *The Tempest* and a number of twentieth-century texts that use Shakespeare's play for anticolonial purposes. "Tempest" in my title alludes to both scenes of inscription, a despecification that matches the setting of the play, an island notoriously unmoored and variously located: a place between north Africa and Italy and yet an Atlantic locale, perhaps indeed situated in the black Atlantic that Paul Gilroy summons up to figure the condition of modernity.[1] This lack of fixity, this multiplicity of unfixed locations, may well be, as Brent Hayes Edwards has suggested to me, a condition of possibility for the reinscription of Shakespeare in numerous sites of colonial translation: into an English that refuses imperial ownership of the tongue, into French and Spanish (and, indeed, into those "foreign" languages first, by Ernest Renan and José Enrique Rodó, prompting later anticolonial reinscriptions). However, in the name of the character who has become a byword for anticolonial riposte, Caliban—a character who is, according to the stage direction, not there, for the island is "uninhabited"—one finds a supposed specificity of locale. "The Caribbean" in my title points to anticolonial writing's aim to write into existence a being first named through an initial misdescription of a tribal solidarity characterized by the act of cannibalism that gives a name to Caliban. "Caribbean" also points to a twentieth-century configuration, itself highly contested and contestatory and certainly not yet realized: the Caribbean as an area that might recognize itself through that name as a way of overcoming the disparate conditions of colonization performed by the English, the French, the Dutch, and the Spanish as they carved out the islands for colonial control. The name "Caribbean" might overcome the ongoing divisions between regimes that cling to these initial linguistic differences and that continue to be riven by the tensions among settlers, descendants of slaves brought from Africa, later immigrants from Asia, and native Indians who managed to survive the holocausts visited in some domains but not in all.[2]

In writing from that past, in this present, to a possible future, I follow

Gayatri Chakravorty Spivak, seeking to read these anticolonial texts as performing more than a reversal still bound within a colonialist binary, embracing Spivak's wariness of a "postcolonial reason" that reinscribes a colonial logic as the global condition.[3] The performative possibilities upon which I fasten are assembled against that position of political despair, a position to be found, for instance, in one of the most frequently cited studies of later uses of *The Tempest,* an essay by Rob Nixon.[4] Nixon reads the rewritings of the play against the dead end of the collapse of movements for national independence in their reinscription within neocolonial domination. This is the plot of global capitalism that David Harvey calls the postmodern condition, an inescapable stranglehold. It is against such despairing reinscriptions of domination, following in the wake of J. K. Gibson-Graham's inspiring model in *The End of Capitalism (as We Knew It),* that this essay is launched, seizing upon possibilities—and actualities—that cannot be reduced to the supposedly invulnerable logic of a unidimensional economic analysis.[5]

I am prompted too by the agenda that Lisa Lowe and David Lloyd outline in their introduction to *The Politics of Culture in the Shadow of Capital,* where they caution against "a homogenization of global culture that radically reduces possibilities for the creation of alternatives." Specifically, they locate in the cultural sphere (in relative autonomy from the political or the economic) a site of "alternative rationalities."[6] Against the denigrations that attach to race, to poverty (to those Frantz Fanon called the wretched, the condemned, "les damnés"), to women, to lesbians, to homosexuals (groups not often solicited by the "classic" texts that reply to *The Tempest* by Aimé Césaire, George Lamming, Kamau Brathwaite, and Roberto Fernández Retamar, but on the agenda in the work of Sylvia Wynter and Michelle Cliff, for example), and without arguing for an equation among the binds of racism, the forces of compulsory heterosexuality, and the immiserations wrought by colonialism and global capitalism, I aim in the pages that follow to articulate connections that hold out the possibility of a future made by new social actors, a future that necessarily will also have broken with an Enlightenment legacy of liberalism and the market that lends ideological support to colonialism, a future that could resemanticize otherwise suspect terms, as Cliff does in titling a 1993 novel *Free Enterprise.*[7]

To delineate the possibilities in the "different kind of creature" made by colonization (whose lineaments I begin to trace in the first part of this study, following arguments and representations offered by Fernández Retamar and by Lamming, whose phrase I quote), feminist responses to *The Tempest,* notably those found in Wynter's inspiring essays and in Cliff's novels and theoretical writing, will prompt rereadings (in the second part of this book) of some classic texts (by Brathwaite and Césaire). These I situate within an expanded framework of social history and queer writing of the Afro-Caribbean diaspora (including texts by Hilton Als, Dionne Brand, Jamaica Kincaid, and Patricia

Powell) that represent alternative conditions of existence. In the final section of this book, the limits of the Enlightenment will be engaged through some consideration of John Locke, Immanuel Kant, and G. W. F. Hegel, as I conclude this inquiry into race, sex, and gender in the Caribbean. Although Shakespeare's play will occasionally be mined for the resources it makes available for this tradition of writing, *The Tempest* is not the inspiring force in this book. It lies, rather, in these diasporic texts and the living possibilities they represent.

ACKNOWLEDGMENTS

I have had the opportunity to offer lectures on this project to a number of responsive audiences. I am grateful to Ann Rosalind Jones for an invitation to Smith College (where it was an additional pleasure to have Julie Graham in the audience); to Garrett Sullivan, for the opportunity to lecture at Pennsylvania State University and to meet with his students and colleagues, including Jeffrey Nealon, who urged me to think more about monsters; to my dear friend Marcie Frank, for inviting me to deliver the 1998 Lahey Lecture at Concordia University, and to her dear brother, Adam Frank, who arranged for me to speak at the University of British Columbia (where I especially valued Paul Yachnin's engagement); to Bruce Boehrer, for inviting me to Florida State University and for extending such warm hospitality; to Richard Rambuss (almost the only person who could convince me to attend the Group for Early Modern Cultural Studies [GEMCS]) for inviting me to Emory, where I appreciated Natasha Barnes's interest (and was overwhelmed by Chuck O'Boyle's culinary genius); to William H. Sherman, for an invitation to the University of Maryland (and for presenting me with a copy of *"The Tempest" and Its Travels* before it was available in the United States); to Peter Stallybrass, for the chance to lecture at the University of Pennsylvania (and to Tyler Smith, for making the arrangements and giving me such a warm introduction); to Robert Cesario, for inviting me back to Temple University (where the pleasure of seeing old friends like Tim Corrigan, Gaby Jackson, Paula Robison, and Alan Singer was matched by the wonderful engagement of Samuel Delany); and, finally, to Carolyn Williams, who kindly accepted me as a fellow at the Center for the Critical Analysis of Contemporary Culture at Rutgers University in 2001–2, during which time I completed the final draft of this book and had the opportunity to present parts of my project to my fellow fellows, among whom I am especially grateful for the suggestions offered by Brent Hayes Edwards.

My thanks to Richard Morrison at the University of Minnesota Press, with whom it has been such a pleasure to work again, for finding such sympathetic and engaged readers; the advice of Josiah Blackmore, Karen Newman, and an anonymous pair of readers has guided my final revisions. Thanks to everyone at the Press who facilitated the publication of this book, especially

Kathy Delfosse, copy editor extraordinaire (and belated thanks to her for her work on *Shakespeare's Hand,* as well as to Rachel Cole for her work on the manuscript). My thanks to Meredith Evans, for her assistance in preparing this book for the press, and even more for her luminous intelligence and congeniality. Thanks to Jonathan Brody Kramnick for his reading of the manuscript; although I am sure I have not handled to his satisfaction all the issues he raised, I know that our friendship does not depend on seeing eye to eye. To Michael Moon, as ever, I owe more than I can say.

I have learned most about the texts I treat in *Tempest in the Caribbean* from discussions with students, undergraduates and graduates, at The Johns Hopkins University and at Duke University, in courses I taught over the past several years. Several are thanked in the notes for specific contributions. One person named there—Andrew Kitchen—cannot receive this small tribute to his immense gifts. Andy was one of the most brilliant students I have been privileged to teach, a person of boundless generosity and wit. His death in August 2002 is an overwhelming loss. I dedicate this book to his memory.

A Different Kind of Creature

A DIFFERENT
KIND OF CREATURE

'BAN, 'BAN, CA-CALIBAN

The role that *The Tempest* has played to articulate colonial relations and,
more important, as a site from which to launch anticolonial responses is,
by now, a well-surveyed field. From the fairly compendious account of "Colonial Metaphors" in Alden T. and Virginia Mason Vaughan's *Shakespeare's
Caliban: A Cultural History* or Rob Nixon's much-cited essay "Caribbean
and African Appropriations of *The Tempest*" to a number of more specialized
treatments, rewritings and deployments of *The Tempest* have been examined
in New World Anglophone and Francophone writing, in Anglo-Canadian, Afro-
Canadian, Quebecois, African American, and Latino texts.[1] My aim in the
pages that follow is not to offer yet another survey but to launch a more limited inquiry centered on some of the foundational revisionary texts produced
in the Caribbean by Roberto Fernández Retamar, Aimé Césaire, and George
Lamming, as well as on some that are less familiar by Michelle Cliff and
Sylvia Wynter, among others, and to open a discussion of questions of sexuality that have not been broached in much of the critical literature on the
topic of deployments of *The Tempest*. Although criticism has moved beyond
seeing the Prospero-Caliban couple as a shorthand for colonizer-colonized
relationships to inquire into the position of Sycorax and Miranda—and even
of a black Miranda—and thereby valuably to raise questions of gender, these
interventions have rarely moved beyond heteronormative assumptions.[2] It
is my aim to suggest the value of positing post- and anticolonial possibilities
and positions that exceed that norm.

While tying such an argument to rewritings of *The Tempest,* I also want
to show that the play can be of use to make such a point. Although I take it
as inarguable that *The Tempest* is shaped by and furthers a (proto)colonialist

discourse and practice, the intentions of the play do not exhaust its potential meanings. For that reason, in the pages that follow, I take up several moments of textual trouble—frequently signaled by bibliographical problems—that, I argue, fracture along the lines of race, gender, and sexuality. Recently, and to my mind, disturbingly, criticism has been moving away from the view of *The Tempest* that prevailed in 1980s and '90s New Historicist and cultural materialist accounts of the play as a colonialist document. An emphasis on the Mediterranean and Old World *Tempest* now all but ignores such readings when it does not seek to deny them (this despite the elegant argument in Peter Hulme's *Colonial Encounters* that showed the uses of Mediterranean discourse for Atlantic ventures and insisted that the literal absence of a straightforward colonial plot in the play was a representational strategy that needed to be interpreted).[3] Thus, in the introduction to their 1999 Arden edition of the play, as in *Shakespeare's Caliban,* the Vaughans demur from the widespread opinion that Caliban's name derives from "cannibal." It would seem, for them, that for the name to fit, Caliban would need to be shown literally consuming human flesh.[4] Such a view ignores an argument like Hulme's, who demonstrates tellingly that the ascription of cannibalism to the Caribs, a claim made from Columbus on, did not rely on empirical evidence. Nor did the similar attribution, in the course of the sixteenth century, of cannibalism to virtually all native inhabitants of the New World.

Indeed, as Hulme shows, not only was the ascription of cannibalism made in the absence of evidence, even the supposed coherence of the group to whom it was at first applied, the Caribs, is equally suspect; it is as likely as not that the name was one given to those resistant to colonial imposition rather than one reflecting some ethnic or tribal solidarity. Like the characterization of cannibalism, such naming occurs in the service of a transformative encounter, an attempt to draw definitive boundaries between colonizer and colonized, groups that only came into being after the moment of contact. The Vaughans' attitude toward Caliban's name must be shaped by their desire to save the play from a colonialist reading (hence their positing of colonialist readings of the play as "metaphoric" and their insistence that Shakespeare could not have intended Caliban to be read as a Native American, let alone as a Black). Yet textual evidence for the derivation of Caliban's name seems overwhelming: Shakespeare borrows verbatim from John Florio's translation of Montaigne's "Des Cannibales," after all, and only to refute its relativist attitude toward "cannibals" (Montaigne's name for Brazilians) with its portrait of a savage Caliban, as Richard Halpern, for one, has demonstrated in an essay that will guide me in the following pages.[5] Moreover, Caliban plays with and reverses the syllables of his name, "'Ban, 'Ban, Ca-Caliban / Has a new master—get a new man!" (2.2.178–79), which, it seems clear, is an invitation to any audience who may have missed it to recognize the anagrammatic play involved in the name of the character.[6]

Yet such instability also might suggest a certain leeway between "Caliban" and "cannibal," spaces of ambivalence and contradiction of the kind that Homi K. Bhabha and those who have followed his lead have taught us to read. The representation of the colonized as savage and unmanageable could, at the least, testify to resistance and the continuing failure of the colonialist enterprise to do its work of "civilizing"/exterminating. On the sheerly negative ground of what the colonialist calls savagery and monstrosity, a platform of refusal could be erected. Insofar as colonialism operates through domination, struggle in these terms seems doomed to be a dialectic caught within colonialist discourse, however deep and broad its ambivalences and fissures might be. Although, as Halpern argues, this may well be the case in *The Tempest,* in many of the anticolonial texts I consider here, that impasse is at the least recognized, and terms that exceed the dilemma are launched, in part by finding unheard-of resources in terms of denigration, even the unthought possibility (from a colonialist's perspective) of embracing precisely what has been reviled. These resources are located especially in supposedly monstrous differences of race and sexuality, not so that they can be transcended in some move "beyond" racial or sexual difference to a universal human sameness but, rather, so that grounds can be enunciated for the "different kind of creature" glimpsed, for example, in the closing pages of George Lamming's *In the Castle of My Skin,* a creature that has refused Enlightenment values tied to the "human."[7] It is toward versions of possible, represented, even lived difference that these pages are drawn.

I take as another warrant for this inquiry, one that supplies at lightning speed the history that connects twentieth-century Caribbean responses to *The Tempest* and the colonial situation it heralds, the striking claim that C. L. R. James proffers in "The Making of the Caribbean People": "[T]he African who made the Middle Passage and came to live in the West Indies was an entirely new historical and social category. He was not an African, he was a West Indian black who was a slave. And there had never been people like that before and there haven't been any since."[8] Thus, in the pages that follow, I subscribe to the program outlined by David Scott in *Refashioning Futures: Criticism after Postcoloniality,* who argues that if "the redemptive project of overcoming colonialism is to return the natives to themselves," this project can be pursued neither under the rubric of the recovery of some antecedent precolonial identity nor under the aegis of some homogenizing and normativizing account of "the native." Rather, Scott continues, the question to be asked is, "Who exactly are these 'natives'? What is their gender? What is their ethnicity? What is their class? What is their sexual orientation? What are their modes of self-fashioning?"[9] Indeed, I would add, following James, new kinds of persons may not be grasped so readily even in the multiple categories that Scott deploys. New kinds of creatures reshape old categories. To reiterate: As Hulme suggests, even a native category like "Carib," which certainly comes to be a name for native belonging and identification, may be a post hoc nomination of groups united only by their ability to irritate and thwart colonialist powers.

O BRAVE NEW WORLD

Among New World responses to *The Tempest* perhaps Roberto Fernández Retamar's is the best-known to U.S. academics (in part because his 1971 essay "Caliban" appeared in English in *The Massachusetts Review* a couple of years later, and subsequently—in 1989—was republished by the University of Minnesota Press in a collection of Fernández Retamar's essays with a foreword by Fredric Jameson). The Vaughans fetch their epigraph from "Caliban" for their chapter on "Colonial Metaphors," citing a crucial sentence from Fernández Retamar's manifesto: "What is our history, what is our culture, if not the history and culture of Caliban?" (Vaughan and Vaughan, 144; Fernández Retamar, however, does not figure centrally in their chapter). And Nixon brings his history of appropriations to its climactic close with Fernández Retamar. For the project at hand, it is crucial to register that Fernández Retamar's tract is, from its first page on, a response to the question ¿Existen ustedes? ("Do you exist?") and that it offers an answer that seeks to describe the novelty of a being hitherto assumed to be at best derivative and at worst a monstrosity to be repudiated. The plurality that Fernández Retamar seizes under the name of "Caliban" is a figuration for this novelty and multiplicity: "our *mestizo* America," as he calls it, citing José Martí's phrase.[10]

The appeal of this argument is perfectly captured by Richard Halpern, who frames his study of *The Tempest* through Fernández Retamar, arguing, as Fernández Retamar does, that the play's utopic and dystopic vision is of a piece. Halpern notes how Fernández Retamar's and Martí's racially mixed figure—bringing together Native American, African, and European into a new configuration—represents a move beyond either accepting or repudiating metropolitan culture. "Our America" is no derivative. Moreover, as Halpern goes on to argue, Fernández Retamar's mestizo "denies unique or delimited points of origin, it replaces a monological conception of cultural discourse with a dialogical or indeed disseminative one" (263–64), providing a theoretical mapping easily assimilated to various strands of poststructuralist thought. Yet, to continue Halpern's point, the force of this gesture is not merely theoretical; it is bodily and historically grounded.

One historical ground for Fernández Retamar is, of course, the Cuban Revolution of 1959, and "Caliban" is its cultural manifesto; another is to reestablish José Martí, the late-nineteenth-century Cuban intellectual and revolutionary, as a precursor to Fidel Castro's regime, and as Fernández Retamar's forebear. From Martí, Fernández Retamar plucks not only his central concept of "our America" (the title of a crucial piece of Martí's cited often in "Caliban"), but also Martí's call for a new futurity linked to the mestizo past. Fernández Retamar's Martí "dreams not of a restoration now impossible but of the future integration of our America" ("Caliban," 20). There is no return to a "pure" origin or a singularity, but there is the possibility of a future for which "Martí is, as Fidel was later to be, aware of how difficult it is even to find a name that in designating us defines us conceptually" (20). These gestures resonate not only with the agendas we have noted in C. L. R. James or David Scott but also with the historical situation of colonialism, as Hulme traces it, as an encounter that changes everything. And indeed, Fernández Retamar's gesture might be said to transcend James's, if only because of its inclusiveness. It reminds us that the history of colonialism is not one thing. There are places in "our America" where the indigenous population was totally decimated and replaced with African slaves; places where Africans and natives were both present and exploited; places where Native American resistance made conquest all but impossible; places, like the Caribbean, where the end of slavery in the nineteenth century marked a new influx of others—Asians—who, as indentured servants, were virtual slaves.[11] It is, moreover, the case that those of European descent born in the New World were often suspect, as if they had been "infected" by the tropics. "Our *mestizo* America" would seem the most economical way to name all these conditions at once.[12]

Yet despite the capaciousness of this gesture, it is founded on some troubling exclusions. Fernández Retamar's desire to make "our America" a unique case, for example, bars the applicability of the term to North America and to the experiences of Native Americans or African Americans there (the United States is, understandably, so much the enemy of the Castro regime that Fernández Retamar seems unable to imagine such forms of solidarity).[13] And although conditions of *mestizaje* can be found in other colonial locales, these, for Fernández Retamar, are merely accidents; they are not essential, as they are in "our America." *Mestizaje* is, rather, "the distinctive sign of our culture" ("Caliban," 4), he affirms. Thus, although it can be argued that everyone is the product of mixture, Fernández Retamar wants the sign of inclusiveness to function instead as one of exclusion and exclusiveness.

Halpern points to one intensely troubling way this is framed: the virtual exclusion of women from the revolutionary view that Fernández Retamar offers. In a role call of New World Calibans, only one woman is named (Violeta Parra, the Chilean songwriter). Halpern is certainly right in noting that Fernández Retamar's imagining of revolution as an entirely male adventure is hardly unique to him. And Rob Nixon, who also notes the masculinism of Fernández Retamar's account, suggests that *The Tempest* itself is another masculinist text, one sign, for him, of the limits of the uses to which the play might be—and, he claims, has been—put.[14] Unlike Nixon, Halpern recognizes that the embodiment of *mestizaje* is gendered and sexualized, and he also sees the limits in Fernández Retamar's view. Fastening on the figure that Fernández Retamar deploys and defends against—of being a "distorted echo" ("Caliban," 3; "eco desfigurado," 23) of European culture—he argues that

Fernández Retamar offers the choice between an Echo tied to the Narcissus of European self-reflection and a revolutionary Caliban, noting that "the implicit opposition of Echo and Caliban clearly genders the resistance to cultural dependence in a troublingly masculinist way" (Halpern, 264 n. 6).

The trouble, however, is not simply that such a masculinism erases femininity (or that it imagines sexual difference on the model of originary maleness and derivate femaleness); it also deplores femininity in men. That case has been made by Ricardo Ortiz in an important essay that seeks common cause with Fernández Retamar in order to further what Ortiz terms "revolution's other histories."[15] Desiring to expand the framework of what counts as "America," Ortiz ends his essay by advocating the work of two gay male Latino American writers, urging recognition of the homophobia in Fernández Retamar's text upon those who have happily embraced the Calibanic vision it offers without noticing this radical exclusion. As Ortiz details, Fernández Retamar's homophobia comes closest to articulation in his dismissive phrase "the neo-Barthesean flutterings of Severo Sarduy" ("Caliban," 36; "el mariposeo neo-barthesiano de Severo Sarduy," 68), where *mariposeo* is almost to say the derogatory slang *maricón*.[16] It's there too in such gestures as references to "writers like Emir Rodríguez Monegal and Severo Sarduy" ("Caliban," 34) or "the likes of Guillermo Cabrera Infante and Juan Goytisolo" ("Caliban," 36). And it is especially there, as Ortiz details, through repeated figurations of penetration: José Enrique Rodó's *Ariel* is described as opposing the "North American penetration" that Rodríguez Monegal welcomes in his "'Nordomania'" ("Caliban," 15), the sign of which is a formalist "emasculation" of Rodó in Rodríguez Monegal's edition of his works; congruently, Domingo Sarmiento's admiration for the United States is characterized as "a neverending historical orgasm" ("Caliban," 25). For Fernández Retamar, those who wish to be penetrated by U.S. or European culture are definitionally nonrevolutionary artists who put themselves in the female derivative position of Echo. Such a cultural position is also a homosexual stance in a cultural milieu that defines "the homosexual" as a man who takes it up the ass.

Ortiz, responding to Fernández Retamar's insistence that his text be read contextually, deftly locates "Caliban" in its immediate history, the virulent homophobia of the Cuban regime, which had in the late 1960s incarcerated male homosexuals. Although it no longer engaged wholesale in that practice by the time Fernández Retamar wrote his manifesto, the 1971 National Congress on Education and Culture, which predates Fernández Retamar's tract by several months (Fernández Retamar quotes Castro's speech on that occasion), made clear that revolutionary intellectuals could not be homosexual.[17] The missed chance represented by a text like "Caliban," when restored to this context, is caught by José Quiroga in *Tropics of Desire,* where he makes the important points that Cuban homosexuals had been early advocates of the revolution and that the revolution, moreover, was inspirational to those on the left in the

United States in the 1960s, including not only those in the Civil Rights movement, which Fernández Retamar seems not to have noticed, but also feminists and gay liberation theorists and activists.[18] In Castro's Cuba, particularly in the 1970s, sexuality was viewed as a merely private, lifestyle choice necessarily antithetical to the aims of revolutionizing society. In the particularly dire economic situation of the early 1970s, gays were a target in a recognizable diversionary tactic of drawing attention away from government and social failures by scapegoating them. Jesse Helms may hate Cuba, but he shares one sentiment officially countenanced by Castro's regime.

What is perhaps most pertinent here is not so much to decry Fernández Retamar's or Cuba's sexual politics—neither is, after all, particularly unique in "our America"—as to offer a more dialectical reading of "Caliban" that might allow one to hold on to what remains inspiring in it and makes it a valuable intervention in the readings of Shakespeare from the modern Caribbean that I seek to investigate here. Following Ortiz, it is necessary to see how much policing activity goes on in "Caliban"—and to question it, precisely in the spirit of the inclusiveness heralded as "our *mestizo* America." Fernández Retamar proposes Martí to replace Rodó, specifically Rodó's 1900 manifesto *Ariel,* which had proclaimed that character in *The Tempest* as the model for a reinvigorated Latin America culture.[19] Rodó associated Caliban with the United States. Fernández Retamar agrees with Rodó's negative estimation of U.S. aggressiveness and materialistic crassness (that is, its capitalist and colonialist ambitions, not least in the southern hemisphere). He regards Rodó's association of Caliban with the United States as a fundamental error, one indebted to Ernest Renan, who had rewritten Shakespeare's play to make Caliban embody everything wrong with democracy (Renan is the figure most often cited in *Ariel,* a text whose mission in the service of "we Latin Americans," "a heritage of race, a great ethnic tradition" [*Ariel,* 73], nonetheless never cites a single Latin American text in its cultural program). Throughout, Fernández Retamar declaims a Calibanic genealogy (from Martí to Castro and Ernesto "Che" Guevara) that excludes Europeanizers like Rodó, including among them Sarduy, Rodríguez Monegal, Carlos Fuentes, Jorge Luis Borges, and their ilk. Although Halpern is right to claim that Fernández Retamar would seem amenable to poststructuralist views, it is these that Fernández Retamar explicitly deplores. Suspiciously French, they register as signs of cultural emasculation; homosexual penetration is intimated.[20] What makes this all the more disturbing, and potentially contradictory to the aims of Fernández Retamar's manifesto, is the fact that his figure for "our America" is also an "alien" figure (as he admits ["Caliban," 16]), elaborated in and admitted to his text—indeed, titling it. "Our symbol then is not Ariel, as Rodó thought, but rather Caliban" (14). "Our symbol," like Rodó's, comes from elsewhere—indeed, from the same place, Shakespeare, an author whom Fernández Retamar adores. He calls Shakespeare "the most extraordinary writer of fiction who ever existed" (5), and precisely because he somehow knows "us" better than we do ourselves: "Caliban is our Carib" (9). Fernández Retamar subordinates himself to Shakespeare by misreading Shakespeare's quietistic exposure of the complicity between utopic dreamer and monstrous Caliban as revolutionary.

This creative misreading is of a piece, however, with the ways Fernández Retamar reads his forebears throughout. Attempting to draw a strict line between Martí and Rodó, he must ignore their shared status as founding texts for Latin American *modernismo*. Indeed, Fernández Retamar's text is in line with a troubling foundational gesture for this movement that sought to win all the prestige and glamor accorded late-nineteenth-century European artistic currents and, at the same time, to purge them of their "decadence" (that is, homoerotics).[21] *Ariel* does not erase its relationship to French texts, and it offers itself as a quasi-Platonic dialogue (an old teacher, nicknamed Prospero, addresses his male pupils) in the service of a delibidinized pedagogy, one nonetheless that aims to plant "seeds" from the master's mouth in impressionable youths who are to shape themselves after the ideal of Ariel, around whose statue they gather: "[A] young mind is hospitable soil in which the seed of a single timely word will quickly yield immortal fruit" (*Ariel,* 32). One could be reading Oscar Wilde's *Portrait of Mr. W. H.,* or his declarations at his trial, when he defended his relationship with Alfred Douglas as a spiritual, Platonic affair like Shakespeare's with his beloved in the sonnets. Or, indeed, one could be reading Martí's essay on Wilde, which similarly displays and defends against its swooning response to Wilde's aestheticism and antimaterialism.[22]

Fernández Retamar, predictably, does not mention Martí's essay on Wilde. He does allude in his preface to *Caliban and Other Essays,* however, to Martí's "great essay on Whitman," which, like the essay about Wilde, as Sylvia Molloy has demonstrated, participates in similar complicated gestures of solidarity with Walt Whitman's vision of male camaraderie and demurrals from the sexuality that Whitman advocates through that dear love.[23] But even the moments in Martí admitted into Fernández Retamar's text are more complicated than he allows. He cites Martí's admirable refusal at the close of "Our America"—"[T]here is no racial hatred, because there are no races" ("Caliban," 24)—but he suppresses the fact that Martí is urging this against a belief that "there is a fatal and ingrained evil in the blond nation" (that is, the United States) and not just in support of the Native Americans and Blacks of Latin America.[24] Martí does indeed value Native Americans and their culture; Fernández Retamar cites from Martí's "Aboriginal American Authors" but fails to note that it is a review of a book by a U.S. scholar about these writers, from which Martí fetches much information and which he praises.

Fernández Retamar, like Martí, imagines "our America" as a "brotherhood" ("Caliban," 37, emended at the end to include "brothers and sisters" [41], which, indeed, goes beyond Martí's masculinist vision), but he does not notice how homoerotically (and misogynistically) charged this is in Martí. Martí writes of Simón Bolívar, for example, that "he sears and enthralls" ("Simón Bolívar," 152): "[W]hile America lives, shall the echo of his name pass from father to son in what is best and manliest in us!" (162). Or of Emerson, he writes this: "Of other men one can say: 'This is a brother'; of Emerson one must say: 'This is a father'" ("Emerson," 235). *Of Emerson.* And also, "Why should man envy woman because she suffers and gives birth, if a thought, in its torments before birth and the satisfaction it brings afterward, is a son?" (223). Emerson is the germinative father figure to his son Martí. "There is a profound truth in Emerson's paradox that demands that nations be judged by the minority, not the majority, of its citizens," antidemocratic Rodó writes (*Ariel,* 60), but so, too, democratic Martí worries about the "sordid masses" ("Our America," 149) and about how to govern them according to the precepts of a "universal" spirit available to those who have risen above the flesh. "Poetry . . . is more necessary to a people than industry itself," Martí writes in the Whitman essay ("Whitman," 245), though any reader might have guessed I was citing Rodó. "No man ever lived freer of the pressures of men or of his moment," Martí writes admiringly of Emerson ("Emerson," 221). "Emerson has made idealism human" (236); Martí writes, fraternally, as if to "another self that is above fatigues and miseries," as he says Whitman is when he writes to and from his alter ego ("Whitman," 253). His reader is his Echo. "He awaits the happy hour in which the material [world] will depart from him, and given up to the purifying airs, he will become germ and fragrance in its swells, 'disembodied, triumphant, dead'" (258).[25] Is Martí Caliban, or Ariel?

I do not tally these resonances to deny that there is a revolutionary futurity to be found and valued in Martí, to devalue his death in battle for Cuban independence, or to erase the profound differences between Martí and Rodó. Rather, I suggest that the roots of revolution are more complicated than Fernández Retamar suggests, drawing his distinction (and not least in the text by Shakespeare that Fernández Retamar venerates). Moreover, however much Fernández Retamar's "Caliban" is a revolutionary manifesto, it is also in many respects in line with its *modernismo* forebears. Take Martí's exclusionary gesture at the opening of "Our America" as he calls for the formation of a revolutionary brotherhood: "Only the seven-month birthling will lack the courage. Those who do not have faith in their country are seven-month men. They cannot reach the first limb with their puny arms, arms with painted nails and bracelets, arms of Madrid or Paris" (139). Those others are effeminate, foreign, as in Fernández Retamar but also as in so many nineteenth-century thinkers (so-called) who wished to taint homosexuality as necessarily foreign, feminine (but whose denunciations inevitably showed how many "natives" had succumbed).[26] They are not "natural" men, the kind of men that Martí praises in "Our America" and that Fernández Retamar endorses: "The natural men have vanquished the artificial, lettered men. The native-born half-breed has vanquished the exotic Creole" ("Our America," 141).[27] This naturalization is, at the same time, a metaphysical, transcendentalizing gesture—the oneness of nature that Martí finds in Emerson or Whitman—inflected to naturalize the fantasy of sons produced by fathers (often without mothers), that is, to naturalize a homosocial/homophobic brotherhood always defended against its own homoerotics.[28]

Fernández Retamar makes an invaluable gesture toward Caliban—indeed, toward Shakespeare's Caliban—when he writes, "To offend us they call us *mambi,* they call us *black;* but we reclaim as a mark of glory the honor of considering ourselves descendants of the *mambi,* descendants of the rebel, runaway, *independendista* black—*never* descendants of the slave holder. Prospero, as we well know, taught his language to Caliban, and, consequently, gave him a name. But is this his true name?" ("Caliban," 17). "Martí surpassed the level of meaning, the verb *to say;* Martí *was,* he was that something, he was Cuban reality." Here, I do not cite Fernández Retamar but Severo Sarduy in an exchange with Emir Rodríguez Monegal.[29] But if, for a moment, my reader supposed it was Fernández Retamar and now asks, "Is this his true name?" it should be clear that the question needs to be asked again in a way that would include those that Fernández Retamar would exclude from "our America."

You taught me language

In the Calibanic genealogy that Fernández Retamar offers, George Lamming is singled out as "the first writer in our world to assume our identification with Caliban" ("Caliban," 12). In 1971, the year "Caliban" appeared, Lamming was set to publish what have remained, to date, his final novels. Over the course of twenty years, Lamming published six novels that, as he acknowledged in a 1973 interview, could be regarded as a single, continuous story.[30] After starting with *In the Castle of My Skin* (1953), a novel of a colonial childhood, autobiographical in its inspiration, in which Lamming also charts the lived (if unrecognized) experience of race and class, he then proceeded to *The Emigrants* (1954), which captures the experience of a generation of emigrants (including Lamming) from the Caribbean to London that took place in the 1950s, and on to *Of Age and Innocence* (1958) and *Season of Adventure* (1960), novels set on the island of "San Cristobal," a locale that condenses various Caribbean places as it depicts the failed attempts at independence in the region. Then, as if completing this trajectory, Lamming returned to its point of origins, in *Natives of My Person* (1972) composing a novel that reads doubly, at once an account of the original colonial venture and the present neocolonial situation of economic domination of the Caribbean, and in *Water with Berries* (1971) returning to what he referred to in an interview as "my old Prospero-Caliban theme" for a full-scale rewriting of *The Tempest.*[31]

In 1971, when Fernández Retamar hailed him, Lamming was on the point of ending his exile in London to return to Barbados to take up the position of public intellectual. Since his return, he has published essays and, equally important, he has appeared at numerous occasions (perhaps most powerfully at the memorial service for Maurice Bishop; he also eulogized Walter Rodney) at which he has spoken about the continuing effects of colonialism on the region. As he did in his novels, he has pointed to the worker uprisings of the 1930s as inspiring events and to the various betrayals of the "peasant" and "folk" by a middle class created by a European educational apparatus that had served to divide the inhabitants without in fact giving the new class any real relationship to the means of production.[32] Like Frantz Fanon in *The Wretched of the Earth,* Lamming decries this "lackey" class. In his opinion, this group has served ongoing imperial powers, most notably, for instance, when the U.S. invasion of Grenada in 1983 was welcomed by any number of so-called independent states. Lamming sees those states' democratic processes as little more than a way of furthering divisions of race and class, assuring exploitation and Caribbean dependence. Against the new imperialism of the United States, Lamming has held up the "miracle" of Cuba, and his speeches are at times dotted with references to Martí and to Castro. Indeed, speaking at the twenty-fifth anniversary of Casa de las Américas in 1984 (in whose journal "Caliban" was published), he alluded playfully to Fernández Retamar, who, as its head, must have been present on the occasion. Like Fernández Retamar, Lamming writes frequently of the role the intellectual must play in revolutionizing society, insisting that "it is the function of the writer to return a society to itself" (*Conversations,* 81). For Lamming, throughout his long career, this has meant to represent the poor, black populations and to loosen the hold of European education in order to allow the reclamation of buried experiences so that the various forms of degradation and alienation that persist as the colonial legacy can be surmounted at an individual and collective level. Like C. L. R. James before him, Lamming too thinks that the Caribbean is a unique place, with unique possibilities lodged there: "I don't think there has been anything in human history quite like the meeting of Africa, Asia, and Europe in the American archipelago we call the Caribbean."[33] For him too it is a place marked by "the signature of that sperm" (*Conversations,* 160), as he somewhat graphically insists on the literality of miscegenation that characterizes "our America." And if this phrasing, like the language of Fernández Retamar, is resolutely masculinist, here and there Lamming has acknowledged this shortcoming, hailing "the women who fathered many a household, nursed man and child without a wage and have remained to this day the last surviving example of legalized slave-labour" (*Conversations,* 220), a view that seems nonetheless to imagine women confined to their household tasks, a point disturbingly confirmed when he lambasts middle-class women for their exploitation of the lower-class women who do domestic work for them.[34]

The Lamming who confirmed in a 1978 interview what is apparent from reading his work—"I am a socialist," he declared (*Conversations,* 269)—would therefore seem an entirely logical name to be singled out by Fernández Retamar. Fernández Retamar, of course, does not allude to Lamming's public, post-1971 career that I have briefly sketched, which has brought them into proximity over the past quarter of a century; nor does he have in mind Lamming's career as a novelist. Rather, he refers to Lamming's *The Pleasures of Exile,* an ironically titled set of essays published in 1960. In these, not only does Lamming make the Calibanic identification that Fernández Retamar underscores, but like Fernández Retamar, he also provides a genealogy. In Lamming's case, it fastens on Toussaint Louverture and the Haitian revolution as the inspiring model for the future, on the recent independence of Ghana as the example from the present, and on C. L. R. James, whose *Black Jacobins* recounts the history of the Haitian revolution, as a prototype for the Caribbean intellectual and, indeed, for the situation of Caribbean intellectuals of that time, since James's book had been out of print for twenty years, a sign of how devalued indigenous intellectuals were (this was the reason for Lamming's emigration). Like Fernández Retamar, Lamming also weighs the efforts of Caribbean writers of his generation who have furthered the work of representation of the poor and racially despised—Roger Mais and Sam Selvon, for example—against the efforts of those who have joined the middle class and adopted European attitudes toward "peasant" experience, notably V. S. Naipaul. Indeed, Lamming lambasts Naipaul's "castrated satire" in a rhetoric of emasculation akin to Fernández Retamar's.[35]

Nonetheless, Fernández Retamar's citation of Lamming in "Caliban" is not entirely laudatory. To quote now the entire sentence: "Although he is (apparently) the first writer in our world to assume our identification with Caliban, the Barbadian writer George Lamming is unable to break the circle traced by Mannoni" ("Caliban," 12). Fernández Retamar says no more but, as is typical throughout his essay, he provides a citation from *Pleasures* that presumably speaks for itself. Its subject is language, the language that Prospero claims to have taught Caliban (in this context it is worth noting that Fernández Retamar's sole citation from *The Tempest* is Caliban's retort "You taught me language and my profit on't / Is, I know how to curse" [1.2.362–64, as cited in "Caliban," 6–7]). Pulling Lamming into the orbit of Octave Mannoni's *Prospero and Caliban,* which argues that the dependency that Prospero induced was based on native psychology—that the native, Caliban, wanted what Prospero had to offer, wanted to be colonized, and then despaired at abandonment—Fernández Retamar allies Lamming with a colonialist (and French) Lacanian psychoanalytic point of view.[36] We know, by now, how to read such a gesture.

Fernández Retamar's ongoing ambivalent response to Lamming is also shown in the rather conciliatory follow-up to "Caliban" that he published in 1986, "Caliban Revisited." It is conciliatory not in backing down from the context in which "Caliban" had been written (the arrest of Heberto Padillo for antirevolutionary writing, taken by many Western intellectuals who had supported the Cuban Revolution as a sign of its increasingly totalitarian nature; the Padillo affair was also entwined with persecution of homosexual intellectuals) but in making friendly gestures to two authors excoriated in "Caliban": Carlos Fuentes and Borges (rather extraordinary concessions, considering their politics). By 1986, Fernández Retamar certainly knew more about Lamming than he presumably did in 1971. Not least, he must have been familiar with the brief introduction that Lamming had provided to a 1984 reprint of *Pleasures,* in which he reminds readers that at the time of his writing the book, the Caribbean was still an entirely colonized region, and in which he hails the Cuban Revolution as the culmination of the promise of Toussaint: "[L]ike a bolt from the blue, Fidel Castro and the Cuban revolution reordered our history."[37] Nonetheless, in "Caliban Revisited" Lamming appears merely as one of those in the Calibanic line; a footnote, adducing the 1984 edition of *Pleasures,* does admit that Lamming deserves more attention than Fernández Retamar accords him. This intertextual history suggests an ongoing conflictual relationship with Lamming; the charge against Lamming serves as an apotropaic gesture of self-distancing.

Like Fernández Retamar, Lamming in *Pleasures* is responding to the question, Do you exist? Like Fernández Retamar, he must answer in the language of the colonizer: "Right now as we are discussing, as I am discussing with those colonizers, how else can I do it except in one of their languages, which is now *our* language, and with so many of their conceptual tools, which are now also *our* conceptual tools? This is precisely the outcry that we read in a work by perhaps the most extraordinary writer of fiction who ever existed. . . . 'You taught me language'" ("Caliban," 5). Here is the passage from *Pleasures* that Fernández Retamar cites as evidence of Lamming's dependency:

> Prospero has given Caliban language; and with it an unstated history of consequences, an unknown history of future intentions. This gift of language meant not English, in particular, but speech and concept as a way, a method, a necessary avenue towards areas of the self which could not be reached in any other way. It is this way, entirely Prospero's, which makes Caliban aware of possibilities. Therefore, all of Caliban's future—for future is the very name of possibilities—must derive from Prospero's experiment, which is also his risk. Provided there is no extraordinary departure which explodes all of Prospero's premises, then Caliban and his future now belong to Prospero. . . . Prospero lives in the absolute certainty that Language, which is his gift to Caliban, is the very prison in which Caliban's achievement will be realized and restricted. (*Pleasures,* 109–10; as cited in "Caliban," 12–13)

It appears that Lamming's Caliban, unlike Fernández Retamar's, is not someone who returns a curse for the "gift" of language, a point that Lamming, in fact, explicitly makes (*Pleasures,* 15). But then again, neither is Fernández Retamar's "Caliban" reduced to cursing, for he too speaks the same tongue, deploys the same concepts. Once again, we face here the problem of distinguishing cultural mixture—*mestizaje*—from mere imitation. Fernández Retamar and Lamming face a shared dilemma. Does the passage from *Pleasures* cited by Fernández Retamar substantiate his charge of colonial dependence?

In the passage Lamming confronts the fact that "Caliban" is not the name of some precolonial creature; it is the name for the colonized, a name provided by the colonizer. The very naming is a performative gesture that ushers "Caliban" into a new form of existence, one, as Lamming underscores in *Pleasures,* that must have been a wrenching experience: "exiled from his gods, exiled from his nature, exiled from his own name" (15). To take, now, the name "Caliban" as one's own is not to reclaim a territory that can be called innate or primordial, but rather to revalue the very being made in the naming. Lamming parts company with Fernández Retamar in denying that "Caliban" is the name of "our Carib" ("Caliban," 9), but it is for the sake of seeing that "our Carib" is also a secondary formation produced by colonialism, a necessarily mixed being composed through the encounter.

It could appear that Lamming is endorsing Prospero's values, the particular avenue toward self-discovery and self-realization that he declares to be "his way" and not Caliban's. This is an admittedly difficult point, but it does speak to the cultural situation that Lamming addresses. The simplest way to put it would be to note that Lamming is a novelist—that is, he works in a form that is definitionally European—and that although he aims to make the novel the repository for kinds of experiences hitherto unavailable to it, he is nonetheless staking out a territory that cannot really be called indigenous but that must retrospectively recast the terms of what counts as cultural production. As he says several times in *Pleasures,* the point is that "English is no longer the exclusive language of the men who live in England" (36); it is also a West Indian tongue.

As Lamming ventriloquizes Prospero's belief—that the language he has given Caliban will only serve to limit him; that it will make him aware of his unbreachable difference from Prospero, of the impossibility of achievements matching Prospero's—he is tracing the contours of a lie, the lie of "that *language* with which Prospero tried to annihilate the concrete existence of Caliban" (*Pleasures,* 180). It was, as he admits (as does Fernández Retamar), a lie lived as slavery and self-hatred, and still lived. The being that Prospero conferred on Caliban, giving him language, was to name him as a deformed slave, a monstrosity incapable of thought. It was to reduce him to the condition of mere labor, to brutish nature, to "the role of Thing, excluded, devoid of language" (166). It was also to offer Caliban an opening to a blocked futurity, and it is Calibans like Lamming who have superseded the block, seen through the lie. "Will the Lie upon which Prospero's confident authority was built be discovered?" (117). It is toward that project and its continual unfolding (since, as Lamming sees it, "the Lie" has not ceased to exert its hold on the Caribbean) that Lamming works.

"Caliban has got hold of Prospero's weapons" (*Pleasures,* 63). If the weapons meant are the ability to wield language, to write, far more than that is at stake. "The old blackmail of Language simply won't work any longer. For the language of modern politics is no longer Prospero's exclusive vocabulary" (158). Indeed, the ability to see through that language and its false pretenses has long been available; it exists in the work of C. L. R. James, in the man he made a hero: "[W]e shall never explode Prospero's old myth until we christen Language afresh; until we show Language as the product of human endeavour; until we make available to all the result of certain enterprises undertaken by men who are still regarded as the unfortunate descendants of languageless and deformed slaves" (118–19). The moment in which Lamming writes is governed by the principle that "colonisation is a reciprocal process" (156). Caliban arises from the colonial encounter, but so too does Prospero. In the discovery of what was made then and what might be made from it lies a future in which Prospero either must cower or with which he must come to terms. What Lamming suggests, moreover, is that the terms will necessarily be new ones, since the old lie of language was based on Caliban's exclusion and oppression. If language has been seized by the colonized and has been seen through as "the Lie," the point is for Caliban not simply to reverse the dialectic but to exceed it and to usher Prospero into a future that he no longer can imagine he controls.

. . . AND THEN I LOVED THEE

Is Lamming nonetheless in the grips of the dependency complex that Mannoni described? Such would seem to be the belief that guides the Vaughans in their chapter "Colonial Metaphors" in *Shakespeare's Caliban,* where they summarize (with utter equanimity and approval) what they take to be the gist of Lamming's argument: "[L]anguage was Caliban's 'prison.' . . . it is Prospero's language and therefore largely Prospero's vision of the future that Caliban must accept" (166). Nixon implicitly answers Fernández Retamar's charge that Lamming is caught in "the circle traced by Mannoni" by claiming that through Caliban Lamming urges decolonization of "the area's cultural history by replacing an imposed with an endemic line of thought and action" ("Caribbean and African Appropriations," 569).[38] Although it is certainly the case that Lamming wishes a revitalization of the Caribbean that involves "endemic" and indigenous cultural traditions (*Pleasures* opens by invoking the Haitian Ceremony of the Souls, for example; Lamming announces that his race is not a chip on his shoulder but a mountain on his back), Nixon's account considerably simplifies Lamming's position and also deploys the terms used by Fernández Retamar, of suspect foreign influence that must be repudiated.

Lamming certainly claims the identification with and as Caliban that Fernández Retamar and Nixon take to be the significance of his work: "I am a direct descendant of slaves, too near to the actual enterprise to believe that its echoes are over with the reign of emancipation," he writes (*Pleasures,* 15). But he makes another claim as well: "Moreover, I am a direct descendant of Prospero worshipping in the same temple of endeavour, using his legacy of language—not to curse our meeting—but to push it further, reminding the descendants of both sides that what's done is done, and can only be seen as a soil from which other gifts, or the same gift endowed with different meanings, may grow towards a future which is colonised by our acts in this moment, but which must always remain open" (15). That is to say: Lamming, like Fernández Retamar, depends upon a notion of cultural *mestizaje;* and if, like Fernández Retamar, this is imagined as a largely male-male enterprise, it is here figured through an impossible act of sexual intercourse, two fathers, Caliban and Prospero, producing this son. Vera Kutzinski has recently charged that Fernández Retamar's "Caliban" works in a similar way: "Fernández Retamar's cultural *mestizaje,* which legitimates him as an Hispanic-American intellectual and as a first-person narrator, is born not from heterosexual violence but from the homoerotic embrace of Caliban and Ariel across their respective race and class differences."[39] In other words, Fernández Retamar's tropes are tainted by his virtual exclusion of women in "Caliban" and his failure to recognize that the *mestizaje* he celebrates literally depends upon violence against native and black women. For Kutzinski, it renders him (homo)sexually suspect.

If a homophobic suspicion is similarly deployed in Fernández Retamar's charge against Lamming's dependency complex, it could be motivated, moreover, by the way Lamming ends his discussion of *The Tempest* in *Pleasures:* wondering whether Caliban's expressions of "ingratitude" awaken in Prospero "the knowledge that he really deserves such ingratitude" (116). Lamming's terms could seem to echo Mannoni, who moves in one brief discussion of *The Tempest* from Caliban's lines on language to "the real reason" for Caliban's antagonism. Mannoni cites the speech from *The Tempest* that Lamming also quotes at the end of his discussion of the play:

> . . . When thou camest first
> Thou strok'dst me, and mad'st much of me; wouldst give me
> Water with berries in't; and teach me how
> To name the bigger light, and how the less,
> That burn by day and night; and then I lov'd thee . . .
>
> (1.2.332–36, as cited by Mannoni)

He goes on to paraphrase it: "[A]nd then you abandoned me before I had time to become your equal. . . . In other words: you taught me to be dependent, and I was happy; then you betrayed me and plunged me into inferiority."[40] Lamming, too, talks of "Prospero's betrayal of love" (*Pleasures*, 114), of how Caliban "haunts" Prospero "in a way that is almost too deep and too intimate to communicate" (99).

Even if remarks like these cause Fernández Retamar to place Lamming into Mannoni's orbit, I think it would be far more accurate to recognize that Lamming's thought runs, rather, along the track laid out by Fanon, in his redescription (and refusal) of Mannoni's thesis in *Black Skin, White Masks*.[41] Fanon repudiates Mannoni's claim of innate dependency and utterly annihilates the racist ruse of a benign colonialism. The native of whom Mannoni talks, Fanon underscores, *"has ceased to exist"* (94); the Malagasy are, rather, the creatures made by colonial exploitation. If they are dependent, it is because they have been made dependent. Although Fanon insists on the actual material, economic circumstances glossed over by Mannoni—the brutalization and immiseration that produced dependency—he is most concerned, as is Mannoni, with describing a colonial psychology. For Fanon, as is well known, the "native" (that is to say, the colonized) has suffered a total psychological destructuration. His ego ideal is white, a condition of impossible identification. (In *Black Skin, White Masks,* "his" is the necessary gendered marker of the colonized; as Fanon writes, he knows nothing about the woman of color [179–80]).[42] Like Fanon seeking "the liberation of the man of color from himself" (8), Lamming too wants to bring to the surface these deep deformations of psyche that are the colonial legacy, the false consciousness of the white mask that he wishes covered his black skin. Both authors seek the contours of a new identity.[43] When Lamming admits the affective intensity of the relationship between Prospero and Caliban, he points beyond the material circumstances of Caliban's robbery (the island taken from him) and the supposed compensatory "gift" of language toward the deep psychological level on which this intensity is based. In this account, his aims are akin to Fanon's, tracing a colonial psychology. Indeed, the psychology Fanon describes is not all that far from Mannoni's—with the crucial caveat that it is not supposed as "indigenous" and is certainly not in any sense validated, as it is in Mannoni.

Moreover, the psychology of *Black Skin, White Masks* is a "deep" and almost unspeakable one: Fanon does not offer ego psychology but a psychoanalytic model. This means, as Fanon insists, that "considerable attention must be given to sexual phenomena" (160). As is well known, these take the form of interracial sexual relations between "the woman of color and the white man" and between "the man of color and the white woman" (the topics of the second and third chapters of *Black Skin, White Masks*). As Fanon describes them, they are necessarily perverse, and chapter 6 details the psychopathology of colonial sexual relations. There Fanon rewrites the Freudian scenario of a child being beaten into that of the white woman dreaming of being raped by the black man. Given the fantasmatic nature of the black man, Fanon opines that ultimately "it is the woman who rapes herself" (179). She has sex with herself—a masturbatory fantasy that perhaps, for Fanon, qualifies as lesbian. The white man similarly dreams about the black man. Fanon keeps discovering and deploring the "homosexual territory" (183) he encounters, notoriously averring that there is no homosexuality indigenous to the Antilles (not even in the cross-dressing men whom he knows about but who, he assures his readers and himself, "lead normal sex lives" [180 n. 44]).[44] The black man, whether with a white man or a white woman, is nothing more than a penis, and a castrated one at that—which is to say, in these Freudian terms, a woman.

Who is this black man in Fanon if not Caliban? This white man and this white woman if not Prospero and Miranda? Although Fanon barely mentions *The Tempest* in his rebuttal of Mannoni, he does in fact credit Mannoni's "Prospero complex," citing Mannoni's definition of it: "[T]he racialist whose daughter has suffered an [imaginary] attempted rape at the hands of an inferior being" (Fanon, 107, citing Mannoni, 110). "Toward Caliban, Prospero assumes an attitude that is well known to Americans in the southern United States," Fanon continues. "Are they not forever saying that the niggers are just waiting for the chance to jump on white women?" This fantasy Lamming too fastens on in his reading of *The Tempest*. He calls the rape charge "The Lie" (*Pleasures,* 102), twinning it with the accusation about language, drawing together thereby the intimate relations that (de)structure Caliban—with Prospero and with Miranda.

WOULD'T HAD BEEN DONE!

This brings us to a point that Richard Halpern has emphasized: There is a major stumbling block—or there should be—to the easy embrace of Caliban as cultural hero and founder of a race of mixed-bloods. It implicitly validates the charge lodged against Caliban in *The Tempest:* that he is a would-be rapist. As Halpern goes on to say, the charge is a trap and an ideological lure. On the one hand, it effaces the much more usual direction of colonial violence perpetrated by white heterosexual males; on the other, it forces anyone who claims Caliban to exonerate rape. "Retamar's choice of a rapist as an anticolonial hero not only betrays a striking indifference to matters of gender, but falls into an ideological trap set by *The Tempest,*" Halpern concludes ("Picture of Nobody," 283). Commentators in the Calibanic line who follow Fernández Retamar (Nixon would be one of them) simply ignore the question of Caliban as rapist. Nixon goes further, however; his own inattention to questions of gender and sexuality leads him in his summary of *Pleasures* to fail to mention the fact that Lamming is indeed aware of the problematic accusation of rape and of the problematic validation of the rapist. As Peter Hulme has remarked on more than one occasion, one of the most extraordinary things about Lamming's *Pleasures* is that it devotes an entire chapter to an anticolonial reading of *The Tempest,* one that anticipates a critical practice that would become familiar among literary academics—almost all of them unaware of the Caribbean tradition of responses to and deployments of the play—fifteen or more years later.[45] In a 1991 essay, Hulme fastens on the page devoted to the rape accusation in Lamming's chapter "A Monster, a Child, a Slave" (in *Pleasures*) as a significant moment in Lamming's anticolonial argument. Taking Lamming's reading of the rape as an instance of his refusal of the notion that Shakespeare might be assumed to be an unquestionable locus of cultural authority, Hulme concludes that Lamming's reading of the play "is decisively better" than that offered by traditional, worshipful readers of Shakespeare. It shows "that Prospero's behaviour towards Ariel and Caliban is indefensible, that his determination to inflict humiliation on Alonso is, to say the least, unpleasant, and that his exchanges with Miranda and Caliban reveal a whole series of psychic anxieties."[46]

Prospero accuses Caliban of attempted rape, and Caliban responds,

> Would't had been done!
> Thou didst prevent me—I had peopled else
> This isle with Calibans
>
> (1.2.348–50)

Hulme cites Lamming's analysis:

> What an extraordinary way for a slave to speak to his master and in his daughter's presence. But there is a limit to accepting lies and it was the Lie contained in the charge which the man in Caliban could not allow. "I wish it were so." But he does not wish it for the mere experiment of mounting a piece of white pussy. He goes further and imagines that the consequence of such intercourse would be a fabulous increase of the population. . . . Is there a political intention at work? Does he mean that he would have numbers on his side; that he could organise resistance against this obscene, and selfish monster. . . . Did Caliban really try to lay her? This is a case where the body, in its consequence, is our only guide. Only the body could establish the truth; for if Miranda were made pregnant, we would know that someone had penetrated her. We might also know whether or no it was Caliban's child; for it is most unlikely that Prospero and his daughter could produce a brown skin baby. (*Pleasures,* 102, cited in Hulme, "Rewriting the Caribbean Past," 180)

Hulme remarks on the "spectre of incest" (181) raised by Lamming's analysis; in fact, this is a specter also raised by Mannoni's reading of the same moment and follows from his understanding of the psychic mechanism of white racism: that Prospero has projected onto Caliban his own desire and has then painted it black, as the desire of the other. This is one way "the Lie" is formed, and it rhymes with that other lie: that Caliban is a deformed, languageless monster who would naturally rape his daughter. Hulme demurs from the sacrilege in Lamming's use of the West Indian vernacular "pussy" in his re-phrasing of Prospero's charge against Caliban: "No doubt, thirty years on, we wish that Lamming had found a different way of making the gesture" (181).

No doubt; for whereas Lamming reads the lines as perhaps implying that Prospero's imputation tells us more about what is on his mind than on Caliban's, the vernacular here seems explosively misogynistic. In part, this comes from Lamming's view of Miranda as a "brainwashed" subject in the grip of her father's "propaganda" (*Pleasures*, 105). Although Lamming imagines that once, in the past, Miranda and Caliban were two innocent children, Miranda and Caliban have been separated by Prospero, he exiled to his languagelessness and bestiality, she to an inviolable purity that is the mirror of her father's belief in his total separation from the monster he has made. As brainwashed subject, Miranda evokes little sympathy in Lamming. Nonetheless, even as he responds to the political purposiveness of Caliban's response—his seeing that miscegenation would be the way to gather strength against Prospero (strength too against Prospero's belief in the unbreach-able divide that separates master and slave)—Lamming demurs, at least momentarily, from the mere reproduction of Calibans that Caliban desires. Hulme omits from his citation these sentences: "But why, we wonder, does Caliban think that the population would be Calibans? Why would they not be Mirandas? Does he mean that they should carry their father's name? But these children would be bastards and should be honoured no less with their mother's name" (*Pleasures*, 102).

In other words, for Lamming—as for Fernández Retamar as well, we might recall—the very possibility of naming the colonial subject is in ques-tion. Lamming seizes upon "bastard" as a kind of honorific, a naming akin to *mestizo* insofar as it suggests illegitimate mixture, a condition not unrelated to Lamming's own claimed genealogy of two fathers and no mother, if only in offering yet another form of sexual union outside of normative hetero-sexuality. Moreover, if Lamming catches Caliban in the grips of a patriarchal fantasy in his belief in a line of Calibans, he perhaps means to suggest that Caliban is displaying one of the effects of colonial education, for Caliban here, like Prospero, thinks of the sexual relationship as a property relationship. Indeed, one reason to focus on the rape accusation (and not just in Lamming) is that it ties together what have recently been seen as alternative possibili-ties in reading *The Tempest*—either as a colonial text or as European. For the bar placed between Caliban's and Miranda's sexual union is meant to ensure for her precisely a marriage with another European royal (to make sure that the kind of marriage forced on Claribel, which has shipwrecked the court party, never happens again). The two plots are knotted at this juncture.[47] It is therefore not only because Lamming is misogynist but also because he sees that Miranda is a kind of pawn in male-male exchanges that she quickly fades from view in his analysis.

What this also means, however, is that more is going on than the incest that Hulme and Mannoni find in this moment. For—to pick up just after the place where Hulme stops his citation—Lamming continues by noting that the specter of the brown-skinned child would mean something made by Miranda and Caliban that lies outside Prospero's control, something nonetheless that is "the result and expression of some fusion both physical and other than physical: a fusion which, within himself, Prospero needs and dreads!" (*Pleasures,* 102).

What is this dread and need? It is, in part, a recognition of bodiliness that is grossly distorted in Prospero's enslavement of Caliban, which has made him into mere body, the bodiliness that Prospero would seem to repudiate for the sake of his self-representation as mind divorced from matter: "It is in his relation to Caliban, as a physical fact of life that we are allowed to guess some of Prospero's needs. He needs this slave" (*Pleasures,* 98). It is the labor that Caliban is forced to perform and that the aristocrat disdains. It is, in these ways, a part of himself that Prospero has cut off and then re-marked in the divisions he makes: between those who are bodies and those who are minds, those who have language and those who do not. (Miranda's virginity puts her on the side of Prospero.) It is the part to which Caliban gives evidence, the "natural generosity" (107) of his gifts—of food, of showing all the wealth and resources of his island and offering them to Prospero in exchange for his paltry teaching, "this original tendency to welcome which gets Caliban into trouble" (114). It is what Caliban continues to house in himself despite all the deprivations and accusations, a spirit of "freedom" (101), an innate "seed of revolt" (98) that is the sign of an "original rooted-ness" (101) that Prospero cannot ever finally deny him. The island is his, but his in a form of belonging that is not the possessiveness and proprietariness of Prospero. Rather this belonging is an originary state before ownership, a state that would make all its inhabitants bastards. In this way, the political gesture that Caliban wrests from the rape accusation resonates beyond even the notion of gathering an army behind him. It is, in a word, that "love" that Caliban says he felt at first and that Prospero has violated. In some other world, some other time, Miranda and Caliban "could be together in a way that Miranda and her father could not. For Prospero is alone. He hates and fears and needs Caliban" (115).

Lamming thus locates the intensity of the male-male relationship that lies beneath the rape accusation in the splitting of Prospero that is the counterpart to his deformation of Caliban, his "Calibanization" (cf. *Pleasures,* 157).

With a forthrightness rarely matched in subsequent anticolonial criticism of the play, Lamming describes Prospero as "an imperialist by circumstance, a sadist by disease" (*Pleasures,* 112); the "monster" in the title of his chapter on the play is not Caliban but this raging "old man," an "obscene and selfish monster" (102). And the sign of his disease is his inability to love, his "loathsome habit of cutting people down" (113). The rape accusation is central to Lamming's analysis because it ramifies everywhere: "Caliban is . . . the occasion to which every situation, within the context of the Tempest *[sic],* must be related. No Caliban no Prospero!" (108). The refusals of Caliban, the charges against him, ramify to Prospero's retirement from rule, showing he never cared for his people; to Antonio's fault, Prospero's doing; and especially to something to which Lamming returns repeatedly, the absence of Prospero's wife, mentioned only once in the play, not even remembered by her daughter (104): "It is likely that he had never experienced any such feeling towards his wife" (113), and "Who, we are left to wonder, was really Miranda's mother? And what would she have had to say about this marvellous monster of a husband who refuses us information?" (115). Lamming connects this absent figure to another one, Caliban's mother, whom Prospero insists on calling "a so-and-so" (116). And, thus, Lamming speculates as to whether Miranda may have been a bastard and whether Prospero's claiming that Caliban is a "bastard" is how he all but tells us about his own relationship with Sycorax. "We ask ourselves why a Duke should debase himself to speak in such a way [about Sycorax]. The tone suggests an intimacy of involvement and concern which encourages speculation" (116). The rape accusation is spoken by a monster who never loved his wife or his daughter. Prospero's "disease," ramifying in every direction, implies sexual failure, sexual anxiety as his hidden truth, as well as the "deepest and most delicate bond" that ties him to Caliban (109), a "fusion" he "needs and dreads" (102). The thread of language; the accusation of rape. "Caliban haunts him in a way that is almost too deep and too intimate to communicate" (99).

Love may be the secret of the bond, but love is not the form the bond manifests. Lamming's Prospero is a "malevolent old bitch" (99), and the veiled accusation of same-sex desire is probably just that, an accusation. Nonetheless, Lamming's bastard vision of a future (which would also connect to the past from which Prospero cuts Caliban—and himself—off) could not be a site of mandatory heterosexuality, of the marriage relationship with its legitimation of property and its making of women into property. The unspeakable desire toward which Lamming points but which he never names is at once an alternative political/social formation, neither colonial nor capitalist, and an alternative sexual formation populated by bastards born of forbidden mixtures: across race, but also athwart gender, queer (male and male producing male).

Might Lamming subscribe to the vision that Fanon has toward the end of *Black Skin, White Masks?*

On the field of battle, its four corners marked by the scores of Negroes hanged by their testicles, a monument is slowly being built that promises to be majestic.

And, at the top of this monument, I can already see a white man and a black man *hand in hand*. (Fanon, 222)

Fanon's sentences are almost impossible to read. As a monument to the lynching/castrating of black men, a black man and a white man hold hands. Is this the terrifying vision of the complicity of the white-masked black man, the abhorrent spectacle (for Fanon) of male-male intimacy that is the coupling of two castrated males, one black, one homosexual? Or is it the vision of a desired future, beyond difference and alienation, of mutual recognition? "Superiority? Inferiority? Why not the quite simple attempt to touch the other, to feel the other, to explain the other to myself?" (231). As Fanon himself has argued throughout *Black Skin, White Masks,* nothing could be more fraught than what he ends by calling simple.

WATER WITH BERRIES IN'T

Lamming may glance back at a past, before colonization, when Caliban was quite other than he is now, and he may hope that something of that native love and generosity may yet serve into the future. In a chapter in *Pleasures,* "In the Beginning," recasting a scene from his 1958 novel *Of Age and Innocence,* Lamming provides a myth of origins, in which property is shared ("lan' didn't belong to nobody" [*Pleasures,* 19]), in which there is an immediate connection to the land, and in which the sexual division of labor is already in place: "Their wife cook and make bed, an' the land begin to take a human shape, turnin' soft, an' sheddin' new food wherever the Boys put down their fingers, tendin' seed an' tiny plant for what we call harvest" (19). No doubt, this serves as a model of utopic futurity, and not least because it is narrated by a group of boys who represent the various racial/ethnic/national strains of the Caribbean: Black, Indian, Chinese (and English in the scene in the novel). The possible future toward which Lamming gestures, however much it may be governed by this (masculinist) fantasy, a group of boys who may replicate the original Tribe Boys, must also be founded on the new kinds of people made by colonialism. Although these are paradigmatically called Prospero and Caliban, the model of the mixed, illegitimate being does not necessitate these gendered terms. To phrase this differently: The coupling of Prospero and Caliban cannot in any simple way produce normatively gendered figures. Even in the utopic originary moment in *Pleasures,* the family unit is extended: "An' it seem that what we refer to as family was not a mere man an' woman with the result thereof, but animals too" (19).

Lamming's 1960 novel *Season of Adventure* depicts further possibilities outside the scope of his more usual masculinist representations. The novel is

about a revolution that would reestablish relations to the land, to the peasant class, to Africa. Throughout, drums gather secret forces; the Haitian
Vodun Ceremony of the Souls is celebrated. Although the revolutionaries are
a cast of male characters—"Boys," in Lamming's privileged parlance—they
are joined by Fola, a woman who seeks to break with her European education
and her middle-class foster father, who holds a position in the "independent"
government. To propel her forward, Fola pursues a "backward glance" toward
the origins from which she has been cut off, a search to discover the identity
of her father.[48] Throughout the novel, it remains undecidable whether he was
white or black. Fola is unavoidably double, and her coming to revolutionary
consciousness is formulated in her recognition that she is "Fola and other
than Fola, meaning bastard" (174). Bastard: Fola shares Caliban's condition; doubly fathered, she also shares Lamming's. In the course of the novel,
this double and unknown father is painted by the artist Chiki as the very
image that draws support for the revolutionary cause. By placing paternity
in doubt, Lamming puts into question the apparatuses of institutionalized
heterosexuality.

Nonetheless, even as Fola is included as one of the "Boys from Forest
Reserve, the original and forgotten bastards of the new republic" (292), she
pays a price for this inclusion, virtual rape by one of the revolutionary lead-
ers (she may become the mother of a bastard). Moreover, Fola's paternity
cannot be established because her mother had sex sequentially with a white
man and a black man, one of whom fathered Fola. The white man was, for
her mother, a fantasy object come true; the black man raped her: "And so
Fola became that beauty and cherished burden which Agnes had always
borne! Fola, now fugitive as the double fatherhood no certainty can separate" (343). Lamming's genealogy for Fola may be meant to expose the way
in which "the Lie" is internalized and perpetuated. Nonetheless, his way of
imagining women outside of normative social/sexual relations involves an
abjection in which he appears to participate (a complaint justly made by
Lamming's feminist critics, one that finds a parallel in criticism of Fanon's
treatment of women of color). I would also argue that it serves as a site for
authorial identification.[49]

That doubled valence can be seen in *Of Age and Innocence,* where Shephard,
the revolutionary leader, takes an instant antipathy to Penelope, a white
woman, and violently repudiates her. Yet Penelope comes to recognize herself
in and through Shephard. Just as he must win through his own racial abjection, she must reclaim her own repudiated sexuality. Penelope is a lesbian.
She formulates the connection: "To be Shephard in spite of . . . To be Penelope
in spite of . . . To be a man in spite of . . ."[50]

Penelope's recognition through Shephard is matched in the novel by that
of another character, Mark, a black man returning to San Cristobal after European emigration. Mark is similarly mesmerized by Shephard. Like Penelope,

he keeps a diary, and his attempts to come to political consciousness are matched by hers to affirm her lesbianism. Mark remains trapped in his attempt to transform buried truths into political action. Penelope is at least able to articulate her situation. Here is a crucial entry from her diary:

> I shall always feel the mark, "in spite of," branded on my presence. Penelope in spite of . . . Penelope in spite of . . . It would be better to lose one's status completely and be seen wholly as a new thing; much better than to have one's status granted with a certain reservation. . . . I believe this is what those people who are called inferior experience, and find resentful and intolerable. . . . The Negro, the homosexual, the Jew, the worker . . . he is a man, that is never denied, but he is not quite ready for definition until these reservations are stated, and it is the reservation which separates him from himself. He is a man in spite of . . . I shall be Penelope in spite of . . . (151)

Penelope's diary entry could be read to mean that she wishes for the "mark" of her stigma to be removed, that she wishes she could overcome the split produced by the "reservation" signaled by the phrase "in spite of," as if being lesbian or black or homosexual or a worker were a condition one sought to transcend in order to be fully human—"a man" no longer divided. But, in fact, her point—and Lamming's—is just the opposite. It is, rather, that this difference must be accepted even if it means one must demand to be seen as a "wholly new thing." When Penelope and Shephard reconcile, it is through the recognition that he offers: "My rebellion begins with an acceptance of the very thing I reject, because my conduct cannot have the meaning I want to give it, if it does not accept and live through that conception by which the others now regard it. What I may succeed in doing is changing that conception of me. But I cannot ignore it" (205).

That Lamming is speaking through Shephard and Penelope is evident from the echo of their words in a passage in "The Negro Writer and His World," a piece first delivered at the First International Congress of Black Writers and Artists in Paris on September 21, 1956, on a podium that Lamming shared with Fanon.[51] Lamming speaks there of the stigmatized position of race that he occupies; fixed in the gaze of the Other, in "a category of men called Negro," the consequence is that "the eye which catches and cages him, has seen him as a man, but a man *in spite of* . . ."[52] The way "out" of this prison (which can be assimilated to the situation of linguistic placement that Lamming develops in *Pleasures*) is to reoccupy this terrain of stigma.

Lamming's point is not that he "is" black in some preordained, essential way (so much is suggested by Penelope's parallel categories, when "worker" is thought of as analogous to a sexual or racial/ethnic position); rather, it is that one must embrace the lived fact of race (or class or sexuality). This is not a matter of mere identity politics, but it is certainly political. Its most stunning realization can be found in the climactic moment toward the end of *In the*

Castle of My Skin (1953), a conversation that the protagonist G has with his friend Trumper, who has returned to Barbados from the United States. Trumper plays G a recording of Paul Robeson singing "Go Down Moses" and identifies with the "people" in that spiritual.

> "What people?" I asked. I was a bit puzzled.
>
> "My People," said Trumper. . . .
>
> "Who are your people?" I asked him. It seemed a kind of huge joke.
>
> "The Negro race," said Trumper. (295)

G is puzzled by this answer; although he understands the racial label, he does not know that it applies to him: "I understood the Negro race perfectly, but I didn't follow how I was involved." Trumper explains: "The blacks here are my people too, but they don't know it yet. You don't know it yourself" (295).

Racial identity in this formulation is something one might partake of and yet not know it; something that others might know and stigmatize a person for without that person even recognizing racial identity as the cause of the stigma. The reclamation of "My People" at this moment stands against the use of the phrase earlier in the novel, "low-down nigger people," "the enemy was My People" (26–27), words that starkly demonstrate the effect of colonial power to divide the oppressed from each other, to lead them to misidentify themselves as the source of their misery. The Barbados of *Castle* is a tense site of unrecognized class and racial division; black supervisors and overseers, a bureaucratic class of middlemen, constantly shield the white landlord from the people, who are mystified about their lack of self-possession and their powerlessness and translate it into attempts to hold on to their small shreds of misguided dignity, some spurious sense of self buried deep within the castle of the skin (as if, somehow, moral bearing explained or would ameliorate their immiseration), while they direct the violence properly due the land-lord against all those who exercise more immediate power over them (any-one positioned differentially, which is to say, potentially anyone). They live the truth that one character states: "[N]o man like to know he black" (104). These divisions of race and class are experienced through a constant sense of being scrutinized that produces self-division and stultification. Trumper cuts through all this when he delivers his "new word" (227).[53]

In other words, lack of knowledge of race and of the role it plays in their oppression functions in much the way that a sexual secret would. In *Castle,* the two are connected. Virtually the first scene of surveillance discovers boys masturbating (30); soon after, there is a brutal scene of violence, as the head teacher beats one of the boys: "'Twasn't what you could call a natural beat-ing" (43). He does not beat the boy for some supposed infraction of the rules of behavior that are constantly being enforced to erect divisions and to cause humiliations or because the boy has failed at some miserable piece of the cur-riculum designed to keep the students forever ignorant of their history. He beats the boy because the boy knows (or is assumed to know, since his mother works for the head) that the head has been beaten by his wife (she is, or is thought to be, promiscuous). For pages, Lamming details the intensities of scenes of watching, of spying out such secrets of sexual/racial/class humiliation. Later in the novel, the mystified matriarch of the village, Ma, assumes that the landlord is selling his land because of the attempted violation of his daughter by one of the boys. The attempt is a lie—"the Lie" in fact—it was a white sailor who tried to rape her. Such bad behavior by "My People" has not in fact motivated the landlord; he has been bought out by Slime, a black man who will do to his people what the colonial powers did before. Earlier in the novel, Slime is mistaken for a Moses or a Jesus. He also is propelled on his career when he is fired by the head teacher because he is suspected either of having slept with the head's wife or of knowing the person who has.

It is against the error of holding on to one's private secrets that Trumper speaks, against the mistaken belief "'bout a thing be what you make it an' think it is" (293). Trumper has a sense of systematic oppression, of external causation and connections that he arrives at through the experience of a racism in the United States more direct than anything he has known before in Barbados. As he explains to G, in the United States, a Black is called a "nigger," whereas at home, he is called "a nigger man"; the absence of one word—"man"—and the turning of the adjective of denigration into a substantive makes all the difference. As long as "man" is said, it could be assumed that there is a commonality; without "man," the fact that the universalizing noun is anything but becomes starkly clear. To embrace "My People" as one's own, as identity, is to know that one "ain't got no time to think 'bout the rights o' Man or People or whatever you choose to call it. It's the rights o' the Negro, 'cause we have gone on usin' the word the others use for us, an' now we are a different kind o' creature" (297). "A different kind of creature": G spends two pages pondering this difference and what it would take to know it. The new name here—Negro—and the new existence it entails is a version of the embodiment called "Caliban."

This embrace of difference, of the reviled self as the product of a condition that is shared, not only explains why a character like Penelope, whose lesbian desires are known to no one, nonetheless experiences her secret as stigma, but also shows how what D. A. Miller terms the "open secret" structures racial identity in a phobic world.[54] (Fortuitously, Lamming uses the phrase "open secret" in *Castle* [25] to refer to the history of slavery that lies right before anyone's eyes—if it could be seen by the villagers—in the sugar fields where they work.) Lamming's novel delivers a colonial psychology comparable to Fanon's in its sense of a subject destructured under the fully alienating gaze of an Other. The mystifications of colonialism, of racial and class oppression, are experienced as an opacity, a buried truth that functions as a sexual secret. And like the open secret, it is worn on the skin and yet not

known, imagined to reside in a "castle of the skin" as secret shame that needs
to be guarded rather than claimed as a site of strength, not abjection.

The demand here is not to "come out" but to be. It translates into more
immediate sexual and gendered terms. For among the divisions of this world
are the separations of men from women that lead to the "masculinism" of
Lamming's vision. For him, as for Fanon, the black woman is virtually unknown. Indeed, paradigmatically, in a scene close to the end of the novel, and
just as G is meditating on the castle of his skin (261), he visits a prostitute.
Rather than having sex with her, he tells her a story about a boy who liked
to give other boys a stick covered with shit. G does not pause to explain the
story to the woman; perhaps he can't. It is a scene of humiliation between
boys, but also of connection precisely through anal abjection, and perhaps a
way of naming a secret of male-male intensity. It is certainly juxtaposed to
a failed or refused scene of heterosexual encounter. Elsewhere in the novel,
colonial powers work to try to regulate heterosexual relations, to "normalize"
them in ways that violate "promiscuous" relations that are themselves also in
part the legacy of slavery. This legacy also produced G's mother, "who really
fathered me" (11). Determined to protect him from "bad" influences, to propel
him (through education) away from the village (and in fact, as he comes to
see, into the position of those who use their distance as a way of maximiz-
ing this minimal difference into a site of power), G's mother is certainly no
revolutionary. Unknowingly working to continue colonial divisions (of gender
and class), she is nonetheless in her doubly gendered position, as a mother
who fathers, the counterpart to the absent and doubled father of a novel like
Season of Adventure.

The conflicted state of consciousness that Lamming represents in his
alter ego G, whose racial identity is a secret to himself but not to those who
are responsible for his systematic oppression, follows W. E. B. Du Bois's crucial
concept of double consciousness and echoes (or perhaps anticipates) Fanon's
configuration of black skin and white mask. Deeply psychologized, it is not
a form of identitarianism that would have at its end self-reclamation or the
reinforcement of normativizing social relations. It could be related to the self-
making enjoined in the stunning sentences with which Fanon concludes *The
Wretched of the Earth:* "Let us waste no time in sterile litanies and nauseat-
ing mimicry. Leave this Europe where they are never done talking of Man,
yet murder men everywhere they find them, at the corner of every one of
their own streets, in all the corners of the globe."[55] Like Fanon, Lamming
aims at a recovery of "the whole man" (*Wretched,* 252), at a "new history of
Man" (254) that will produce the "new man" that Fanon hails as the final
word of *The Wretched of the Earth* (255). And while this recovery involves, it
appears, a wholesale repudiation of Europe, that is not quite Fanon's point.
His point is, rather, a refusal of a mimicry that would repeat the crimes of
European civilization (the prime example would be the repetition of exploi-

tation in the newly formed "independent" states run by the bourgeoisie, exemplified in *Castle* by Slime and in *Season of Adventure* by Fola's stepfather Piggott, whose nickname is "Piggy"), a refusal of European mimicry but not necessarily of what Fanon calls "the sometimes prodigious theses which Europe has put forward" (*Wretched*, 254). For Fanon, like Lamming, has been shaped by and continually engages this inheritance (call it Marx or Hegel or Lacan or Sartre). We approach, once again, the mestizo condition enunciated by Fernández Retamar, but not, it is worth noting, as it appears in his latest formulation of the Calibanic condition.

In "Caliban Speaks Five Hundred Years Later," originally delivered as a talk at U.S. universities in 1992, Fernández Retamar widens the scope of what it means to speak as Caliban and embraces "a post-Western society, authentically planetary, brotherly and sisterly, of human beings."[56] After the massive exclusions of "Caliban," it is welcome to find him speaking of "the discovery of the total human being"—which he believes was made possible by the "indispensable encounter" of 1492. This totality embraces "man, woman, pansexual, yellow, black, redskin, paleface, *mestizo,* producer (creator) rather than consumer, inhabitant of humanity, the only real mother country ('Patria es humanidad,' Martí said, restating a Stoic idea), without East or West, North or South" (171). If this sounds momentarily like Penelope's list, now extended even further, its utopic call is not made in the name of some "new" and "different" form of "humanity," as Lamming's and Fanon's are, but in a rapturous assimilation of difference into a universal sameness. This new history, if it is that, Fernández Retamar announces as "the end of pre-history and the beginning of the almost virginal history of the soul," a terrain avowedly poetic, lodged in the imagination. The conflict between Caliban and Ariel is overcome: Fernández Retamar hails Che as "the most Calibanesque of the Ariels I have ever personally met and loved," and he ends his exhortation invoking "Saint Teresa the illuminated" (171). Fernández Retamar tells all: Marxist humanist, spiritual pluralist, a multiculturalist at home in the United States.

Has Fernández Retamar become what he claimed to see in Lamming? At the least, he demonstrates something Lamming has never ceased to insist upon: that colonialism is not simply over. Here is how Lamming put it in a 1973 interview, in the context, in fact, of a discussion about *Water with Berries,* the novel in which he rewrote *The Tempest* and to which I turn in conclusion in the pages that follow:

> [T]he colonial experience is a living experience in the consciousness of these
> people. And just because the so-called colonial situation and its institutions
> may have been transferred into something else, it is a fallacy to think that
> the human-lived content of those situations are automatically transferred into
> something else, too. The experience is a continuing psychic experience that has

to be dealt with and will have to be dealt with long after the actual colonial situation formally ends.[57]

Lamming fetches the title for *Water with Berries* from the lines from *The Tempest* that he cites at the close of his discussion in *Pleasures:*

> . . . When thou cam'st first,
> Thou strok'dst me, and made much of me; wouldst give me
> Water with berries in't; and teach me how
> To name the bigger light, and how the less,
> That burn by day and night: and then I loved thee.
>
> (1.2.332–36, as cited in *Pleasures,* 117)

Water with Berries also answers some of the questions posed in *Pleasures.* Returning to his old theme of Prospero and Caliban, Lamming substitutes Prospero's wife for Prospero. Lamming has discussed this alteration in interviews, claiming that through Mrs. Gore-Brittain he represents the "impotence" of empire; claiming as well that the violence directed against her (she is killed by Teeton, one of three Caliban figures in the novel) really is meant for Prospero.[58] This attempt at ameliorating violence that is nonetheless directed at a female character—and she is not singular in this respect, since no woman in the novel is treated any better—rings hollow. So, too, those who have followed Lamming's analysis, and read the novel as a colonial allegory, have been able largely to evade what Peter Hulme, for one, notes in his discussion of the novel, that Lamming is significantly like Mannoni in highlighting the component of colonialism Hulme calls "sexual anxiety."[59] Hulme thinks the conjunction of Lamming and Mannoni fortuitous (implicitly taking up thereby a position in the charged field of Fernández Retamar's accusation). In *Water with Berries,* sexual secrecy is all but coincident with the highly sexualized structure of occlusion through which Lamming regularly represents the colonial condition.

Dependency is Teeton's condition. He lives in a room in Mrs. Gore-Brittain's house in the London suburbs, and as the novel opens, we are told "he loved this room."[60] From its first page, Teeton is trying to find a way to tell the Old Dowager (the name most usually applied to Mrs. Gore-Brittain) that he plans to return to San Cristobal. It takes him two hundred pages to get up the nerve to break up a living arrangement characterized by highly elaborate and evasive games, protocols in which as little is said as possible: an "unspoken partnership" (14), "their friendship had achieved the force and delicacy of a secret," "that concealment which continues to work when everything is known; remains transparent to all" (38). Teeton believes the old woman loves him like a son (he calls her "Gran" affectionately). She, however, sees her dead husband ("Prospero") in him; he makes her feel young. Teeton is bound to her in a guilty, shame-provoking way that he recognizes after he has told her he will leave: "[H]e was ashamed, felt sunk in shame. And it seemed to him, in the extreme lucidity of the moment, that this shame was an atmosphere in which he had always lived" (205).

Teeton comes to recognize his dependency; moreover, he comes to see it as of a piece with his entire life, beginning with "the earliest, invisible fungus of birth" (205). The shame is connected to a sense of hiding and secrecy, which he seeks now to break in returning to San Cristobal and continuing actively to pursue the work of the Secret Gathering, the revolutionary group to which he belongs and with whom he has been meeting in London during his seven years of exile. Although this secret political membership is one that Teeton guards from the Old Dowager, it is not the ultimate secret of the novel. Perhaps, by casting the Caliban-Prospero relationship as a male-female couple, Lamming invites us to read the cross-sex relationship as a dissimulation of a same-sex relationship. He certainly invites comparison of the relationship to the other sexual relationships in the novel. For each Caliban in *Water with Berries* has a troubled relationship with women.

Teeton, Roger, and Derek are Calibans in the register of *Pleasures*, Caribbean artists who fled to England: Teeton is a painter finally abandoning his career to sell his paintings to finance the Secret Gathering. Roger, a composer, copies scores. Derek, an actor, plays the part of a corpse in play after play, reduced to a mute. Although once, at Stratford, they had some success—Derek playing Othello, Teeton painting sets, and Roger providing occasional music for a scene—they seem successful no longer. As the sole citation from *The Tempest* included in the text suggests, they have been playing the part of the dead Indian that Trinculo and Stephano discuss (2.2.27ff., cited 159–60), monsters on display to make men.

In the course of the novel, as Teeton struggles to find a way of telling Mrs. Gore-Brittain that he is leaving, Roger wrestles with his wife Nicole's pregnancy. He believes, or claims to believe, that he is not the father of the child. In a privileged moment of access to Nicole's thoughts, we are led to believe that Roger's Othello act is similarly delusionary. Rather, it appears that Roger, an Indian, cannot bear the thought of the "impurity" that would be evident in the child that his white American wife would bear. Roger's fear of racial mixture is thereby a version of Teeton's dependent affection for Mrs. Gore-Brittain: Roger left San Cristobal in part because "he had inherited this horror of impurity" in revulsion against a place that "seemed to take a mad delight in celebrating the impure" (70). Nicole flees Roger—to Teeton's room—where she is discovered dead, presumably a suicide.

The discovery of Nicole's corpse precipitates Teeton, in the care of Mrs. Gore-Brittain, to fly north. Her corpse doubles one that is revealed to him in the middle of the novel, and that revelation makes apparent the structuring secret of the text, that the characters are in the grip of the (rewritten) sexual plot of *The Tempest*. Midway in the novel, Teeton has a meeting with Jeremy Rexnol Vessen-Jerme, a cultural attaché from San Cristobal. Teeton thinks Jeremy is hoping to ferret out some secrets about the Secret Gathering, as he tries to lure him (and by extension, the other Calibans) back to San Cristobal, an appeal labeled a "tropical variation of the treason of the clerks" (92). The scene abjects Jeremy. His "enigma of colour" (86), his presumed attempt to pass, his lackey relation to the spuriously "independent" regime—all abject him through the various charges lodged in his elaborate name: royalism, pseudo-British/aristocratic hyphenation; vassalage; disease ("germ"). Jeremy has not come to find out about Teeton's political affiliates, however; rather, he has come to deliver the news that Teeton's wife, whom he left when he left the island, has committed suicide.

This is the corpse that Jeremy delivers. Teeton's wife is named Randa, a truncated "Miranda." His history of abandonment of her coincides with his "desertion" (18) of the Secret Gathering. Seven years before, he had been apprehended and faced long-term imprisonment, perhaps death.[61] Randa had saved him by sleeping with the American ambassador; he had fled from her "betrayal"; he had betrayed his comrades. Thus, Teeton's political relationship, his guilt about it, is related to his guilt about Randa, whereas her "guilt" (sleeping with the enemy) would seem to replay Miranda's threatened cross-coupling (as well as Nicole's supposed adultery). Teeton has never talked about his wife to anyone. No wonder, then, that Mrs. Gore-Brittain sees her husband in him, for he too was someone who never minded his wife (as we know and as Lamming underscores in his reading of Prospero's character). Moreover, her Prospero got his perverse sexual thrills by putting his wife in a coffin and glimpsing her naked body beneath the funeral veils (182). Jeremy delivers such a corpse to Teeton; Nicole deposits hers in his room.

The heated atmosphere of these sexual revelations goes even further. For however much Lamming has claimed that Jeremy should be read as a figure of all that would be repellent in someone who sold out politically, he is also a figure of intense interest.[62] The scene with Jeremy, like many elsewhere in Lamming's works, is fraught with the unspeakable, evasive remarks, intense stares: "Teeton couldn't keep his eyes away" (87). "'I'm glad to see you again,' said Teeton, and immediately regretted what he had said" (88). There is an old "friendship" between them (87) adding weight to Jeremy's sentence "You never wrote me" (96). As Jeremy delivers the news of Randa's death and forces Teeton to speak about his wife's sexual relationship with the American ambassador, Teeton lashes back at Jeremy, accusing him of having had sex with the German ambassador. Jeremy admits he was tempted but denies the charge (his overdetermined name, however, seems to deny the denial).

What is the force of this homosexual accusation? In part, it functions the way scenes of abjected sexuality do in Lamming's 1954 novel *The Emigrants*. The malaise of new Caribbean immigrants in London is registered sexually;

in unhappy marriages, infidelities, and, especially, in nonheterosexual forms of behavior: for example, a white man who can only get excited when in bed with a black man; his female partner in this ménage à trois who prefers women; lesbianism that leads to murder. In the usual plotting device of a kind of national romance that has been often noted in so-called Third World novels, sexual relations gone awry allegorize the sociopolitical situation. (Lamming, however, never writes a novel in which normative monogamous heterosexual relations signify national health; the marriage plot is not his).[63] But in the case of Jeremy, more than abjection seems involved:

> The pearl was about to find its owner. Teeton heard some previous knowledge return; and recognised, for the first time, the echoes of sexual torment he had aroused by hinting at an intimacy which Jeremy had shared with the German ambassador. Teeton felt a trifle embarrassed. (101)

If these sentences mean that Teeton sees Randa's behavior in Jeremy's, the charge against Jeremy recoils onto Teeton. But the sentences do not quite deliver that equation; they remain opaque even as they claim to offer a recognition and a restoral of the pearl to its owner. Whose sexual torment has been aroused? Do the sentences imply that Jeremy would have slept with the enemy, as Randa had, in order to save Teeton? That the "friendship" of Teeton and Jeremy was a sexual union? That Jeremy betrayed Teeton by his attraction to the German? Is Teeton recognizing how far astray he went when he abandoned his wife, his friend, and his comrades and fled to England and the bosom of Mrs. Gore-Brittain?

Teeton's response to Jeremy is further flight, to Hampstead Heath. There, in a hallucinatory scene in which he recalls meeting Randa at the Ceremony of Souls and in which Jeremy's face bears down upon him, he meets another woman with a past. She is Myra (named much later in the novel), the other half of Randa, and her story furthers *The Tempest* connection. She tells of her years on the island, her father's tutelage, the arrival of a stranger, the attack and murder of her father, the attack upon herself organized by her father's "servant" (neither the name "Prospero" nor the name "Caliban" ever appears in the novel), and her gang rape, including rape by his dogs.

Myra's abjection moves Teeton; he identifies with her story, recognizing in her motherlessness his own fatherlessness (147). Aroused by her, he nonetheless refuses to give in to sexual impulse: "[H]e would abandon the ordinarily accepted role of masculine initiative. It was a foolish notion at any time" (148). Lamming has it both ways, of course: engineering the scene of Myra's abjection as well as of her redemption (or, more to the point, Teeton's) through a "sacred" act of abstention. Myra would seal their nonsexual union by thrusting Teeton's hand into her womb, she thinks, guiding it "cruelly into the barren grave of her cunt so that he might discover for himself the future of skeletons which he was now so eager to idolise" (153). There is no going back, nor can they go forward through a heterosexual embrace.

What follows are even more revelations about the skeletons in the closet. After Mrs. Gore-Brittain carries Teeton off, he learns that Myra had been abducted to San Cristobal by her father in retaliation for his wife's adultery. To Miranda's question in *The Tempest,* Lamming answers no: He was not her father; his brother was. The brother, who pilots Teeton and Mrs. Gore-Brittain on their northward flight, is named Fernando, at once "Antonio" and "Ferdinand." Not only has he slept with his brother's wife and fathered the bastard Myra, but Myra has slept with him. Fernando retells Myra's story to Teeton, adding more lurid details:

> Perhaps you can imagine how they made the hounds violate her sex. The animals. The very creatures which had been her fondest pets. Those monsters stirred up the animals' lust for her; and let them loose over her body. Just as they had seen their master do with some of them. His own field servants. Oh, yes, my brother, come from the same blessed loins, the same privilege and blood; my brother himself had made this devil's crime a common sport upon his servants. Male and female alike. Trained his hounds to mount a human sex. That monster. (228)

The sliding syntax of Fernando's speech attempts to make what "Caliban" did to "Miranda" a reenactment of Prospero's own perversity, as he made his servants—male and female alike—have bestial, sodomitical sex, the devil's crime. Fernando's accusation is akin to other explosions late in the novel, racial reviling, for example, that stings Derek because he had not been prepared for it (215). As in *Castle,* Lamming delays the surfacing of the violence that underlies the tense opacities of the situations in which his characters move as if in a fog. Derek, it should be noted, ends his act as a corpse by coming alive on stage and attempting to rape an actress there.[64]

The recoils in Fernando's speech, the loops of abjection and monstrosity that catch Prospero and Caliban and that are enacted on the body of Myra, parallel the scene with Jeremy, the crosshatching of his homosexuality with Randa's abjected act of sexual betrayal/salvation. The abjection of such desires as monstrous cannot be separated from the terrifying appeal of untoward couplings. Fernando's speech traces the circuits of monstrous contact that circulate through the body of the violated woman who serves as the conduit joining Prospero, his brother, and the natives. Here, Prospero and Caliban are one, monstrously alike. This monstrosity is, arguably, another way of naming the different kind of creature more hopefully embraced at the end of *Castle.* It glimpses, however horrifically, a different future, a world where fathers are indeterminable, in which female desire, ravaged and rampant, is not bounded by marriage. The production of bastards, cross-race and cross-species couples, and the lesbianism of a Penelope are among the possibilities of such a future.[65]

In such highly conflicted ways, Lamming makes it possible to imagine the generation of Caliban outside of normative modes of social/sexual reproduction. If Caliban was born in the relationship with Prospero, and made in abjection, bondage, and slavery, the future cannot simply reclaim a time before colonialism nor aim for its simple reversal; rather, it seeks a reordering that, from the point of view of colonial powers, must appear as the very refusal of the terms of colonial order and a rejection of the abjection and stigma that it places on alternatives. In Lamming's works, these alternative social and sexual arrangements follow from the union of Prospero and Caliban, love offered and refused, and are manifest in the Secret Gathering of the Boys, or the even more secreted lines of identification with figurations of violated female sexuality. This futurity has a past that Lamming is reclaiming and rewriting; it is found in *The Tempest*.

CALIBAN'S "WOMAN"

CALIBAN'S "WOMAN"

. . . THE SON THAT HE DID LITTOUR HEERE

Fernando names "Prospero" a monster in *Water with Berries* (as does Lamming in "A Monster, a Child, a Slave" in *Pleasures of Exile*), invoking the word used most often in *The Tempest* to describe Caliban. The transfer to Prospero is heard faintly in the play when Alonso responds to Prospero's punishing torments with "it is monstrous, monstrous" (3.3.95). The thirty-four uses of "monster" in *The Tempest* are unprecedented in Shakespeare's corpus; no other play has more than half a dozen.[1] This repeated nomination makes Caliban an apt site for monster theory (to recall the title of an anthology edited by Jeffrey Jerome Cohen), since the character embodies many of the points Cohen elaborates in the seven theses on monster culture that he offers.[2] Monster difference may begin with the illegibility of bodily shape, but it quickly attaches itself to racial and sexual difference and to violations of gendered norms and licit forms of coupling.

In *Shakespeare's Caliban,* the Vaughans respond to the repeated use of "monster" and the descriptions of Caliban that associate him with a variety of nonhuman forms by asking whether Caliban is human.[3] It is a question with obvious pertinence to the discussion G has with Trumper in *In the Castle of My Skin:* Is "the Negro" human, a man, or "a different kind of creature" altogether? In Fernando's virulent characterization in *Water with Berries,* inhumanity is associated with bestiality, with forms of sexual coupling across species and without regard to gendered, heterosexual propriety. Such accusations, prompted by *The Tempest,* are sites across a wide range of twentieth-century Caribbean texts for revaluing the possibilities of the new kinds of persons (outside the orbit of the human) created by colonial encounters.

Maintaining that Shakespeare's Caliban is human despite the vilification

41

to which he is subject throughout the play, the Vaughans adduce as proof the lines in which Caliban is first described in *The Tempest,* as Prospero and Ariel discuss the circumstances of his birth. It was in fact their discussion that drew my attention to a hitherto uncommented-upon crux in the Folio text of the play, its sole authoritative source. The Vaughans print the Folio lines as follows:

> . . . Then was this Island
> (Save for the Son that [s]he did littour heere,
> A frekelld whelpe, hag-borne) not honour'd with
> A humane shape

depending for the bracketed *s* in "[s]he" on an emendation, which, they note, Nicholas Rowe first supplied in 1709.[4] The Vaughans take these lines to establish that Caliban (unlike his mother, presumably) is the first "humane shape" to inhabit the island. The lines are somewhat more equivocal, however, as Hulme points out in *Colonial Encounters,* since they admit Caliban's humanity by way of "an eminently misreadable double negative."[5] Moreover, as Hulme argues, when Miranda tallies how many other humans she has seen, Caliban counts as human the first time (at 1.2.446) but not the second (3.1.50–51), leaving Caliban in the position of being "a man and not a man according to Miranda's calculations" (107). Hulme's phrasing echoes Lamming's: "Caliban is Man and other than Man."[6]

What is further striking in this context is the fact that, at least as printed throughout the seventeenth century, Caliban's birth is ascribed to a mother who has become male in gender in the lines describing the moment of parturition (elsewhere there is no question of her gender). If Caliban is born human, he is born from a mother who is not. Sycorax lacks a "humane shape," and littering is not a human form of giving birth; her inhumanness would seem to be underscored by the gender change. Were one to take the male pronoun seriously, it would necessarily call into question at least one biblical definition of the human: man, born of woman. Caliban's humanity would not be assured if his mother was not a woman. A monster begets a monster.

That it is possible to take the Folio line seriously (that is, not simply to regard "he" as a printer's error that Rowe corrected) is attested by the textual history of the play as seen in the subsequent seventeenth-century folios. For if this is merely a mistake, it is remarkable that it was not until Rowe that it was caught. As Matthew W. Black and Matthias A. Shaaber argue, "[T]he three later folios are not imperfect reprints of F1, F2, and F3 respectively, but critical editions in exactly the same sense that Rowe's is a critical edition."[7] The anonymous editors of 1632, 1664, and 1685 each consulted the previous folio for the basic copytext, much as Rowe based his text on F4. Each, moreover, was unlikely to have had much, if anything, in the way of authoritative textual material in support of emendations to the previous texts. That is, in most cases, changes in the subsequent folios (when they are not new errors) are emendations, many of which modern editors happily accept, that can be chalked up to common sense, to what Black and Shaaber refer to nicely as "the fitness of things" (25). A "mistake" of the kind that appears at this moment in the Folio text of *The Tempest* is exactly the type of error one might have supposed would have been caught in one of the later seventeenth-century folios, which, Black and Shaaber argue, were especially good at catching obvious typographical errors (even if some new ones inevitably were introduced as well) and correcting the kind of solecism the misgendering of Sycorax would seem to represent.

Here are the lines as they appear in the seventeenth-century folio editions:

> Then was this island
> (Save for the Sunne that he did littour heere,
> A frekelld whelpe, hag-borne) not honour'd with
> A humane shape.
>
> (F2 [1632])

> Then was this Island
> (Save for the Sun that he did littour here.
> A frekelld whelp, hag-born) not honour'd with
> A humane shape.
>
> (F3 [1664])

> Then was this Island
> (Save for the Sun that he did littour here.
> A frekel'd whelp, hag-born) not honour'd with
> A human shape.
>
> (F4 [1685])

The fullest modern collation can be found in Frank Kermode's 1954 Arden edition: "282. son] Sunne F2; Sun F3, F4. she] Rowe; he F, Ff,"[8] and it barely suggests what the seventeenth-century texts reveal: that these lines were not printed unchanged from edition to edition. Although the pronoun "he" does remain constant, instead of correcting that "obvious mistake," a new "mistake" was potentially introduced in the lines, the replacement of F1's "Son" with the "Sunne" of F2, modernized in spelling to "Sun" in F3 and F4. If the change from "son" to "sun" was an attempt to relocate birth from a mortal male to an appropriately mythological level (Zeus gives birth to Athena, for instance, as does Adam to Eve), that response would seem less to register the "wrongness" of the gender than to want, somehow, to accommodate it. More to the point: Changes in punctuation (which serve, in fact, to confuse the sense of the lines, another sign that the "obvious" mistake of "he" for "she" was not perceived as such), in capitalization, and in the spelling of "frekelld," "hag-borne," and "humane" make it evident that these lines were not merely reset from folio to folio. Each time, changes were made; in every instance, therefore, there was the opportunity to correct "he" to "she." That Rowe first did it, then, is not quite to be ascribed to common sense.[9]

How, then, to account for the persistence of this "error" in seventeenth-century editions of *The Tempest*? Perhaps by appealing to the "fitness of things" that Black and Shaaber invoke, the fitness, that is, that necessitates that the monstrous offspring of a witch (in these lines, bestially born [whelped and littered] and freakishly marked [freckled]—a maculate conception) must be prodigiously and unnaturally mothered, but perhaps, too, by seeing that this gendered change has its counterparts elsewhere in the play. Stephen Orgel has described some lines from Prospero's narration of the past to Miranda earlier in this scene as articulating a birth fantasy: Miranda's saving presence on board their vessel of exile is turned by Prospero into the instrument by which he gives birth:[10]

MIRANDA: Alack, what trouble
Was I then to you!
PROSPERO: O, a cherubin
Thou wast that did preserve me. Thou didst smile,
Infused with a fortitude from heaven,
When I have decked the sea with drops full salt,
Under my burden groaned, which raised in me
An undergoing stomach to bear up
Against what should ensue.

                    (1.2.151–58)

"*Burden,*" Orgel notes, "is the contents of the womb," and "*groaning* is a lying in." Throughout the play, Orgel argues, Prospero does his best to efface and to denigrate women and to appropriate their powers.[11] (In some tension with this erasure and appropriation, Miranda is in the angelic position, spirit to his matter, strength and fortitude to his tears; she seems not merely responsible for "infusing" him but also for his final erection, as he reports himself "raised" and bearing "up.") The lines, therefore, much as they appropriate femaleness (or, more specifically, maternal function),[12] also would seem to be giving and taking maleness to and from Miranda. Orgel explains it this way: "The women of Shakespeare's plays, of course, are adolescent boys" (57)—hence Shakespeare's identification with nominally female characters. Such gender dislocations as these, Orgel suggests, might be relocated by remembering the fact that Miranda was played by a boy and that thus these exchanges between genders are nonetheless exchanges between persons of the same gender.

In the context of such an argument, the gendering of Sycorax as male at the moment of her delivery of Caliban might mirror Prospero's seizure of female territory, or the stage that, Orgel reminds us, only appears to offer a world of "he's" and "she's." Rowe's emendation, then, especially as it is printed by the Vaughans—"[s]he"—nicely brackets and subordinates the female to the male. Their proper bibliographic form is Prospero's plot in small. If, as we have seen, modern readings of *The Tempest* from an anticolonialist position are "masculinist," they might be said to repeat the masculinist plot of the play—a plot, as we have seen (and will be seeing further), that requires interrogation rather than emulation.

And yet nowhere, save in the line Rowe emended, is Sycorax anything but female. If the Folio line is not a mistake, its "fitness" would lie not in the naturalizing of gender that would remind us that all of Shakespeare's actors were genitally male but in the "fitting" of monstrous birth to monstrous womb, which would suggest a different plot altogether. This is not to deny Orgel's suggestion that Prospero indulges in a birth fantasy and, by extension, encroaches on female/maternal powers. That suggestion is not merely borne out in the lines from act 1, scene 2 cited above but can also be seen in many of the assumptions of his power, whether he is delivering Ariel from a tree (something Sycorax, he claims, could not do, and in which he acts as a midwife in a scene reminiscent of the birth of Adonis from Myrrha, his incestuous mother: "It was mine art, / When I arrived and heard thee, that made gape / The pine and let thee out" [1.2.291–93]) or uttering lines in the monologue in act 5, scene 1 (originally spoken by Ovid's Medea), lines that mark his closest moment of identification with Sycorax. If, then, the male gendering of Sycorax is to be explained, one route might lie through the identification of magicians in the play, cutting across the denials that structure Prospero's assumptions (or those of Kermode's introduction to his Arden edition, with its detailed discriminations of black and white magic).

It has to be remembered, however, that Prospero has two seemingly opposing but actually congruent gender strategies in the play. One involves strongly marking gender difference and denigrating females (this is especially the case with Sycorax, but it is there when Prospero turns on Miranda and calls her his foot); the other is through the erasure of gender difference, the subsumption of women into his part, as in the lines we have already considered, in order to produce identification—or the "brainwashing" Lamming reads in Miranda's vilification of Caliban (or in her falling for the man her father has chosen for her). Hulme struggles in *Colonial Encounters* to drive a wedge between Prospero's play and *The Tempest*. In much the same way, to read the crux about the gender of Sycorax only as another instance of the appropriation of female under the sign of male and the erasure of gendered difference is to fold one play into another and thereby to subscribe to a patriarchal phantasm.[13] If one were to treat the Folio's "mistake" as not mistaken, it would be with the aim of preserving and exploring what is monstrous in this moment rather than seeing it as part of the way Prospero's seamless power overrides all opposition, including gendered difference. Such a critical gesture would be congruent with an anticolonialist seizure of the territory of denigration as a site of reclamation.

Equally important would be this: The genital identification between adult male actor and boy actor is not necessarily a bottom line; that boys could play women's parts has everything to do with the fact that there was a strong identification between boys and women that depended not on genitals but on congruent positions of social subordination. Boys are not simply male but neither are they female.[14] This gender lability, secured by social hierarchy, may reflect on the monstrosity of Sycorax and her son, but it is certainly not equivalent to Sycorax's monstrosity, nor does it explain it. Hence, Sycorax's violation of the biological function that differentiates males and females cannot be equated with Prospero's appropriative violation of that same boundary from the opposite direction.[15] At the moment that Sycorax performs the uniquely female act of giving birth, she encroaches on territory that Prospero claims for himself; her monstrosity is registered as gender change and recorded in the form her offspring takes. Were she to serve as a mirror of Prospero at this moment, it would not bolster the assurance of male power, the subordination and incorporation of the female within the male. Rather, it would suggest something quite different: not the opposite of female monstrosity (for that opposition is included in the masculinist plot) but a monstrosity whose excess is registered in female masculinity and in the equivocal shape of its progeny. I return to the initial question: *Is* Caliban human? Is he *properly* male?

I do not know whether such questions vexed Sir Arthur Quiller-Couch and John Dover Wilson in their editorial labors for their 1921 Cambridge edition of the play,[16] but Dover Wilson is quite adamant about the inappropriateness of the lines we have been considering. Here is how they appear in the Cambridge edition:

>   Then was this island,
> (Save for the son that she did litter here,
> A freckled whelp, hag-born) not honoured with
> A human shape.
> ARIEL: Yes: Caliban her son.
> PROSPERO: Dull thing, I say so: he, that Caliban
> Whom now I keep in service.

And here is Dover Wilson's comment on them:

(1) This passage is a violent digression. (2) Omit it and the context flows straight on. (3) The F. has a comma after "in service," which is absurd. . . . Is it possible to avoid the conclusion that these five lines are an addition, a piece of patchwork, designed to compensate for a rent elsewhere in this section? The reason for their introduction is not far to seek; Caliban is to enter at l.321, and this is the first mention of his name! (83)

Dover Wilson maintained (unconvincingly to most subsequent editors) that F1 preserves a text of *The Tempest* reworked for court performance and that this is especially apparent in act 1, scene 2, where Prospero's prolix narrations replace an earlier play that dramatized what he narrates. Nonetheless, this is the only passage that Dover Wilson explicitly and vehemently declares to be not merely an awkward covering over of the earlier text but a spurious segment in need of excision. Although his comment does not address the *she/he* problem dutifully noted elsewhere in the edition, I assume that Dover Wilson is exercised by the monstrous birth of Caliban in this passage. He would have the discussion flow "straight on" without introducing the birth of Caliban as an object of contention between Prospero and Ariel. "Omit it"; then there could be no echo of the birth of Caliban in the birth of Ariel from the tree. Then, one could not hear that Prospero's threat to "rend an oak / And peg thee in his knotty entrails" (1.2.294–95) reverses and echoes Sycorax's delivery. The tree to which Prospero would return Ariel is gendered male; the spot in which Ariel would be confined, "his knotty entrails."

What exercises Dover Wilson here is perhaps revealed in the gloss he supplies for 2.2.163–64 (Cambridge edition lineation): "*An abominable monster!* Exclamation perhaps caused by a glimpse of Caliban from behind, as he bends to kiss Stephano's foot." The Vaughans, we recall, cited the lines describing Caliban's birth in order to argue that however monstrous Caliban is, he is nonetheless human, and they detail for pages the various configurations that haunt this claim: Caliban as tortoise or fish as well as, more generally, Caliban as bestial, as being of demonic origin, and the like, not to mention the stage traditions in which Caliban has appeared in various non- or subhuman forms. Nowhere, however, does the play seem to suggest that Caliban is particularly monstrous when seen from the rear, and although what Dover Wilson presumably has in mind is the degradation and abasement of his offer of service to Stephano (as compared, presumably, to the propriety, in the Cambridge editor's eyes, of his service to Prospero), this political abjection is described in charged physical terms. This is Dover Wilson's fantasy, his glimpsing of a monstrosity that I would be willing to credit, not as a "fact" but as a consequence of the line of associations that I have pursued here: Caliban born from a male mother, a witch, born monstrously and as a monster, born in a manner that is echoed in the threatened return of Ariel to his origins in the entrails of a tree; Caliban, in short, as sodomite.

Fernando, in *Water with Berries,* had been an imprisoned spectator forced to watch "this devil's crime" enacted on Myra's body. It is just such a crime that Dover Wilson glimpses in the offing, as Caliban abominably, monstrously debases himself. This association is perhaps not all that surprising given colonialist discourses of Shakespeare's time. For as often as it was assumed that all natives were cannibals, another charge was leveled: "[T]hey are all sodomites."[17] Charges against "natives" are multiply determined (by political and theological discourses). Insofar as "evidence" for sodomy was produced, it seized upon a sign of inhumanity akin to the *he/she* crux: various indigenous forms of male cross-dressing, which, we might recall, Fanon reports in the Martinique of his youth. Fanon's remark begins to suggest that the claim that all natives are sodomites is not a charge simply to be relegated to the early history of New World colonization. As M. Jacqui Alexander suggests in her important essays on the role of laws regulating sexuality in the modern Caribbean, the accusation remains foundational, and its deflection persists in the minds of legislators bent on claiming heterosexual propriety, limiting women's rights and agency within marriage, and cordoning all forms of nonmarital and nonheterosexual behaviors to a zone of the criminally unnatural.[18]

As Alexander demonstrates, 1990s legislation outlawing as "sodomy" consensual relations between adult same-sex couples is a form of neocolonialism, and not just because it continues colonialist denigrations of same-sex sexuality. Legislators seek to tie the legitimacy of "independent" states in the Caribbean to a male-dominated, heterosexual, middle-class fantasy of a norm that is not merely domestic but imbricated in economic relations to international capital: "Making the nation-state safe for multinational corporations is commensurate with making it safe for heterosexuality," Alexander argues ("Erotic Autonomy," 67). These ongoing socioeconomic consequences also point back to the period when *The Tempest* was written. Witches were invariably poor women, often single women removed from male supervision.[19] And although sodomy accusations may have spectacularly lighted on the bodies of aristocrats like the Earl of Castlehaven in 1634, they were, as Alan Bray suggests in "Homosexuality and the Signs of Male Friendship in Elizabethan England," most likely to fall upon those of lower-class origins who were thought to have been raised to power in illegitimate ways (Gaveston in Christopher Marlowe's *Edward II* would be a most telling literary example). "Sodomy" was a way to police social mobility against a rising class.[20] It was also an accusation ready to seize on foreign bodies; in *Homosexuality in Renaissance England,* Bray reports the case of "Domingo Cassedon Drago a negro" and assumes that "the colour of his skin" made him a likely suspect.[21] Valerie Traub has found similar instances surrounding the "tribade."[22]

"Sodomy," in these examples, functions as a proto-racial marker, as does the claim that "they are all sodomites." Modern Caribbean repudiations of the sodomite are, in this context, akin to the remark of the character in

Lamming's *In the Castle of My Skin* who avers that "no one like to know he black"—a response that arises when Blacks are represented as "low-down nigger people" and believe this to be true.[23] Similarly, when same-sex sex is represented as rape and as degradation that is claimed to be indicative of native nature and being, identification with so-called sodomites would seem impossible. The point here—as with the accusation that Caliban was a would-be rapist, which, in *Water with Berries,* is entangled with the ascription of sodomy/bestiality in the scene of Myra's rape—would be to imagine these forms of sexuality apart from their colonialist representation as monstrosity. Much as *mestizaje* is not *necessarily* an act of unacceptable violence or one of supine passive acceptance, being black is not some sign of moral failure, a stigma one would wish to have removed. The alternative, in all these cases, is to erase the "in spite of," to refuse the regulatory colonial/sexual norm, and to embrace the term of denigration. These possibilities, as we shall soon see, are available in twentieth-century Caribbean texts.

A FREKELLD WHELPE, HAG-BORNE

The *he/she* "error" in Prospero's speech comes in the midst of his vehement attempts to fix in Ariel's mind the condition of imprisonment in which Prospero discovered him, to remind him of something that Ariel says he cannot forget, "the foul witch Sycorax" (1.2.257). "Witch" is, of course, the accusation made over and again, "this damned witch Sycorax" (1.2.263), and her monstrous maternity is on Prospero's lips a moment later when he demands that Caliban appear: "Thou poisonous slave, got by the devil himself / Upon thy wicked dam, come forth!" (1.2.319–20). The damned "dam": As with "litter," Sycorax's maternity is demonized as animal procreation.[24]

Just as the *he/she* "error" exceeds the normative limits of gendered difference in conjuring up the monstrosity of Sycorax's maternity, similar tactics of the unspeakable surround her powers:

> This damned witch Sycorax,
> For mischiefs manifold and sorceries terrible
> To enter human hearing, from Algiers
> Thou know'st was banished.
>
> (1.2.263–66)

Thus Prospero "reminds" Ariel (of what Ariel had in fact told him), holding back from the audience what "mischief" she had performed or what she did that remains too terrible to hear. Albeit late in the play, Prospero does name some of her powers: She "could control the moon, make flows and ebbs, / And deal in her command without her power" (5.1.270–71). These specifications are perhaps only possible once Prospero has, earlier in the same scene, in the lines derived from Ovid's Medea, claimed such powers as his own (5.1.33–57).

But more often, the power of Sycorax remains unspeakable, as are the acts, whatever they may have been, that Ariel refused to perform: "[T]hou wast a spirit too delicate / To act her earthy and abhorred commands" (1.2.272–73). Likewise, her ability to escape the death punishment that her deeds appeared to warrant in Algiers hangs on an elusive "one thing she did" (1.2.266).[25] When, retrospectively, Caliban is introduced, the "one thing" seems to translate into "she was pregnant" (as Orgel glosses the line), and Sycorax's ability to conceive is brought into the orbit of things that cannot be mentioned rather than being recognized as something that women uniquely can do.[26]

When the witch Sycorax is brought into the domain of the unspeakable, she would seem to enter the charged terrain of sodomy, a crime definitionally not to be spoken of among Christians.[27] To understand further the logic at work in *The Tempest*, one wishes that the conjunction of witchcraft and sodomy had been the subject of sustained historical scrutiny. Arthur Evans's *Witchcraft and the Gay Counterculture*[28] has these ambitions, but it is deeply flawed by its desire to prove a transhistorical identity between witches and homosexuals as part of an ages-long subversive counterculture. While there is little to be said for this thesis (neither witches nor "homosexuals" constituted a self-conscious collectivity), some of Evans's references to moments when the two crimes coincided are indisputable. For example, the inquisitors in Avignon in 1582 condemned as "sodomy" fornication between men and succubi and between women and incubi.[29] As Jeffrey Richards notes, by the mid–thirteenth century, "homosexuality became an inevitable concomitant of accusations of heresy and witchcraft," no doubt thanks in part to the Papal bull *Vox in Rama* (1233), from which he quotes this description of the witches' Sabbath: "[T]hose present indulge in the most loathsome sensuality, having no regard to sex. If there are more men than women, men satisfy one another's depraved appetites, women do the same for each other."[30] E. William Monter, in his several studies of the Inquisition in various locales during the sixteenth and seventeenth centuries, has supported these linkages, noting, for instance, that of fifty-eight witches convicted in Fribourg in the early seventeenth century, eight were condemned as sodomites (there seems to have been no distinction between male witches and sodomites). Accusations of witchcraft, sodomy, and infanticide, Monter further concludes, circulate differentially, as ways of policing the category of the "unnatural."[31] What makes this connection easy can be gleaned from one description of a sodomite as someone "committing heresy with his body,"[32] for it suggests how the bodily act of witchcraft—sex with the devil—that preoccupies Prospero and many other commentators might easily overlap with the category of sodomy (not least because witchcraft was most usually a charge leveled against women, sodomy against men). Paul Brown has commented on Prospero's sexual obsessiveness and his desire to regulate others' sexuality, and this feature of the character—the way his "project" plays out in the realm of sexual behavior—perhaps bears comparison with the fevered imaginations

of those who described the supposed goings-on at the witches' Sabbath. As
G. R. Quaife summarizes, these scenes regularly included "anal and oral sex,
homosexuality, bestiality, mutual masturbation, group sex and incest."[33]

These connections were not confined to the Continent or to the fantasies
of the Catholic church. As Retha Warnicke has pointed out, the first person
condemned under the sodomy statute passed in England in 1533 (the statute
that made sodomy a felony rather than a matter of church control), Walter
Lord Hungerford, was found guilty not only of having had sex with his male
servants and with his daughter but also of having plotted against the king
with the help of witches.[34] This particular configuration is, in certain respects,
no surprise, insofar as sexual crimes in the period are regularly linked to
state crimes. Warnicke summons up the 1540 case against Hungerford in the
context of her study of the fall of Anne Boleyn, arguing that the queen's delivery of a monstrous, abortive fetus sent Anne Boleyn to the block. Warnicke
details the "sexual heresy" that surrounded these events, in which charges
of incest, adultery, and sodomy (between the queen's supposed lovers) followed upon this monstrous birth. The fetus, that is, did not just represent
the queen's infidelity to the king, and therefore her treason; the other sexual
charges followed upon it and served to explain the monster. We are close here,
I think, to the imagination that links the witch Sycorax with the monstrous
Caliban.

We are also in a position to see that the charge explicitly lodged against
Caliban—the attempted rape of Miranda—would not, in these contexts (as
it would be presumed to do in a more modern instance), obviate a charge of
sodomy. The category "sodomy" was capacious enough to include virtually
any form of sexual union that exceeded the regulatory norm of procreative
sex between married partners. Indeed, as Alan Bray has stressed, sodomy is
thought of as an uncontrollable excess of sexual desire, a debauchery that
is not defined by the gender (or species) of the object chosen.

I would not argue for an equation so much as for a relay from witchcraft
to sodomy in the monstrous conception and birth of Caliban. The connection
was a point of some contention in the literature on witchcraft. For although
the witches' Sabbath often was viewed as a feverishly sexual event, there was
much debate about whether actual physical union between a (mortal) witch
and the devil was possible, and, if so, whether such unions were capable of
producing offspring. (Reginald Scot, in arguing against these sexual possibilities in *The Discoverie of Witchcraft* [1584], nonetheless provides a fair sam-
pling of the arguments made on both sides.) When such unions were deemed
possible, the sex acts of witches (as well as acts of bestiality performed by
sodomites) were thought to result in monstrous births.

Bray pursues these associations in *Homosexuality in Renaissance England,*
pointing both to the ways sodomy overlapped with demonism (in terms of assumptions about destructiveness, heresy, and the like), especially in the "per-
sistent motif that the child of the witch's diabolical union is a sodomite" (21),

and to the ways witchcraft and sodomy diverged. One of his main examples for the latter point is, significantly for the discussion here, Michael Drayton's "Moone-Calfe." The term, of course, is applied repeatedly to Caliban in *The Tempest* to indicate his monstrous, abortive appearance. In Drayton's poem, the devil fathers monstrous offspring, twins who are masculine-feminines, androgynes and hermaphrodites.[35] The male twin is explicitly a sodomite, and the devil, frightened by the monster (line 170), appears to share the divine disgust at the sin of Sodom (lines 317–24). Bray argues that Drayton's devil expresses a commonplace; insofar as demonic offspring were nonetheless the product of heterosexual unions, sodomy suggested a form of sexual relationship that exceeded what was already a kind of demonic parody of proper sex. This point is made in the *Malleus Maleficarum,* that handbook of beliefs about witchcraft, where it is claimed that "nowhere do we read that Incubi and Succubi fell into vices against nature," for sodomy is a sin of such "very great enormity . . . that all devils, of whatsoever order, abominate and think shame to commit such actions."[36] Sodomy and witchcraft cannot be equated; they touch at a border of abomination and of the unspeakable.[37]

In this context, it is worth recalling, too, that the pregnant wombs of condemned witches were opened to reveal within them horrific and deformed spawn. These assumptions are most fully in play around the trial of Anne Hutchison in early seventeenth-century New England. Charges of heresy are materialized in her body as well as in her followers', who are also revealed as witches by their abortive and monstrous offspring (one of whom, like Caliban, is described as having horns, claws, and scales). "Mistris Hutchison . . . brought forth not one . . . but . . . 30. monstrous births or thereabouts, at once; some of them bigger, some lesser, some of one shape, some of another; few of any perfect shape, none at all of them (as farre as I could ever learne) of humane shape."[38] Next to the birth described by this Puritan minister, Sycorax's "littering" is almost demure, and the equivocal declaration that her offspring bears a human shape is almost humane. Yet he is also insistently called monster and mooncalf, just as his mother is never anything but a witch, one whose crime Prospero cannot name.

Sex with the devil, the accusation Prospero *can* utter, may therefore euphemize what remains unnamable and unspeakable about what Sycorax did, what she brought forth. A "demi-devil," Prospero ultimately calls Caliban (5.1.272), only half a devil, and thus "a bastard one" (5.1.273). "Bastard" names that horrific condition of mixture; but of what? "This thing of darkness I / Acknowledge mine" (5.1.275–76). Is Caliban born of Prospero and Sycorax, as Lamming speculated? (Orgel, in his gloss to 1.2.266, notes of Prospero's "one thing she did" that "the problematic element in the passage is not its meaning, but the obliqueness of Prospero's reference to it," as if, perhaps, he has something to hide.) Or is he born of the devil and Sycorax, as Prospero charges? And what of the remark that Sebastian makes as Prospero whispers to him and Antonio that he knows that they plotted together to kill Alonso. How does he know? Because he put the idea in their heads? Because Ariel told him? "The devil speaks in him" (5.1.129) is Sebastian's response to Prospero's preternatural knowledge. Has Prospero encroached so far (even into the treasonous and sodomitical plotting of Sebastian and Antonio) that, rather than being in control of the unspeakable, he has come to embody it, as Lamming's Fernando suggested when he saw "Caliban" and his dogs doing to Myra what "Prospero" had done to his servants, male and female?

The relay from sodomite to witch may remain a subject for further historical scrutiny. But one path of connection between Sycorax and Caliban that ramifies into the present survives. As Makeda Silvera points out, in Jamaica the term for "strong women," for independent women, and for women who love other women is "man royal" or "sodomite." The former term masculinizes; the latter, Silvera assumes, is fetched from Genesis, applied from colonialist religious discourse of condemnation of the "natives" to a word spoken by Jamaicans in disparagement of other Jamaicans. "Dread words. So dread that women dare not use these words to name themselves. These were the names given to women by men to describe aspects of our lives that men neither understand nor approved. . . . How could a Caribbean woman claim the name?" she asks, and not merely rhetorically.[39]

If Dover Wilson's recoil at the "abominable monster" is, then, a recoil at what is most abominable—the sin beyond all others—he turns from asskissing (metaphorically, to spell out what foot-licking means at 2.2.143) to even more unspeakable acts, literalizing in his presumed view of Caliban's bottom the horror that he sees him performing. (Ass-kissing is the devil's kiss, the sign the witch makes of her devotion to her master, a sign of political allegiance, just as Caliban's is.) There is, however, another moment in the play that prepares and makes "fit" Dover Wilson's reaction to the abominable monster. Here is how Prospero describes what Antonio did:

> bend
> The dukedom yet unbowed—alas, poor Milan!—
> To most ignoble stooping.
>
> (1.2.114–16)

Dover Wilson's gloss on Caliban inadvertently glosses these lines, and the implications here are complex, not least because "Milan" is at once the name for both Antonio and Prospero in the substitution that has as yet not quite differentiated one from the other. (As Prospero is the rightful holder of the dukedom, it is in his interest not to make that distinction.) The lines thus represent the submission of Milan to Naples as either Antonio's voluntary or Prospero's enforced violation. Here Dover Wilson's reading of Caliban's abject position finds a more immediately plausible object: this scene of "ignoble stooping" does invite a view from the rear; indeed, it suggests that Milan has been taken from behind, mastered anally. The connections between sodomy and treason make this implication utterly unexceptionable.[40]

Dover Wilson's reading of the scene of Caliban's submission to Stephano thus ramifies another way in which betrayal of political propriety is registered in the play as sodomitical submission. It also connects back to the equivocal description of Caliban's birth. Finally, it connects to an episode in the play in which Caliban is represented as anally receptive and as anally productive. In act 2, scene 2, Trinculo creeps under Caliban's gaberdine. "Misery acquaints a man with strange bedfellows" (2.2.38), he remarks as he does so, using a word that can refer to same-sex sleeping partners. Stephano comes across this four-legged figure, and assumes that "this is some monster of the isle" (2.2.63). Yet the monstrosity here (the reiterated use of "monster" begins in this scene), although initially registered by Trinculo in terms of the animal/ human nature of Caliban and by Stephano in terms of the Mandevillian man of Ind, lies in what Stephano finally sees, Trinculo and Caliban making the beast with two backs, "an incarnation of the monstrous in lovemaking," as David Sundelson comments, not distancing himself from what he takes Stephano's attitude to be.[41] Stephano euphemizes the situation when he regards the four-legged creature before him as doubly mouthed, though he marks one mouth as forward and the other as backward. His exchange of mouth and anus fits nicely with a figure whose name respells "cannibal" or with colonialist allegations that all New World inhabitants are cannibals and sodomites. At the moment when Trinculo emerges at Stephano's command to "come forth" (2.2.98; the line echoes Prospero's delivery of Ariel as well as his first command to Caliban [1.2.315]), Stephano asks, "How cam'st thou to be the siege of this mooncalf? Can he vent Trinculos?" (2.2.101–2). In witnessing an excremental birth, Stephano seems to imagine that Caliban has swallowed Trinculo and now is delivering him whole. Alimentary canal and birth canal meet in a fantasy of anal delivery that we have already seen in Prospero's threat to return Ariel to the entrails of the tree from which he was delivered. This scene of venting realizes the "mistake" about Caliban's origins that the seventeenth-century folios repeated and that Rowe "corrected." Here a male mother, the mooncalf who is the abortive and monstrous child of the witch, gives birth anally. Orgel is one of the few editors to record that "siege" means "excrement" and "vent," "defecate." Only George Steevens, in a note to the line in his 1778 edition of the play, registers (phobically, to be sure) any sense of what is going on here: "*Siege* signifies *stool* in every sense of the word, and is here used in the dirtiest." Is it any wonder that when we last see Caliban in the company of his coconspirators Stephano and Trinculo, they have been mired in a pool of "horse-piss" (4.1.198)? It is a fitting end for the "foul conspiracy / Of the beast Caliban and his confederates" (4.1.139–40); exit pursued by dogs.

So RARE A WONDERED FATHER, AND A WIFE

As we have seen, it is not Caliban's birth but his alleged rape attempt that is the charged site in anticolonial readings of *The Tempest* for mixtures that may entail new—and monstrous—combinations. Significantly, a recognized (and much discussed) crux in *The Tempest* speaks to this charge; it can also be connected, or so I would argue, to the problematic "he/she" of 1.2.282. I refer to the line spoken by Ferdinand at his betrothal to Miranda and to "a reading whose time has come," to cite the final words of the "bibliographic coda" to Orgel's "Prospero's Wife" (64). Orgel endorses the bibliographic evidence presented by Jeanne Addison Roberts to the effect that Ferdinand's lines during the masque in act 4, scene 1, "So rare a wondered father, and a wise, / Makes this place paradise" (the reading to be found in virtually all previous twentieth-century editions of the play), originally read "So rare a wondered father and a wife / Makes this place paradise" (the reading adopted in Orgel's edition at 4.1.123–24).[42] Orgel summarizes Roberts's findings in his note to line 123: "[E]arly in the print run, the cross-bar of the f broke off, transforming 'wife' to 'wise'. Several copies of the Folio show the letter in the process of breaking." This explains why most copies of the Folio read "wise," why the variant "wife," when recorded, has seemed merely a variant, and hence why most modern editions of the play read "wise." Orgel's endorsement of Roberts's work is not made only on the bibliographical grounds that "wife" is what F1 read originally and authoritatively; it is also part of a "collaborative" effort of the kind that he remarks throughout his essay, the understanding that what makes for the "rightness" of a reading is never simply the facts but the climate in which they are available and visible. Orgel's reading marks a time when feminist readings allowed one to see things that were formerly invisible, and the restoration of "wife" in these lines thus restores Miranda to the scene of celebration. It marks her presence, whereas the traditional reading had absented her from Ferdinand's rapt response, which begins, after all, "Let me live here ever" (4.1.122).

This commendable endorsement of the feminist impulse arguably to be found in Roberts's essay (it is not stated explicitly) requires some further consideration. One must keep in mind that Ferdinand's response at this moment in the betrothal masque might serve to measure him against Miranda's "suitor" who has been summarily rejected as a rapist, that it is the Caliban in Ferdinand who has been charged as a usurper and demeaned to do servile labor and whose own rapacious sexual impulses for Miranda (graphically registered even as they are ostensibly repudiated at 4.1.23–31), and for the city-state she represents, have been legitimized by this betrothal. As Mark Thornton Burnett remarks in an essay on the discourse of monstrosity in *The Tempest*, Prospero's warnings to Ferdinand about his potential to violate Miranda hold up the specter of the "loathly" issue of such illegitimate intercourse (4.1.21), thereby recalling Caliban's projected progeny of Calibans as well as the monster birth of fecal matter in the scene when he vents Trinculo.[43] Miranda herself enthusiastically endorses the terms of her marriage to Ferdinand, as is suggested by her response in the chess-playing scene to her future husband's empire building. (The "masculinization" of Miranda in Prospero's account of her saving powers may find its terminus in her willingness to call whatever false power grabbing Ferdinand pursues "fair play" [5.1.175].) The "feminist" gesture that would include Miranda more visibly in this marriage would in these respects further the marriage plot that casts Caliban (and with him, non-Europeans and nonaristocrats) as an impossible, monstrous mate.

In "Prospero's Wife," Orgel claims that the variant "wife" was lost before Roberts found it: "[A]fter 1895 the wife became invisible: bibliographers lost the variant, and textual critics consistently denied its existence until Roberts pointed it out" (64). The variant is occasionally recorded (for example, in Morton Luce's 1901 Arden edition and in Northrop Frye's Penguin text);[44] it is simply not adopted. Frank Kermode has it both ways: He places a question mark after noting the variant and recommends "further inquiry," but he ends his gloss by commenting that "the true reading may be *wife* after all." Kermode did not have before him the evidence that Roberts presents. He relied, instead, on the easy mistake of confusing *f* and long *s* in the printing process, and lacking hard evidence, he only allows "wife" in his note, not in the text. Howard Horace Furness, in the 1892 variorum edition of the play, cites with approval one Grant White, who opines that to print "wife" here would "degrade the poetical feeling of the passage" and then goes on to make the revealing comment that in his own copy of F1 he cannot tell by looking whether the line reads "wife" or "wise."[45] How he comes to print *wise* fully supports Orgel's contention that we see only what we are prepared to see: "Personally," Furness writes, "seeing that I much prefer *wise,* I incline to believe that it is 'wise' in my copy." Presumably editors after Furness who print "wise" have shared his preference.

What preference is this, however? Not the one Kermode records in his note: "[W]e may think that in this Adam-like situation, Ferdinand must have said *wife,*" nor the preference to be found in all eighteenth-century editions from Rowe on, which, in fact, print "wife." Rowe probably did not emend the line on the basis of consultation of a copy of F1 that read "wife"; his emendation was made on what Orgel calls "logical grounds" ("Prospero's Wife," 63), the logic, presumably, that Kermode suggests: that it is difficult to believe that at the moment of his betrothal, having declared a desire to live in paradise forever, Ferdinand would omit Miranda.

It is this logic, however, coupled with the fact that eighteenth-century editors invariably printed "wife," that must lead us to ask what time has come when the line reads "wife" in Orgel's edition. Eighteenth-century editors, who assumed that Shakespeare wrote "wise," were not restoring his intended meaning but modernizing the text, and indeed, doing so in ways that I would argue parallel the normalizing of gender that Rowe performed in assigning a feminine pronoun to Sycorax at the moment of her delivery of Caliban. The eighteenth-century readings of the play, that is, are not feminist interventions. They put "wife" there to assure the domestic relationship and the propriety of Ferdinand's remarks. They make his future wife present in order to police the male-male relations between Ferdinand and Prospero. Ferdinand's celebration of his "father" is only saved from excess within the context of marriage. This must be granted at least as a caveat against the assumption that restoring "wife" restores a woman to the text; "wife" is not Miranda's name but her function. Although she has been given the illusion that she has freely chosen Ferdinand, she marries him as part of her father's designs. (Ferdinand is Prospero's choice, and it is his desire that his daughter enacts and makes legitimate.) As Orgel astutely argues, Prospero's aim in marrying them is to legitimize what Antonio did, placing Milan beneath Naples; now Milan will not fall to "ignoble stooping" because of the marriage alliance. What this further assures is the propriety of male-male relations, and it manages the hierarchy between Naples and Milan through the homosocial configuration that Eve Kosofsky Sedgwick identified in *Between Men*.[46] What Rowe and his followers presumably heard in Ferdinand's espousal of his "wise" father was the possibility that his desire for Prospero repeated Antonio's for Alonso.

This "danger" is not entirely removed when the correct reading is restored. "And a wife" is, at best, an addition, and "so rare a wondered" seems primarily, if not exclusively, to refer to Prospero. As "wife," Miranda is clearly in a subordinate relationship to her husband-to-be and to her father. Moreover, as Orgel notes, as do other editors as well, "wondered," as an adjective describing Prospero, echoes Miranda's name, an object of admiration subject to such punning elsewhere in the play. If "wondered" means someone who can produce wonders, then Prospero's magic show and his magical daughter are equated. They are both wonders that he produces. What Ferdinand is celebrating in the lines is Prospero's art and his production of a child, his male maternity. Miranda is, as it were, already in the phrase "rare a wondered," and her separation out in "and a wife" is almost as redundant and self-referential as the line would be if it read "and a wise." Putting "wife" in the line—as presumably Shakespeare did—hardly ensures her independence or her existence outside the patriarchal arrangements being celebrated here as Prospero hands her over to his chosen son-in-law.

The difference between eighteenth-century texts and the original F1 reading "and a wife" is that Rowe and his followers presumably believed that by supplying "wife," the intensity of the male-male bond had been diluted and made acceptable; F1 does not quite have those guarantees. In the sex/gender system in which Shakespeare writes, the choice between male and female lovers is not as supposedly exclusive as it comes to be imagined in the eighteenth century. The facts that in these lines these two relations come together as one and that the emphasis is on the father (he gets the adjectives; he comes first in Ferdinand's utterance) are also marked by the verb form "makes": Father and wife are here a single entity. Rowe and subsequent eighteenth-century editors emend "makes" to "make"; this separation, the grammatical propriety of making father and wife two subjects, furthers the work of heterosexual propriety. Shakespeare's more fluid grammar cannot be taken unequivocally to be making father and wife a single subject, but it cannot be ruled out either.

Hence, the modern reinsertion of "wife" in this line does not by itself mean that some time of enlightened gender relations has necessarily arrived. Rather, as Orgel argues, it is only within a certain climate of reading that the line would have feminist force. But to my mind, it is not enough simply to get Miranda back into this line. A feminist reading of the lines might well involve a critique of the limits under which Miranda appears here (as that appendage called wife) and of the kinds of class and racial proprieties being secured. Such a reading might seek to underscore the work that this heterosexual arrangement is being called upon to do: making acceptable male intimacy that might otherwise give (homophobic) critics pause. The lines, of course, have a further caution for the critical project I pursue: To note that F1 here marks the difference between the properly homosocial and the overcharged and dangerously sodomitical (which it seeks to situate everywhere but in Prospero's relations with men) through Miranda's body means that one cannot simply celebrate Shakespearean sexuality for the ways in which it takes male-male and male-female relations in stride, as complementary and not as mutually exclusive. There are hierarchies of power in these lines: between father and child, between men and women. Some men (above all, Caliban) and some women (Sycorax) stand outside all these forms of "order" as sites of "monstrous" inhuman excess. The elucidation of the possibilities of gendered/ sexual relations has already bracketed what remains unspeakable.

To Ferdinand's ecstatic lines, Prospero replies, "Sweet, now, silence!" (4.1.124), a gentle and affectionate command at which some editors have balked (Dover Wilson assigns the line to Miranda), although Orgel quite usefully points out that men do call each other "sweet" in Shakespeare. Dover Wilson reassigns the lines, but like all other modern editors, he prints "wise" here too (the "variant" "wife" does not appear in the Cambridge edition). This returns us to a question raised above: Why have modern editors preferred "wise" to "wife"? It is not, presumably, because it allows the eros of the situation between Prospero and Ferdinand to be registered. Indeed, when Grant White claimed that printing "wife" would constitute a "degradation" of "poetic feeling," one can see that the presence of "wife" for him would necessarily introduce a sexual element and thus mar "poetic feeling" between men, which presumably cannot ever be supposed to have an erotic component. Here Kermode's remark on the "Adam-like situation" of Ferdinand-in-paradise could be further glossed. In this line, Prospero is, as it were, the sole source of Miranda, just as in the biblical myth woman comes from man. This is the paradisial version of what, were Sycorax male, would be the abomination of Caliban's monstrous birth, and it is a component of the version of the misogyny that led Andrew Marvell to write, "Two Paradises 'twere in one / To live in Paradise alone"[47] and, indeed, also of the ages-long Christian tradition that lays the blame for the Fall on woman and that yearns for the time before the creation of Eve, when Adam's only playmate was his creator. White's recoil at "wife" is a response to these yearnings for a paradise of male solitude. Kermode's more tempered remark about Ferdinand in paradise participates in eighteenth-century normativizing heterosexualization. The time that has come, when "wife" appears in these lines, certainly disputes the virulent misogyny of White; however, it remains in danger of simply reproducing heterosexuality and thus also insisting upon limits for women (they were meant for marriage) and for men (relations between them could never be sexual ones).

It thus seems necessary to recognize the limits of interventions in the name of feminism or of gay affirmation that can be made by way of the Shakespearean text and to recognize, moreover, that these adjudications tacitly suppose that the sexuality of a Sycorax or of a Caliban would be beyond the pale. Nonetheless, within its modest limit as a political move, Orgel's restoration of "wife" and his declaration that it is a reading whose time has come would seem utterly unexceptionable. Could anyone after Orgel print "wise"? The answer, of course, is yes. In the single-volume Shakespeare produced for Oxford by Gary Taylor and Stanley Wells at the same moment that Orgel was preparing his Oxford edition of *The Tempest,* 4.1.123 of *The Tempest* reads "wise." John Jowett provides the explanation for that decision in the 1987 textual commentary for the edition. His note is worth reprinting here:

> Roberts . . . showed that there was progressive damage to the crossbar of "f" during printing. Error is none the less so easy that the matter does not end there. Whereas previous critics were divided as to what F actually read, almost all preferred "wise" as the more convincing reading. F's pararhyme is suspicious; *wise / paradise* is a Shakespearian rhyme. "Wife" gives trite sense and demands two grammatical licences: that "So rare a wondered" is extended to qualify "a wife", and that "Makes" has a plural subject.[48]

This is an extraordinary note. Though it seems to start by accepting Roberts's findings, it immediately introduces an unspecified sense of "error." One presumes that Jowett has in mind something like Kermode's note on how easily *f* and long *s* can be confused in the printing process. What is extraordinary here, then, is that Jowett appears to accept the fact that F1 originally read "wife," but he also wants to entertain the possibility that it did so in error (presumably as a compositor's error). Thus, he in essence argues that even though what Roberts saw really did happen, that is beside the point. What would normally be accounted a strong bibliographical demonstration is policed, I assume because of the context that Orgel adduces: that Roberts's work supports a feminist agenda. (It hardly needs to be pointed out that the field of bibliography has been and remains heavily male-dominated.)[49] Although Jowett's category of "error" is the closest he comes to making a bibliographic objection to Roberts, the logic of his claim leads to an undermining of any bibliographic protocols. If any reading of a text could be in error (and, of course, any can), then the textual/bibliographic evidence, even when it appears incontrovertible (that F1 originally read "wife"), can only be subject to interpretation. It is, then, presumably (though this is unstated) the "bias" in Roberts's presumed interpretive stance that Jowett questions.

Having established "wife"/"wise" as variants (rather than "wife" as the reading and "wise" as a variant produced by mechanical breakdown), Jowett appeals to "previous critics" who have found "wise" more "convincing." Here, as with "error," who or what is involved goes unspecified. It is not really a matter of criticism that is being determined here; rather, it is a matter of editorial practice and of the overwhelming numbers of editors ("almost all") who can be mobilized on the side of "wise." "Convincing" is of course a question-begging term: convincing in terms of the bibliographic evidence? Surely not, unless the fact that more copies of F1 read "wise" than "wife" (which must be true) is taken as constituting a bibliographic fact. Convincing from some critical predisposition? Presumably, but that is not where the note concludes. It concludes, rather, on questions of what is genuinely Shakespearean at the level of writing practice.[50] Yet one must suspect any claims to know what is Shakespearean, especially, as here, when the rhyme is so heavily loaded semantically. Things that rhyme should, and "wife" does not.

Speaking as some masculinist embodiment of the law, Jowett takes extraordinary license, although he is probably right that "rare a wondered" does not extend to "wife." This is the only moment where Jowett's reading coincides with my own, and it points to the limits, as I have remarked, of reclaiming the line and "wife" in the name of feminism. Indeed, it just might be that Jowett will not have "wife" because if the word were there, it would show that Shakespeare did not have a properly modern, liberal, and egalitarian view of women. I have already addressed the point about "makes." It is amazing that a Shakespearean editor has not noticed how often Shakespeare's subjects and verbs do not agree—has not noticed, that is, that Shakespeare had not learned eighteenth-century grammar. For of course, what is remarkable about Jowett's note is that it goes beyond the eighteenth-century editors in demanding from the lines grammatical propriety of the kind Rowe and his followers provided by changing "makes" into "make." In short, much as

Jowett's reading is motivated by an animus against Roberts and the collaborative efforts that Orgel endorses in positing the time that has come, his
eighteenth-century editorial procedures (he does not rely on F1 as his copytext here; rather, he relies on the weight of tradition; he expects Shakespeare
to use modern grammar) are *also* aimed at a propriety of gendered relations.
Because a wife should be praised at least as much as a father-in-law and
should be an independent subject (and not just grammatically), the line
must read "wise." Otherwise, Shakespeare might have been a misogynist and
a patriarchal poet. Jowett's reading, then, is *also* a product of the time that
has come.

That time may have passed. For the Vaughans' 1999 Arden edition of *The
Tempest* (as well as the 1999 Pelican edition) prints "wise." Although the
Vaughans indicate that they "would like to read the word as 'wife'" and that
they believe Shakespeare probably intended that word, "wise" is neverthe-
less, they claim, what F1 reads, perhaps because of a handwriting error in
transcribing the text; perhaps because of a compositor's error in reading the
manuscript; perhaps because of a slip of the compositor's hand as he went
to fetch an *f* and instead drew a long *s* from the neighboring box; perhaps,
indeed, because an *f,* so easily indistinguishable from a long *s,* had been
misfiled.[51] Still, as far as they are concerned, F1 reads "wise," and they must
follow their copytext: "We opt for the Folio's 'wise' because there is no compelling reason to alter a word that is as plausible as the alternative in syntax
and logic, more feasible in rhyme and more compatible with the technology of
Jacobean type-founding" (138).

The last item on their list points, in fact, to why they have been led to reject Roberts's claims. In his introduction to the second edition of the *Norton
Facsimile of the First Folio of Shakespeare,* Peter Blayney has asserted that
the two copies of F1 in the Folger collection (numbers 6 and 73) that Roberts
claimed had "wife" do not:

> As a typographer I cannot agree that what resembles a crossbar in Folger cop-
> ies 6 and 73 is in fact part of the type at all, or that the marks in the supposedly
> intermediate copies were impressed by the remnants of the crossbar. But the
> way in which ink is deposited by metal type on damp paper is too specialized
> a subject to examine in detail here, and proper resolution of the matter must
> await a much more thorough discussion.[52]

Orgel had announced a reading whose time had come. But in the face of
Blayney's assertion of expertise, time seems to have stopped in awe at the
male's mastery and at the secrets he guards. Where Roberts had seen a bar
breaking, Blayney sees "blotted ink" (as the Vaughans summarize his claim,
137). What we see is not a neutral "matter" awaiting "proper resolution."
There is no way of knowing what the particular piece of metal responsible

for the *f*/*s* quandary may or may not have done. But, as Stephen Orgel has remarked to me, the fact remains that to anyone's eyes two copies of F1 in the Folger appear to read "wife," a material fact that may well have extended beyond those two copies. Bar or blot? Miranda married or marred? Is Blayney's argument compelling because now, to have Miranda there as "wife," she would be smirched, blackened, Sycoraxed?

I NEVER SAW A WOMAN / BUT ONLY SYCORAX, MY DAM, AND SHE

The bibliographical dilemmas in *The Tempest* around "he"/"she" and "wife"/ "wise" suggest how complex a mapping of sex and gender will necessarily be in the volatile contexts of the play's writing and rewritings. These dilemmas reveal that the charge of "masculinism" variously and justifiably deployed (against Fernández Retamar or Fanon or Lamming—or Shakespeare) is not one charge. The grids of intelligibility of the homosocial multiply as it fractures along the lines of an excoriated homosexuality (tantamount to a racialization when tied to Caliban and to the figuration of male maternity attached both to him and to Sycorax) and a facilitating homoerotics. In this light, the paralleling offered by Lamming's Penelope as she extends her self-understanding to include "the Negro, the Jew, the homosexual, the worker"[53] can only be a preliminary gesture in mapping such complexities, since it supposes discrete categories rather than complex relationships between and among them. The bibliographical dilemmas intimate, rather, that the meaning of any differential or diacritical term will be subject to its relationship to other terms. "Correcting" the "he"/"she" "error" to "she" does not remove all the ways in which Sycorax is positioned in the play to fail to represent a normative instance of femininity: a monstrous mother, engaged in illicit sex, not coupled with a known father. Nor does it make it possible to imagine that Caliban, however "masculine" his rape attempt is, can be comprehended along the lines of what is permissible to Ferdinand, that he ever could be invited into the relationship affirmed at the betrothal. Restoring Miranda to the text as "wife" will potentially assure her the normative position denied to Sycorax, but it will not quite do what various forms of feminism might wish: grant her personhood or autonomy, usher her into an egalitarian, unsubordinated position. Hailing Miranda's inclusion as "wife" therefore speaks to the form of feminism that would have a woman in the text, no matter what the cost might be—a demand for "representation" that is sounded frequently in criticisms of *The Tempest* that deplore feminine absence in the text, as if presence were itself a guarantee of recognition.[54]

It is such an absence that Rob Nixon underscores in the conclusion to his essay "Caribbean and African Appropriations of *The Tempest*" when he explains why "the plot ran out" after the 1970s ushered in "independence" and attendant neocolonialism:

The play's declining pertinence to contemporary Africa and the Caribbean has been exacerbated by the difficulty of wresting from it any role for female defiance or leadership in a period when protest is coming increasingly from that quarter. Given that Caliban is without a female counterpart in his oppression and rebellion, and given the largely autobiographical cast of African and Caribbean appropriations of the play, it follows that all the writers who quarried from *The Tempest* an expression of their lot should have been men.[55]

Nixon's argument seems to preclude what nonetheless has happened: engagement with the play by feminists, who see more possibilities than he can imagine.[56] In the pages that follow, such possibilities will be mapped. These are prompted by the figure of the sodomite and witch in *The Tempest* and lead to the "monstrous" possibilities of nonnormative sexualities to be found in the work of a number of Caribbean writers and theorists (and in various forms of Caribbean social/sexual arrangements).

Let us begin with a striking intervention—one that complicates the terms of feminism—exemplified by a stunning 1990 essay by Sylvia Wynter that attempts, as the title of her essay puts it, to move "Beyond Miranda's Meanings: Un/Silencing the 'Demonic Ground' of Caliban's 'Woman.'"[57] Wynter's essay appeared as the afterword to an important inaugural gathering of work by Caribbean feminists, and her intervention means to serve as a caution to an enterprise that she reframes. Rather than assuming that feminism is given or available to or desirable for Caribbean women, Wynter moves toward an identification with "Caliban's 'woman,'" eschewing the terrains of various kinds of absence—Caliban's father or mother, most pointedly—in favor of a figure she wishes to disentangle from "Luce Irigaray's purely Western assumption of a universal category, 'woman'" (355). Wynter's argument hinges on the claim that the absence of a "mate" for Caliban in *The Tempest* is of a different order than the absence of his mother or father. She conjures "Caliban's 'woman'" into existence (indeed, writes *as* her), thereby actively rewriting the play. The scare quotes around her designation signal a distinction between "Caliban's 'woman'" and Miranda as a representative of "woman," a dehomogenization of terms that could be compared to the textual cruxes we have examined in *The Tempest*. Wynter's is a feminist reading that nonetheless resists those feminist readings of the play that would forge identifications with Miranda. For however much Miranda is Prospero's tool, she is also Caliban's accuser and reviler. As Wynter puts it, the displacement of gender as the ultimate ground of explanation is shown in the play through "the relations of enforced dominance and subordination between Miranda, though 'female,' and Caliban, though 'male'" (358). Miranda, that is, is doubly placed, and her gender signifies doubly: in relationship to her father and future husband, on the one hand, and to Caliban, on the other.

The position that Wynter takes has disturbed other feminists. Indeed, the "beyond" of her title is a gesture she has made in relationship to other discourses, with equally abrasive effects. In "Beyond the Categories of the Master Conception: The Counterdoctrine of the Jamesian Poiesis," for example, she challenges the usual readings of C. L. R. James by insisting that Marxist paradigms of class and economic determinism will not explain the full complexity of his project.[58] In "On Disenchanting Discourse: 'Minority' Literary Criticism and Beyond," an essay for an issue of *Cultural Critique* devoted to the question of "minority discourse," Wynter's "beyond" is tantamount to a refusal of a term ("minority") that, like "feminism," nonetheless enables her movement "beyond."[59] That this "beyond" communicates with positions we have been mapping is suggested by her "Beyond the Word of Man: Glissant and the New Discourse of the Antilles": "This new terrain and perspective was to define the Antillean educated elite, opening them/us onto the possibility of a new intellectual front, outside the orthodox 'fronts' of Marxism, liberal nationalism, and feminism."[60] This new space and location is as much an outside as it is a "demonic ground," an unrecognized foundation instantiated by a figure like "Caliban's 'woman.'"[61]

Wynter comes to the positions she takes through a career that parallels that of many Caribbean intellectuals of her generation. A year younger than Lamming, she, like him, left the Caribbean for Europe. For her, as for him, the 1930s worker uprisings were decisive events. As she puts it in an extraordinary interview conducted by David Scott, "that movement determined everything I was going to be or have been" (hence, her break with Marxism nonetheless conserves it as well, although not in some entirely doctrinaire form).[62] Her 1962 novel *The Hills of Hebron* traces various post–World War I social movements that were precursors to the uprisings of the 1930s. Her time in Europe was, as it was for Lamming, a period of discovery of "what it was to be this new thing: a Jamaican, a West Indian" ("Interview," 130). Like Lamming, she quickly came to see the ways in which social uprising was co-opted by the emergent black bourgeoisie and nationalist groups. Like Lamming's Trumper, she came to understand the contours of "race" better by comparing the U.S. system of stark black/white opposition to the more complex equilibrations of color and class in the Caribbean. Wynter refers often to Lamming and to other notable figures of her generation, such as Fanon and Edouard Glissant; conversely, she was recognized immediately by her contemporaries as a major intellectual force in her own right.[63]

Although Wynter has been a playwright and a novelist (as well as a dancer and an actress), she has also (unlike Lamming) briefly worked in the government in her native Jamaica. Her central career has been in academia: At the University of London, she specialized in Spanish Golden Age literature; subsequently she took up a teaching post in that field at the University of the West Indies in Jamaica. In the 1970s, she came to the United States, holding positions first at the University of California, San Diego, and then at Stanford, from which she retired after teaching there for some twenty years. The move to the United States enabled her to branch out from her "field" (in which she has published a number of essays) and into the broader terrain mapped in the numerous essays she has published since the 1980s as she has pursued a project whose aim is nothing less than "to rethink the origins of the modern world, and with it, the origins of different categories of people."[64] For her, the novelty she seeks to articulate is, as it is for Lamming or C. L. R. James or Fernández Retamar—or, indeed, for Glissant, as she quotes and glosses his project—based in colonialism: "[B]ecause Antillean societies 'did not pre-exist the colonial act, but were literally the creation of that act,' one cannot 'speak of structures disturbed by colonialism, of traditions that have been uprooted'" ("Beyond the Word," 643). This refusal of pristine precolonial traditions, however, is not a refusal of Africa or of "race," since the springboard for a beyond follows from the new beginning of the colonial venture, which, Wynter never forgets, was also the beginning of a new era of denigration institutionalized in slavery and the plantation system. Extending Glissant, Wynter takes Shakespeare's Caliban "as a symbol of the first 'native' or nihilated (*néan-tisé*) peoples." She seizes upon Trumper's "new word" in *In the Castle of My Skin* and upon his articulation of a position beyond and outside the position of "man" as her platform for a thinking beyond the categorical and on to the new ground of the *"radical alterity"* announced in the refusal of the rights of man.[65] Her search, by means of "Caliban's 'Woman,'" is for "a new 'model' projected from a new 'native' standpoint" (BMM, 364), launched, that is, from a site of negation that is literally unimaginable in *The Tempest*, "Caliban's physiognomically complementary mate" (BMM, 360). Phrased that way, it might appear that Wynter is merely demanding representation of the black woman, that the plot she seeks opposes mixture and would further racial division and heteronormativity. But in fact, her "model" exceeds all those normative assumptions. Indeed, in "'A Different Kind of Creature,'" Wynter challenges *créolité* and proponents of *mestizaje* as insufficiently radical, by which she seems to mean that such programs, *unrooted* from the nonnormative position of negation, aim at a false homogeneity akin to the "neoliberal humanist piety of *multiculturalism*" that she deplores and that does not mark out for her a path to a position "beyond."[66]

To understand Wynter's radical thought and the place of her reading of *The Tempest* in it, it is crucial to see that she reads the play as an index to a global transformation that begins for her in the Renaissance.[67] In "Beyond Miranda's Meanings," she is intent on one piece of a complex system that she has sketched in numerous essays, mapping how racial difference came to be installed as a categorical difference that overrode, rewrote, and re-placed gender difference: "Caliban, as an incarnation of a new category of the human, that of the subordinated 'irrational' and 'savage' *native* is now constituted as the lack of the 'rational' Prospero, and the now capable-of-rationality Miranda, by the Otherness of his/its *physiognomic* 'monster' difference" (BMM, 358). This is why Miranda's gender is no guarantee of difference in terms of racial positioning.[68] As Wynter understands it, the medieval binary of spirit/flesh was easily assimilable to the binarism of gender, just as it was also allied to divisions between the clergy and laity. For her, the "discovery" of Columbus is very literally a global event of vast displacements in which the "non-homogeneity of the human," first mapped in distinctions between spirit and flesh or man and woman ("1492," 36), underwent a crucial secularizing permutation. She insists that when Columbus broke with a vision of the limits of the habitable world and Copernicus similarly declared that the world was made for the sake of humans (rather than for God), a new terrain of the human arose, one that divided persons not so much by gender as by rational capacity: "[W]ith the shift to the secular, the primary code of difference now became that between 'men' and 'natives,' with the traditional 'male' and 'female' distinctions now coming to play a secondary—if none the less powerful—reinforcing role" (BMM, 358). She in turn links this development to the kinds of self-realization—detached from assurances of noble blood that had supported earlier distinctions—that empowered the emergent bourgeois class. A series of nonrational "native" Others arise as the placeholders of an alterity that guarantees the differentials that secure the norm. As Wynter sees it, the process is completed in the fully racialized schema that follows upon Darwin and social Darwinism, in which the "wretched of the earth" are produced as the final filiation of all that is not "Man," a "dys-selected" group that barely can be thought of as human.

Against this stark developmental pattern of what is ultimately a systems theory approach to human history indebted to the early theorizations of Gregory Bateson and to the more recent work of Humberto Maturana and Francisco Varela, Wynter looks to "a new contestatory image of the human" ("1492," 50) as a way of completing the unfulfilled promise of humanism (the promise lay in breaking into an expanded sense of the secular; its failure lay in the proliferation of categories of irrational savagery ultimately capped by the utterly irredeemable "nigger"). David Scott, in his interview with Wynter, positions her between humanism and the antihumanism of Michel Foucault (whose archaeology of "Man" in his *The Order of Things* is crucial for Wynter). Scott reads Wynter's project as one seeking to "re-enchant" humanism. Yet Wynter places so much pressure on the figure of "Man" that secures humanism and liberalism that her desire to rethink the "human" must ultimately lie outside the orbit of "humanism" even if it is somehow its fulfillment (this rhythm, as we have noticed, also shapes her relationship to feminism and to Marxism). "'Nigger,'" she insists, is the "ultimate conceptual other to 'Man'" ("Columbus," 153). Although Wynter wishes to overcome all forms of alterity, and to reach, from her "demonic position," a space beyond difference that can be called "human," such a position would necessarily break with the very binaristic mode that, she insists, has been the underlying principle behind all invidious distinctions that have secured the human (as "Man") against non-human Others. Even more pressing, binarism is the very principle by which categories are formed. Wynter seeks nothing less than a move beyond the categorical: "A science of human systems which takes the laws of figuration of human systems as its objects of inquiry must, therefore, adopt a synthetic rather than a categorized approach to its subject" ("Ceremony," 44). In this difficult project, the figure of "Caliban's 'woman'" stands for and in the "ontological absence" (BMM, 360) in which this future possibility resides. Where she "is," no "Man" has been before.

If, through the figure of Miranda, Wynter addresses feminist criticism that too easily universalizes a notion of "woman" and inevitably whitens and Europeanizes its subject, she is equally insistent that "patriarchy" (as a universalizing concept) misses the political dimension of the play: Prospero is not simply a father; he is also a monarch, and his actions need to be read in the context of European state consolidation and colonial expansion. Thus, she takes Irigaray to task, presumably for Irigaray's focus on classical and psychoanalytic texts whose dehistoricized categories of gender are blind to the historical transformation that Wynter seeks to outline. "If, before the sixteenth century, what Irigaray terms as 'patriarchal discourse' had erected itself on the 'silenced ground' of women, from then on, the new primarily silenced ground . . . would be that of the majority population-groups of the globe" (BMM, 363). Replacing the "ground" of "woman" with "the majority population" indicates one reason why Wynter is not happy with the designation "minority." Further noteworthy in this formulation is the way "Caliban's 'woman'" serves as an alternative to the structure of desire in *The Tempest,* where every male character's desire—whether he be a prince, a plebe, or a native—is, as she puts it, "soldered" (BMM, 361) onto Miranda. Wynter thereby suggests that the desire for "Caliban's 'woman'" would not be assimilable to the desire for Miranda articulated in the play—including by Caliban when he incites Stephano and Trinculo by comparing the incomparable to what he can compare her to, his mother:

> I never saw a woman
> But only Sycorax, my dam, and she;
> But she as far surpasseth Sycorax
> As great'st doth least.
> (3.2.98–101)

This alternative desire is based in the history of slavery as it unfolds in Shakespeare's era, when it was considered more expeditious to reproduce "natives" through replacements of live Africans for dead ones than to foster conditions of life in the New World that would enable sexual reproduction.

From this, Wynter implicitly fetches the strong sense that "reproduction" is not only or always a matter of sexual reproduction. As a figure for alternatives to the heterosexual plots of *The Tempest,* "Caliban's 'woman'" figures new populations, new alliances, and new ways of thinking, possibilities "beyond the 'master discourse' . . . and its sub/versions. Beyond Miranda's meanings" (BMM, 366). The orthographic play of the slash in "sub/versions" expresses Wynter's sense of the complicities of (white) feminism with male and colonial dominance, while the "beyond" here beckons beyond binaristic overturning, beyond the reoccupation of the same terrain by those formerly excluded (a process, Wynter argues, that always produces new exclusions), toward something genuinely new, the "wholly new thing" glanced at in Penelope's diary ruminations, the "different kind of creature" that Trumper announces.

In refusing the identity politics that attach themselves to race or gender or sexuality, Wynter does not mean to deny their pertinence to the struggle she imagines and articulates. Rather, she wants to drive all such local "-isms" to a recognition of the new population of which "Caliban's 'woman'" forms a vanguard, a population that certainly would include those oppressed by race, class, gender, or "sexual preference" (BMM, 359). Stunningly, these constitute the "majority population groups." In the history that Wynter traces, racial exclusion serves as the primary site for the worldwide social suffering that she sees as the result of the discourses she traces—the "'industrial waste' . . . of the Black and Latino lives of the United States' inner cities, as well as of American Indian lives on the reservation . . . and their global counterparts, the jobless/welfareless denizens of the shantytowns/*favela* archipelagoes of the Third and Fourth Worlds" ("Columbus," 147)—and as central to the intellectual project of Othering that she seeks to dismantle. Its privilege lies in the fact that "race" explains the contours of modernity best, as the endpoint of the transformations that Wynter traces.

In her theorizations, Wynter draws from and extends the work of figures like Fanon, Césaire, and Lamming (and Elsa Goveia, an important social theorist and historian of the West Indies who is rarely mentioned in the same breath with these founding figures).[69] Her reach toward synthesis is remarkable, embracing a bewildering set of theorists of every kind and of many disciplines (Foucault and Jacques Derrida, but also social scientists, biologists, systems theorists, and historians) and formulated in sentences of remarkable length and in vocabularies that shift from clause to clause as they enact the desire to go beyond the regime of "Man." Understandably, one can find her lacking in specificity about forms of difference, can feel disabled as she refuses to ally herself with specific groups, and can worry that her attempt at a new regime of the human may fall prey to a suspect universalism.[70] Nonetheless, the impulse "beyond" in Wynter is recognizably one that points to the social movements of the 1960s, where recognitions of oppression were imbricated with each other.[71] The call from the colonized and the racially oppressed extended to women and to gays; Wynter's work reinvigorates that desire for connections.

In terms of my own project, certainly a far more limited one than Wynter's, the crucial connection lies in her linking of the modern racial binarism to notions of biological difference and of the natural, which leads her explicitly to call into question again and again "allegedly 'natural' erotic preference" (BMM, 365).[72] Through "Caliban's 'woman'" Wynter posits "an alternative sexual-erotic model of desire" (360). Wynter is not writing as or from the position of gay politics any more than she is positioning herself as a feminist; from her "demonic" standpoint, one in line with the argument being advanced in these pages, Wynter affirms the ontologically untenable ground of a "'monster' difference" (358) that exceeds even Caliban's (he is, after all, represented). "Caliban's 'woman'" is so unthought as not even to be imagined as the irrational opposite of a monstrous mother or demonic father; she is an unimaginable outside, an unimaginable site of desires, an unimaginable object of desire.

What Wynter seeks to describe through this figure is not an individual but a population, a social production that is itself productive. Thinking her way toward and as "Caliban's 'woman,'" Wynter also displays the thinking of a Caliban that would override gendered identification. She aims for a radical alterity, a utopic no place that is at least conceptually possible, a thinkable site to rethink the era of "Man," impelling "both the Antillean and the human subject beyond our present 'order of discourse' and episteme into 'realms' beyond 'conventional reason' . . . a shift from ontogeny to sociogeny, from *l'Etre* to *l'étant,* and the new frontiers of being and knowing that such a shift opens . . . the gift of that Other America" ("Beyond the Word," 645–46). Wynter writes "towards the epochal threshold of a new post-modern and post-Western mode of cognitive inquiry; one which goes beyond the limits of our present 'human sciences,' to constitute itself as a new science of human 'forms of life'" (BMM, 356).

In this overarching project "beyond," one can be overwhelmed by Wynter's systems of multiplying binarisms and can mistake them for a series of parallels. It is thus crucial to register that as these continually replace each other, they also displace each other. Miranda's "woman" can function alongside Prospero's "man" since both consolidate as "Man" against the position of "native." But "native" too, as the Other of "Man," does not have a place for "Caliban's 'woman,'" who is not merely outside the gender category but is even displaced when she is unmarked and included/subordinated and made invisible in the racializing category. (Wynter does not pause over the disappearance and disavowal of the black woman and her desire in Lamming and Fanon, but she nonetheless marks out the possibility of seeing that exclusion.) Gender fractures into new differences that are not themselves symmetrical with previous binarisms; the call from the position of "Caliban's 'woman,'" however much it is prompted by Lamming's Trumper, is nonethe-less one of radical alterity, a beyond even beyond the "Rights of Man" that Lamming posits from a race/class position that is also, as we have seen, lim-ited by his masculinism.

Wynter's reading of C. L. R. James is probably the best place to see her mobilizing the differentials, for she maps how "a system of color value ex-isted side by side with capital value, education value, merit value, and labour value" and insists that "to single out any of these factors was to negate the complex laws of the functioning of the social order" ("Beyond the Categories," 69). The result was "multiple permutations" that give rise to "multiple iden-tities" that go under the singular/plural name "of being a Negro—of being Caliban" (68):

> Given the pluri-consciousness of the Jamesian identity—a Negro yet British, a colonial native yet culturally a part of the public school code, attached to the cause of the proletariat yet a member of the middle class, a Marxist yet a Puritan, an intellectual who plays cricket, of African descent yet Western, a Trotskyist and Pan-Africanist, a Marxist yet a supporter of black studies, a West Indian majority black yet an American minority black—it was evident that the Negro question . . . could not be solved by an either/or. (69)

From these multiples emerge, for Wynter, the possibility of a praxis that seizes upon them and that grasps the totality arising from "the experimental categories of the coerced, the non-norm" (83).

THIS ISLAND'S MINE

"Caliban's 'woman'"—or, as Wynter often refers to "her," his "mate"—offers a figure of nonnormativity: Beyond gender as a Western formation, this "woman" cannot find a place under the definition of "woman"; located beyond the normativities of gender that place Miranda as the endpoint of male de-sire, this "woman" might be the object of desires not to be aligned with the sanctioned forms of heterosexuality that support exchanges of property and power; as "mate," this "woman" even might be "male" and the object of homo-sexual desire outside the orbit of homosocial relations.

Wynter does not privilege the sexual terms that her analysis prompts. Although her figure of "Caliban's 'woman'" is not explicitly prompted by the sodomite and witch in Shakespeare's play, it nonetheless seems to me congru-ent with those cross-gendered, racialized "monsters." I turn now to the work of another Caribbean writer whose deployments of *The Tempest* come closer to the figures offered by the play. Michelle Cliff, like Wynter, is a Jamaican (although some fifteen years younger than Wynter) and has been located for many years in the United States. Her writing will be a leading example throughout the remaining pages of this part of *Tempest in the Caribbean* because it best realizes the productive energies to be found in the excoriated sodomite and his mother.[73] Like Wynter (or Toni Morrison or Paule Marshall or Gloria Naylor, for that matter), Cliff is not an author considered in the usual surveys.[74] Nonetheless, she too can be understood to widen the terms of identification that have been supposed possible in relation to *The Tempest*.

Beside Wynter's evocation of "Caliban's 'woman'" could be put the figure Cliff identifies in the title of her 1991 essay, "Caliban's Daughter: The Tempest and the Teapot."[75] As "Caliban's daughter," Cliff takes her place within the majority population group that Wynter imagines. Cliff's genealogical project involves several forbidden mixtures. Cliff labels the portion of her life that culminated in her achieving an M.Phil. at the Warburg Institute (for a thesis in Renaissance history and culture) as "Ariel," the fulfillment of the destiny written on her light skin as the "child who was chosen ... to represent the colonizer's values" ("Caliban's Daughter," 40). Repudiating the eloquence that required her to negotiate "six Western languages—five living, one dead" (38) and renaming that accomplishment "speechlessness," Cliff moves to reclaim an identity she was taught to reject (to recall the title of her first published volume of prose and poetry, *Claiming an Identity They Taught Me to Despise* [1980]). The name for this racial/sexual subject position is "Caliban."[76] Drawing upon and citing Fernández Retamar's "Caliban," Cliff takes from it a dialectic that, as we have seen, Fernández Retamar does not always sustain, summoning the multiple and incommensurate parts that form her identity as an "Afro-Caribbean," which includes, as she elaborates, "Indian (Arawak and Carib), African, European," "both Caliban and Ariel" ("Caliban's Daughter," 40). Thus, in this formulation, Cliff's genealogical project is similar to Lamming's double paternity: Caliban's daughter is also Ariel's. Indeed, going further, this daughter, crossing gender identification, and multiplying herself, *is* "both Caliban and Ariel. And underneath it all, the granddaughter of Sycorax, precolonial female, landscape, I(s)land: I land" (40).

The island that is hers she claims in Caliban's gesture, claiming it is his/hers thanks to Sycorax. The genealogy that Cliff traces is ultimately a maternal line; although no male counterpart for Sycorax is named, her identification is through Caliban (and Ariel), although here no mother is provided for this daughter. This is, therefore, a genealogy that only looks heterosexual. Eliding heterosexual couplings, it nonetheless glances at the violence these elisions register. For, as Cliff makes clear, Clare Savage, the autobiographical heroine of her first two novels, *Abeng* (1984) and *No Telephone to Heaven* (1987), names the crossroads of the complex terrain of identity mapped in this genealogy. "Clare" signifies the light-skinned privilege that affiliates her with the colonizer; "Savage," her heritage in a "wildness" she has been asked to "bleach" out. That bleaching is in fact the sign on her skin of the sex forced on black female ancestors by white male rapists. Cliff proposes an analogy between "the past which has been bleached from her mind" and "the rapes of her grandmothers [that] bleached her skin" ("Caliban's Daughter," 45). So behind the figure of Clare Savage lies the miscegenation that *The Tempest* misrepresents as something Caliban would have done (Lamming's "Lie"), the fundamental misrecognition of sexual violence that, as we have noted, can get elided in too easy celebrations of the mestizo. The broken genealogy Cliff offers breaks with these violent beginnings of the colonial subject to imagine and remember other affiliations, blackening what has been bleached.

These identifications cross gender, and not only in this daughter of Caliban who nonetheless is Caliban. For the grandmother who serves as the site of primordial identification—"the forest, . . . Sycorax, the precolonial female" ("Caliban's Daughter," 39)—is an "old woman . . . liberated from the feminine role" (even though she is a grandmother) who "may claim masculinity as hers" (47). Hence, in a parallel move, reviewing her childhood reading, Cliff asks provocatively, "What does it mean when the Jamaican tomboy says, 'I am Heathcliff?' Or finds herself drawn to Bertha when she is told to identify with Jane?" (43–44), scenes of reading and "wrong" identification reiterated in *Abeng* when the twelve-year-old Clare argues with her father that Ivanhoe should have chosen the dark, Jewish Rebecca rather than the fair, Christian Rowena, or when she wonders, reading *Great Expectations,* whether she should identify with Miss Havisham or with Magwitch, that is, whether she should see herself in terms of gender or racialization. Caliban, Sycorax, Bertha, Heathcliff, King Kong: All are sites in "Caliban's Daughter" for the monstrous identity that Cliff reclaims crossing gender and species to claim her dark self. As she notes, the child chosen to represent colonial values was meant to affirm the difference between "male and female" (40), a colonial propriety violated as Cliff seeks the mixed origins that account for her "own peculiar self" (40), an individuality composed of "everything I am and have been, sometimes civilized, sometimes ruinate" (40), an individual indivisible from the multiple. The I that lands is a plural singularity: I(s) land.

The primordial black woman ("Sycorax") with whom Cliff makes her most profound identification and who (like Shakespeare's character) cannot be confined within gendered definitions could be contextualized by recalling Lamming's nomination of G's mother who fathered him, in *In the Castle of My Skin.* It has been the task of many women writing after Lamming to represent more fully what he merely gestures toward, the experience of women in privation nonetheless carving out new spaces of possibility. These fathering mothers are not just figures of speech. It is commonplace, for example, to note the matrifocality of Caribbean households, a partial reflection of the fact that some 70 percent of children born in the region are not the offspring of legally constituted marriages.[77] Lower-class women are often involved in nonmarital sexual relationships with men. Middle-class married men often father children on the side, and, indeed, fathering children (not necessarily supporting them) is a prerequisite for normative masculinity across classes. The "bastard" condition that Lamming hails through Caliban is, legally speaking, that of most Caribbeans. Thus, many grow up in households headed by such "fathering mothers." Equally to Cliff's point, mothering in these situations is not confined to the biological mother; extensive networks of women raise children. This begins to account for the elision of the "actual" mother in the genealogy of Caliban's daughter.

Rhonda Cobham, in "Revisioning our Kumblas," studies three foundational texts by Caribbean women—Merle Hodge's *Crick Crack, Monkey* (1970), Erna Brodber's *Jane and Louisa Will Soon Come Home* (1980) and Paule Marshall's *Praisesong for the Widow* (1983)—for the ways they represent social rather than biological mothering. The social norm of the nonnuclear family is furthered by these extended networks of women. And although some of these women may be or may have been mothers, the mothering that these novels depict also is a fathering, "eroding boundaries between gendered attributes" ("Revisioning," 307), much as Cliff's claims to identity embrace both Caliban and Sycorax. To account for this, Cobham points to the figure that is so important for Cliff's theorization as well as for her representational strategies in the novels about Clare Savage: the old woman "past childbearing age when, according to many West African traditions, the gender distinction between men and women no longer matters" ("Revisioning," 309). The survival of African social organization is one explanation for this figure, but Cobham also follows Angela Davis on the experiences of African women enslaved in the New World. Precisely through their nonpersonhood—the refusal to them of normative femininity, both in their domestic roles (often raped into motherhood) and in their roles as laborers alongside the men—these women elided the boundaries between male and female. The importance of such discursive claims to African tradition and the history of enslavement is that they deny the Western assumptions that would associate such nonpatriarchal forms of domesticity with cultural failure.[78]

This erosion of gendered boundaries, as Cobham emphasizes, entails the elision between heterosexual and lesbian activity and makes moot the question of sexual identity. Such elisions can be socially precarious: Economic survival often is at stake, and stigma can be launched against "aberrant" sexual activity and refusals of gendered behaviors tied to compulsory heterosexuality. As Cliff puts her version of this point—"to be masculine in this context, in the context of the Caribbean, is not to be 'mannish' but to have access to self-definition" ("Caliban's Daughter," 48)—she answers the notion of gender propriety that can be voiced, especially by those claiming middle-class neocolonial positions, by separating "masculine" and "mannish." If masculinity is definitionally a form of self-possession whereas femininity, in its most normative mode, is a form of dependence, it is in the relations between women that refuse such dependence that a selfhood can be formed, one that risks the label "mannish." This self-identity in Cliff can be compared to the self-identity of the women in the stories Makeda Silvera recounts in her essay on Jamaican "man royals" and "sodomites." Silvera recalls above all her great-grandmother, her grandmother, and her great-aunts as models for the "strong," self-defining woman she becomes. As she interviews her mother and grandmother, they tell her of the many women they knew growing up who had sex with other women but who also raised families, women who slept with other women as well as with men.

Silvera's experiences echo further: Patricia Powell, a novelist who has published three novels in the past decade, each of which focuses on aspects of same-sex behavior and identity in Jamaican settings (Powell's place of origin), has remarked in an interview on the role that her great-aunt played in her upbringing.[79] In Powell's first novel, *Me Dying Trial* (1993), which was originally her honors thesis at Wellesley College, the focus is on a woman trying to be "strong," attempting to find sexual fulfillment both in marriage and outside it, trying to be a mother, but also seeking independence economically and intellectually; all these are in conflict. In the course of the novel, in order to advance toward these goals, Gwennie abandons her children for various periods of time. One of them, her daughter Peppy, the product of a brief and passionate extramarital affair, is sent to live with her great-aunt Ma Cora, who runs a rum shop. Although Ma Cora has been married and has had children, in her shop she trades drinks and gossip with the male clientele. Ma Cora has raised numerous children, an example of the social mothering Cobham describes. Moreover, she has spent her entire life working. She raises Peppy in the rum shop; at the age of four, she is drinking and cursing; by age five, she is behind the counter, selling. Housework is not her domain. When Peppy approaches adolescence, Ma Cora attempts to restrain the tomboy; as in Hodge's *Crick Crack, Monkey,* such restraint puts boys off limits, and although its aim is sexual propriety, it can nonetheless further nonheterosexual choices.

Powell dedicates *Me Dying Trial* "For Aunt Nora," making the autobiographical connection between her great-aunt and Ma Cora all but explicit. Among Ma Cora's teachings to Peppy is instruction that the Bible is not the last word on female sodomites; indeed, when she tells Peppy, of a villager, that "Miss Clementine was sodomite" (96), she does so nonjudgmentally. By the end of the novel, Peppy is still alienated from her mother, but she has also found a female lover, something the novel presents in a muted way. Open declarations of lesbian identity would certainly not lead to reconciliation with her mother, whose attempts at self-realization and respectability in the United States are articulated in part through homophobic outbursts. The problematic path that Gwennie chooses toward self-respect (and a sexual relationship with a man) is contrasted with Peppy's choice.

For Silvera and Powell, the female homosociality highlighted in novels like those of Brodber and Hodge (both focus on a young woman's development in a colonial society in extended family situations, with various models for female behavior) points the way toward a "lesbian" identity that might be said (following Cobham) to characterize women in the Caribbean more generally, especially lower-class women for whom the institution of marriage and the parameters of normative heterosexuality seem remote—are, in fact, a class sexuality derivative of colonial society. Femininity is so tied to these norms that for Cliff (whose novels locate Clare's dilemma inside just such a colonial marital framework), for a woman to be "masculine" means the repudiation of colonial gender and translates into the ability "to claim that part of the self associated with the nonfeminine, whatever that might be" ("Caliban's Daughter," 48), a hesitation in definition that leads Cliff to the ways Charlotte Brontë figures Bertha's nonfemininity as transgressive of gendered and human definition: "I find myself thinking of the notion of the lesbian as monster, marauder; the man/woman in the closet" ("Caliban's Daughter," 48).

Cliff rewrites Sandra Gilbert and Susan Gubar's *Madwoman in the Attic* and its normative femininity as she considers what female identification with the figure of the black woman entails, what it means "to love another woman—psychically and physically—in the Caribbean landscape" ("Caliban's Daughter," 48). Of some interest here—and certainly a sign that Cliff's thinking moves well beyond the analogies offered in Penelope's diary entry about the Jew, the homosexual, the Negro, and the worker in *Of Age and Innocence,* and furthers the project represented by Wynter's intervention—is that Cliff has no desire to call what she is describing *lesbianism.* That term for sexual arrangements she marks as denoting a particular Western form of female-female sexuality. This serves to dehomogenize notions of homosexuality, to deny universality to such social formations—a belief that almost always assumes that homosexuality Western-style is homosexuality *tout court.*[80] Hence—by way of Brontë and Shakespeare, through various forms of identification that resist gendered boundaries and proprieties of identification— Cliff moves toward a "native" sexuality that does not fit within the Western terms "heterosexual" or "homosexual." Forcefully, she repudiates the notion that "one woman loving another woman" can only emblematize "Western decadence," that such relations only serve to show "the seduction of the tropics by Europe" (48).

It is just such a charge that Silvera reports when she describes telling her grandmother that she is a lesbian. It is "a white people ting," her grandmother says, but as Silvera coaxes her to tell stories of the women she knew years ago, she displays the fact that such a statement "was a strong denial of many ordinary Black working-class women she knew" ("Man Royals," 97), women for whom lesbian experience was commonplace. Cliff's intervention speaks clearly to the charge of "Western" imposition to be found in Fanon's *Black Skin, White Masks,* and it also seeks to reclaim what Fanon denies, that explicit forms of same-sex sexuality exist in the Caribbean. As Alexander points out ("Erotic Autonomy," 85–86), Caribbeans who claim that same-sex sexuality is not native to the region are often repeating a colonial plot: In answer to the charge that "they are all sodomites," colonial regimes and their neocolonial extensions seek a form of Western legitimacy based in the repudiation of same-sex sexuality. The nostalgic glance in contemporary Caribbean rhetoric to a time before Western imposition of sexual decadence is often nothing more than a sign of continuing colonization, a narrative that Silvera interrupts by insisting that her grandmother recall stories about women she knew rather than biblical injunctions about world-destroying sodomites.

To find a name for this existence, Cliff jokingly proposes *"Trinidadian"* ("Caliban's Daughter," 49) rather than "lesbian." Although Trinidadian culture is far more open to alternative forms of expresson than is Jamaican, Cliff does not have in mind the cross-dressing institutionalized in Carnival, for example; rather, she points to the Trinidadian writer Dionne Brand and cites approvingly Brand's invocations, in her sequence of poems "Hard against the Soul," of the figure of the grandmother as a site of desire and of identification.[81] Although Cliff does not register this, native names do, in fact, abound. Audre Lorde, pointing back to the island of Carriacou, from which her mother emigrated to the United States in the 1920s, seizes upon the term "zami" to rename herself: *"Zami. A Carriacou name for women who work together as friends and lovers."*[82] These women are those "who survived the absence of their sea-faring men easily, because they came to love each other, past the men's returning" (*Zami,* 14). Silvera adds "zami" to her lexicon of "man royal" and "sodomite" in her story "Baby": "'I know what I am,' continued Baby, 'I'm a lesbian. A zami. A sodomite. A black-skinned woman.'"[83] This conjunction of race and sexuality parallels Cliff's move to decouple "lesbian" from "Trinidadian." It echoes Lorde's discomfort when her white lesbian friends in the 1950s claim "we're all niggers" (*Zami,* 203), not because Lorde seeks to hierarchize difference but because she knows that differences of race and sexuality cannot simply be translated one into the other.[84] Within the lesbian culture of the period she describes, only white women were capable of playing "femme"; black women were supposed to be "butch." Lorde finds herself as sister/outsider to these arrangements of lesbian culture even as she seeks to affirm her lesbianism and her race, and she finds herself opposing mandatory role playing as she affirms her desire "to be both man and woman" (*Zami,* 7).

Indeed, Lorde seeks to extend "lesbian" identity even to her mother, from whom she fetches her sense of strength and anger, if not her mother's way of expressing it, which was often to inflict upon her children the demands of oppressive racist powers she could not resist. This provides yet another frame for understanding the absence of the mother from Cliff's genealogical project (it is even more legible in *Abeng*). Brand too has written about the effects of maternal self-hatred passed on to daughters in *In Another Place, Not Here*

(230–31). It has often been the mother's task to take up (often against self-interest or the realities of social positioning) the work of social division that sends "chosen" daughters—or sons—on a colonial path. This is a situation we might recall in Lamming's representation of G's mother, promoting G's estrangement from the other villagers as his passport to success but also thereby ushering him into the kind of complex identity-crossing situations that Wynter analyzes in the work of C. L. R. James, situations that only multiply in the writing and experiences of black women in the Caribbean.[85]

If Cliff cannot provide a "native" name for her racial/sexual identity, it is in part because such "native" names have been excoriated. In *Coping with Poverty,* Hymie Rubenstein reports of the villagers he studied in St. Vincent that "sexual activity in Leeward Village takes only one socially approved form, with *bulling* [male homosexuality] and *zammie* [lesbianism] considered *nasty*" (257). Although he details the many nonmarital forms of sexual contact, including strong homosocial groupings, as among these socially approved forms of heterosexuality, he takes the villagers' dismissal of "nasty" behavior as the last word on the subject—as if there were no "bullers" or "zammies" in their midst, failing to consider the possibility of their coincident existence with approved forms of same-sex bonding. "Madivine. Friendling. Zami. *How Carriacou women love each other is legend in Grenada, and so is their strength and beauty*" (Lorde, *Zami,* 14). Against Rubenstein, against the village suppositions—which, as Silvera's interviews make clear, can be dismantled by an interrogator who *wants* such truths to be articulated—Lorde suggests networks of women, crossing islands from Carriacou to Grenada and beyond, to the Harlem where she grew up.

"Zami" is a creolization of French "ami," indeed of the elision in the plural, *les amies,* "the friends." "Zami" names in the singular an inevitable pluralization, relationships between women that cannot simply be called lesbian and that cannot automatically preclude a sexual tie either.[86] Its social meaning can be situated through the only ethnographical work of which I am aware—conducted by Gloria Wekker—that has investigated the sexualization of ties between women in the Caribbean.[87] Wekker studies "mati work" among poor black urban women in Suriname. "Mati" means "friend," "mate"—the term Wynter applies to "Caliban's 'woman'"—and may have originated as a term for male shipmates. "*Mati* are women who typically have children [as do both Lorde and Silvera], who may be in a variety of relationships with men (e.g., marriage, concubinage, visiting relationships) and who also have sexual relationships with women" ("One Finger," 336). The sociality she studies, Wekker opines, may have African roots ("One Finger," 332), or it may have been developed with the beginning of the slave trade ("'What's Identity,'" 122). It is attested in early-twentieth-century anthropological literature ("Matism," 149) and, Wekker affirms, continues as a strong and unstigmatized possibility in Suriname, where, she notes, following Lorde, the strength of female homosocial bonds could allow one to claim that all women might be termed "lesbian" ("Mati-ism," 153). Like Cliff, Wekker contrasts this to a form of "lesbianism" among middle-class women, who affirm an identity and class politics that derive from Western models. Unlike such women, Wekker claims, mati do not understand themselves as exclusively "lesbian" in identity or in orientation, and they regard the "self" as a more multiple, nonindividuating, communal, and non-gender-exclusive phenomenon ("One Finger," 331). Mati thereby oppose not only Western-style "lesbianism" but also forms of normative femininity that presume female dependence upon men, "middle-class values like legal marriage, monogamy, the heterosexual contract, one man fathering all one's children" ("'What's Identity,'" 123). Mati sociality resists the heterosexualizing political economy that Alexander studies in the neocolonial regimes of the Caribbean, remaining as a sign of a "counterhegemonic memory of an insurgent sexuality" ("Erotic Autonomy," 86) that legislators now, like colonialists in the past (or like Shakespeare in *The Tempest*), seek to foreclose and abominate.

Although Wekker limits her focus to one group of women in one locale, it certainly seems possible to generalize from her example to that of other poor black women in the Caribbean. Nonetheless, these forms of sociality were not likely to have been readily available to an author of middle-class origins like Cliff, who seeks to break the bounds of her colonial formation, or to someone like Brand, whose affirmations by way of the old black woman are countered by the ways economic deprivation serves to divide women from each other. In Brand's writing, marked by intense alienation from any locale—from her native Trinidad as well as from Toronto, where she has lived since her adolescence—political purpose in support of the poor, especially poor black women, cuts across and overrides the possibility of same-sex ties. Overwhelmed by the despair of heterosexual imperatives and capitalist economies, Brand often represents lesbianism as simply "not enough" and not an answer. For her, femaleness is so marked by privation as to make it seem impossible for there to be female socialities capable of any political effectiveness. Brand's politics are the bleak counterpart to an utter obliviousness, like Fernández Retamar's, to gender and sexuality as counterforces; they echo with the 1950s of Lorde's *Zami,* where "politics," Lorde suggests, meant opposing McCarthyism, and neither race nor sexuality had, in that sense, a politics.

The difficulty Brand faces speaks to the current replay of that earlier era: neocolonial regimes in the Caribbean; neoconservative politics in the United States and Canada; ongoing black nationalist exclusions of women and gays (a point that Silvera, for one, makes eloquently); the failure of many gay male, feminist, and lesbian feminist groups to encompass the question and experience of race. Brand's is not ultimately the stance that Cliff takes, however much she may hail her as sister outsider. Brand's writing positions herself as victim, despite the kind of assurance she voices, for instance in a recent interview: "I think for me the voice is unshakeable: it can say anything it wants, with certainty," where she points to the women of her youth as inspiration, "the kind of women who drink, socialize openly and are completely frank about their sexuality," as the interviewer puts it. "I grew up with these women; my aunts were those women,"[88] Brand replies, and it is to her aunts "Phyllis and Joan—to their big hands, to their bigger laughter" that *In Another Place, Not Here* is dedicated. Brand cautions that such strength should not be confused with power, downplaying what she says her writing can do. Cliff certainly does not shirk these difficulties, yet she continues to find possibilities. In the essay "Object into Subject," Cliff insists on revaluing the agency of black women, and in *Free Enterprise,* she rewrites the history of black resistance to include actual women who often have been ignored, to draw them together across historical and geographical divides. Brand seems to leave her subjects objects.[89]

. . . BY SYCORAX MY MOTHER

Cliff conjures her most powerful image in "Caliban's Daughter," of a "demonic ground" of female masculinity and "lesbian" monstrosity, through the figure of Nanny, the Maroon revolutionary reported to have routed the British in Jamaican revolts. She "could catch a bullet between her buttocks and fire the lead back at her attackers. She is the Jamaican Sycorax. The extent to which you can believe in the powers of Nanny, that they are literal examples of her Africanness and strength, represents the extent to which you have decolonized your mind" (47). That Nanny's anus epitomizes these powers should not be overlooked, for this suggests that it is not biological reproduction that serves to reproduce racial knowledge or self-knowledge. A connection formed this way cannot be heterosexual either, as is evident in the genealogy Cliff provides, at once historical and mythic, from Sycorax and Caliban, from a Sycorax who *is* a Caliban to a Caliban who *is* a Sycorax.[90] However much Cliff reclaims a primordiality associated with an ur-mother and an ur-nature, she does so in the spirit of a "deconstructivist, wild colonial girl" (42), as she puts it, and the de-essentializing impulses in her essay forge the links that allow movement across gender difference and recognition that conventional gender is Western and colonializing. In this respect, Cliff's telling of Nanny's prowess could be contrasted to G's story to the prostitute, late in Lamming's *In the Castle of My Skin,* about boys sharing a shit-smeared stick. G's (and Lamming's) reticence about sex and meaning, about the stigmatized links between boys that might nonetheless house anticolonial and "native" energies, is overcome by Cliff's Nanny, returning bullets shot from her buttocks.

But such a reclamation of identity is only hard-won and partial in Cliff, as can be seen in *Abeng,* to which I now turn. Timothy Chin, in an essay on homosexual representation in Caribbean literature, points to the linkages between Nanny and the character Mma Alli in Cliff's first novel. Mma Alli "had never lain with a man," only with women, yet her sisterhood embraced "Black men" resisting colonial rule, thereby "inscribing a 'proto-lesbian' figure within the reconstructed mythology of an Afro-Caribbean past" that Clare Savage must reclaim against the depredations of her upbringing as a "colonized child."[91] As Chin points out, the relationship between Nanny, the woman who "could catch a bullet between her buttocks" (*Abeng,* 14), and Mma Alli, who made love to women (including Inez, the woman that a Savage ancestor keeps as his forced mistress) as one way to "keep their bodies as their own" (35), is not a biological one. Clare's origins are not only a matter of literal ancestors. Hence, late in the novel, the narrator says of Kitty, Clare's mother, that she "should have been the daughter of Inez and Mma Alli, and Nanny too" (128). In one respect, Kitty *is* their descendant: She is a black woman who attempts not to deny her racial identity. Nonetheless, she has handed Clare over to her father as a child who, inheriting his green eyes and light complexion, can pass as white. (As the novel makes clear, no one whose history stretches back as far as the Savages could ever be white, and racial differences in Jamaica, unlike in the United States, are a complex set of taxonomies that juggle skin color, economic status, and other markers of social difference, like education.) Kitty has succumbed to colonial imperatives. Indeed, her marriage was forced upon her, the result of an out-of-wedlock pregnancy; Clare is the fruit of that union. "What choice did I have" (147), she asks her mother, a question that is not just personal but ramifies to the class and color regimes of Jamaica. At least within the family, Kitty has given up the possibility of identifying with her black ancestors for the sake of furthering racist regimes. At twelve, as she is beginning to come to understand her complex identity, Clare yearns "to suck her mother's breasts" (54), as Mma Alli does Inez's. It is not only the broken mother-daughter relationship she seeks to restore; it is also a relationship between black women imagined as stretching back to Africa and the Maroon revolts headed by Nanny.

Kitty is estranged from her daughter, but she is also the product of estrangement from her mother, Miss Mattie, the potent grandmother of the novel. Miss Mattie, daughter of a white woman who ran off with a black servant, has a history of enforced labor, one in which attempts at economic survival often precluded maternal concerns. "All her life Mattie Freeman had fended for herself. Even in marriage" (142). In the countryside of St. Elizabeth, she is regarded as a rich woman, owning a few acres of land and presiding over a sharply divided social world of women who can enter her parlor and participate in her prayer services and the poorer women who gather outside. The designation "black woman" splits along the lines of class and property. Clare spends summers with Miss Mattie, confined to the household, avoiding these meetings in the parlor as she yearns to break out of the rigid confines of gendered inactivity. (Miss Mattie allows her only a few tasks, none that would sully her middle-class aspirations.) "Strength" goes hand in hand with the enforcement of privileges. Yet Miss Mattie does have power—she is a kind of "sorceress" (14), even if her powers are mundane—and Nanny too was a "sorceress" (14). Miss Mattie has strength, but at a cost: the divisions between her and the poor women of her community, between her and the granddaughter being cultivated for a life beyond country confines, between her and her daughter Kitty, herself divided. Kitty yearns for connections with Blacks, had once dreamed of setting up a school in St. Elizabeth that would have dispensed with the colonial curriculum, a dream cut short after her marriage. She reaches out to black strangers but pushes aside the daughter who will advance whiteness, as Kitty herself had, by marrying Boy Savage, and reproducing him in Clare.

Handed over to Boy, Clare functions as an honorary son (8). Her light skin is tantamount to a sex change. In Miss Mattie's eyes, this explodes as an accusation when Clare steals a gun from her house in a misguided attempt to seize male prerogatives. Clare is, Miss Mattie mutters, "[a] girl who seemed to think she was a boy. Or white" (134). The novel poses as a genuine dilemma the crossing between the masculinism of white privilege and the "masculine" attempt to refuse the white privilege of a dependent femininity. These gendered regimes are those of a middle class, or of a would-be middle class. (It is Clare's skin and her education, not actual economic status, that mark her as middle-class.) These aspirations are most manifest in the novel in the vicious racism of white "ladies" or of those positioned thanks to their skin color or education in this "white" position (Clare's teachers, and the woman she is sent finally to live with). This model is held up to Clare by Kitty and Miss Mattie. She endlessly hears reiterated the sentence, "'Is jus' no fe gal pickney, dat's all.' She had heard this before—spoken in different ways" (57), repeated injunctions policing her femininity. Refusals of this racialized, classed, gender position prompt Clare's search for the kind of strength associated with Nanny or Mma Alli and still dimly to be found in her grandmother. Yet it is by no means simple to imagine how a girl with fair skin and green eyes, a star pupil in the prestigious colonial school she attends, can find her way to positions that are marked as black, lower-class, and nonfeminine. The novel holds out Nanny or Mma Alli as its prized exemplars, but it is adamant in insisting that such possibilities remain unknown and occluded for the colonial Clare. She nonetheless moves along the pathway to such a self-discovery, through her contentious reading, through her identifications with Anne Frank (and through her to questions about blackness and femaleness displaced and crossed in the experiences of the Holocaust), and above all through her relations with Zoe, a poor black girl, given to her as a playmate by Miss Mattie.

Zoe is the daughter of Miss Ruthie, a marketwoman whom Miss Mattie

allows to squat on her land. Clare dreams of a relationship that will overcome differences, binding the two girls together. She inducts Zoe into her
fantasy life and attempts to realize it as she enlists Zoe in her plan to steal
her grandmother's gun and shoot a wild pig. Zoe makes Clare see all the
divisions (of color and class) that divide them. Clare wants to be someone—
someone individual, free of constrictions—but her very desires are bound to
the privilege attached to her social status. She may think she is confined
at her grandmother's house, but she is on holiday, away from her parent's
home in Kingston, away from school. These positions, this movement, suggests her future: emigration to the United Kingdom or the United States.
Zoe is genuinely confined; her life course will repeat her mother's. To Zoe,
Clare is "Kingston smaddy. White smaddy" (118), somebody attached to place
and privilege. Clare's idyll of country friendship is a game played with consequences for Zoe, who cannot leave the land she does not own, and who is
likely to suffer for Clare's gun-toting, masculinist transgressions.

Cliff, however, invalidates neither Clare's desire to break with racist regimes of femininity, to undo the differences between a poor black girl and a
middle-class girl who, thanks to her skin and her schooling, can pass as white,
nor the form that desire takes, as the two girls lie naked beside each other on
a rock, in a masturbatory scene in which Clare yearns to touch Zoe's breasts,
and in so doing, to reach through her body to her mother's as well:

> The two girls closed their eyes against the rise of the sun to noon overhead
> and touched hands. Brown and gold beside each other. Damp and warm. Hair
> curled from the heat and the wet. The warmth of the sunlight on their bodies—
> salty-damp.
>
> Pussy and rass—these were the two words they knew for the space-within-
> flesh covered now by strands and curls of hair. Under these patches were the
> ways into their own bodies. Their fingers could slide through the hair and deep
> into the pink and purple flesh and touch the corridor through which their ba-
> bies would emerge and into which men would put their thing. Right now it could
> belong to them. (*Abeng*, 120)

Such a moment certainly is "lesbian"; it recalls the scene in the novel
between Mma Alli and Inez. Nonetheless, "lesbian" only begins to name the
complications here. Does Clare desire Zoe, or does she desire her dark skin?
Both are forbidden desires. Either might mark a woman as not a woman
in violating the regimes of gendered propriety. In Miss Mattie's mother (a
white woman who runs off with a black man) and in the sister of the woman
to whom Clare is consigned (a woman who has gone "mad" after giving birth to
a child she had with a black man—mad not through her "error" but thanks
to the punishments of deprivation and stigma she was made to suffer), the
novel offers examples of nonnormative heterosexual behavior, a desire for
darkness that may parallel Clare's "lesbian" desire. As in Wynter's work,

a desire for what is thought impossible—the desire for or *as* "Caliban's 'woman'"—may obviate distinctions between heterosexual and homosexual. It may suggest other forms of sociality, the kind, indeed, to be found in Clare's name, although she does not know it. Whereas to Boy, her name recalls Clare College, where one of his ancestors went, for Kitty it is the name of a black girl, Clary, who had safeguarded her and seen her through a life-threatening illness. Abandoned by Miss Mattie to the hands of this girl, Kitty secretly names Clare for this nonbiological "mother" and "sister" who had saved her life. Reaching out for Zoe, Clare is also reaching for herself.

Clare is a child divided by race, by gender; divided by her parents, by her school, by city and countryside. The novel ends with her menstruating, arriving into womanhood. Everything is left open as to whether she will find a way to negotiate the halves and to forge bonds that will enable her to claim an identity that will be black and female, yet not that of a lady or of someone bounded by the restrictions of middle-class proprieties. These proprieties have marked her off for the kind of educational career that Cliff herself had, for instance, or for marriage to a light-skinned man. The claiming of her body seems to hinge upon the possibility of assembling—out of every form of desire that she has been led to believe is wrong and counter to her privilege—an identity worth reclaiming. This is by no means assured or easy. As the narrator notes, Nanny Town exists, but it remains "difficult to reach" (14). It is available in numerous practices: in knowledges of the soil and its produce that poor women have, that even Kitty knows from Miss Mattie; in the garments that women weave, unknowingly resuming African arts. And it is occluded in numerous obfuscations, impossibilities of naming like the kinds that cross in Clare's name, with its open secret of affiliative lines between women. Clare's name is itself criss-crossed. Clare Savage is white and "native," yet her whiteness is the Savage claim, Boy's ancestry that stretches back to the plantation owner who burned his property—that is, his slaves—rather than free them. Her mother, bound to these colonial arrangements, was once a Freeman.

At the end of the novel, Clare is punished for stealing a gun and firing it, accidentally killing Miss Mattie's bull. Her father thinks that her wildness shows her still untamed blackness, and he sends her to live with a white woman whose racism is nakedly held out to Clare as the model for her to adopt. Her mother, however, sees Clare's misbehavior as a sign that she has acted on the privilege she accrues from her father's claims to whiteness. Neither parent, no one in the novel, comments on the fact that Clare fired the gun when a male intruder came upon her and Zoe lying naked upon the rocks. Two naked girls; they had done what girls were not supposed to do, something Clare's male cousins did, displaying themselves naked. Clare had desired Zoe. Her desires are the deepest level of the unspoken in a novel where the unspeakable history of slavery, of race and class and gender differences, is

speakable, if only in euphemisms. Clare's transgressive desire, crossing identification and desire (the wish both to be and to love the black woman), on all
these counts, has no name and apparently has no forms of lived embodiment.
But on the other hand, it has a history stretching back to Nanny and is still to
be found in the bonds between women that are native to her person and her
island.

Abeng is written in fragmented narrative sequences. A strong narrator
knows and sees much that is occluded and unspoken but also leaves much
unsaid and unsayable. The narratives that I have assembled here are presented piecemeal throughout the novel.[92] Judith Raiskin notes that through
Clare, Cliff represents the search of a (potential) Caliban-Sycorax poised
between the recognition that the "challenges to the hierarchical systems of
race and sex"—which, as Raiskin argues, are central to Cliff's project—are
"no match for the force of these systems once set in motion," and the promise
that Lauren Berlant, for one, has identified in a moving meditation on Cliff's
work: "[I]t closes off nothing but the already exhausted futures we call the
present tense."[93] Clare's situation does not promise resolution—its mapping
of the crossings of categories of race, color, class, gender, and sexuality is a set
of disalignments—except in the kind of multiple/singular category-defying
composite that is announced by way of the rereading of *The Tempest* offered
in the persona of "Caliban's Daughter."

. . . MY DAM'S GOD SETEBOS

In Cliff, identity is non-self-identical. Gender is interrupted by race. (The controlled and heterosexualized female body is properly gendered, ladylike; it is
therefore "white," whereas the out-of-control female body, like that of Clare's
classmate Doreen Paxton, who suffers an epileptic seizure and is thrown out
of school for such misbehavior, reveals itself as "black" despite efforts at its
schooling/whitening.) Race, in terms of the female body, is inextricable from
gender; gender is divided along the axes of sexuality. (Cross-racial desire,
whether the desired one is male or female, is stigmatized if the object is
"black" and approved if "white.") Negotiating these often unspoken but nonetheless powerful regimes, reassembling a valued identity out of abjection and
across and through the various dislocations that mark and place Clare, is the
difficult project of the novel and of Cliff's work more broadly.

In part by way of contrast, Cliff's project could be compared to Edward
Kamau Brathwaite's, which is as alert as hers is to the fragmentations and
dislocations of the Caribbean subject. "Caliban," a poem in Brathwaite's
Islands (1969) is mentioned by Fernández Retamar in "Caliban" as "dedicated,
significantly, to Cuba" (Fernández Retamar, "Caliban," 13). Nixon endorses
this reading of Brathwaite's "Caliban" and argues that its allusions to *The
Tempest* serve as repudiations of Shakespeare.[94] The Vaughans, in their chapter "Colonial Metaphors" in *Shakespeare's Caliban,* claim that Brathwaite's

poem can be compared to the reclamation of Caliban by Fernández Retamar and Césaire as another example of texts that "avidly adopted Mannoni's imagery" (155); they offer a bland summary of the poem in their chapter "Modern Poetic Invocations," in which they affirm that in its middle section, Caliban "experiments like his Shakespearean original with the language Prospero taught him," another sign for them that colonial texts are bounded by the colonizer's culture, inevitably included within "Shakespeare's unmatched universality" (171). Yet, as Nixon notes, the "earth music of the carnival and the intercession of black gods" (574) locate other possibilities in the poem, as Gordon Rohlehr's reading in *Pathfinder* confirms by way of the numerous references and allusions to African deities and their attributes and to the limbo dance as it reenacts and refuses the condition of the confinement of slaves on ships across the Middle Passage. For Brathwaite, as for Cliff, resuscitation of African and New World resources is vital.[95]

Neither Nixon nor the Vaughans mention another Brathwaite poem, also titled "Caliban," that appeared first in *Black + Blues* in a 1976 Casa de las Américas imprint, presumably because the "caliban" of that poem is caught in inanition; he is "blind," "tortured," "twisted & bent," a "victim" in a "wilderness."[96] Whereas the Caliban of *Islands* is possibly a ragtag performer of the kind that Paule Marshall presents in her "Brazil," as "o grande Caliban," a worn-out nightclub performer, the "caliban" of *Black + Blues* is even more hopeless, a product of Prospero's (un)making. Whereas Nixon might have included the poem to show how the plot ran out in the postemancipation period, Brathwaite in fact continued to deploy *The Tempest* through the 1990s. He "has never professed to love the tortured fellow," Cynthia James notes, as she maps the various uses to which Caliban has been put in Brathwaite's oeuvre.[97] On the one side, he stands for the Maroon revolutionary and rebel, a prophet and terrorizer who can be the poet's persona, but he is also a traitor, a mulatto, an opportunist, a mindless dancer, and a terrorized victim. This double Caliban can be seen in the use that Brathwaite has made of the figure in historical essays tracing plantation personality types. Caliban, in "Caliban, Ariel, and Unprospero in the Conflict of Creolization" (1977), is a "would-be rebel or house slave," a typology repeated in *Barabajan Poems* (1994), where Caliban is first called a rebel and then immediately recharacterized, "or more accurately wd-be rebel."[98] Brathwaite's project bears comparison with Cliff's insofar as he looks back to the Maroons (as she does through Nanny), to difficult recoveries of identity, and to possibilities that lie buried in histories that need to be unearthed. Moreover, the double Caliban that Brathwaite offers is potentially attuned to the fact that "Caliban" cannot simply name native energies; his name and part are also Prospero/Shakespeare's doing, and the denigrations buried in the name also inform the lived experience of Blacks in the Caribbean. Brathwaite's Caliban, like Cliff's Clare, needs to discover possibilities undreamed of in the monster/clown of *The Tempest*. However,

for Brathwaite, unlike Cliff, such discoveries and recoveries involve a repudiation of the doubleness that is, arguably, the condition of the subject made
in colonialism; racial recoveries in his work reinscribe sexed and gendered
normativities.

This goal is realized in poems that are remarkable as assemblages of frag-
ments, broken words and lines meant to unleash unheard-of energies, as in
the 1969 "Caliban," where Caliban's declaration of self-nomination and independence from Prospero in *The Tempest* is rewritten:

Ban
Ban
Cal-
iban
like to play
pan
at the Car-
nival;
dip-
ping down
and the black
gods call-
ing, back
he falls
through the water's
cries
down
down
down
where the music
hides
him
down
down
down
where the si-
lence lies.
("Caliban," *The Arrivants,* 193)

Elsewhere, Brathwaite trades in "calibanisms," words written in what he
calls nation language, creolizations that express New World sensibilities and
native possibilities of creation.[99] Brathwaite testifies in his autobiographical
"mehri" to his belated inspiration when, as an adult, he read *In the Castle*

of My Skin, a work by his almost exact Barbadian contemporary (Brathwaite was born in 1930, three years after Lamming), underscoring the prescience of Lamming's depiction of a lived misery that lacked terms for its enunciation. Like Wynter, Brathwaite points to Trumper's discovery as one that he made his own and that has guided his vast output over a long career.[100] The embeddedness of his poetry in African mythology and New World reworkings has been unfolded by his critics, especially in the patient and exacting work of Gordon Rohlehr; at the same time, its dazzling rhythms, as his poems attempt to go beyond the meanings that Rohlehr unfolds, produce sounds that exceed ordinary sense in the extraordinary resources of improvisatory creation and re-creation (Brathwaite's texts often exist in numerous forms and rewritings), as has been examined by Nathaniel Mackey, among others.[101]

Biographically, Brathwaite's life follows a familiar curve: from Barbados to England—where he studied at Cambridge—and a return to the Caribbean, to Jamaica, where he taught history at the University of the West Indies (UWI), Mona, for many years until he moved to New York University. He returned by way of Africa; Brathwaite spent eight crucial years in the newly independent Ghana. For the discussion at hand, one way of framing this movement of exile and return can be seen in the transformation of a poem that appeared first as "X/Self's Xth Letter from the Thirteen Provinces" in *X/Self* (1987) and was later recast and significantly renamed as "Letter SycoraX" in *Middle Passages* (1993), where it was reset in "Sycorax video style," a computer-generated set of typefaces that Brathwaite has adopted for much of his publication since the 1990s.[102] Even if Brathwaite has aimed at writing calibanisms, he has been just as intent at reclaiming a maternal inheritance that he (like Cliff) associates with Africa. As early as "Hex" in *Mother Poem* (1977), he alludes to "black Sycorax my mother" (47). Elaine Savory has hailed this aspect of Brathwaite's work, claiming that he has been "moving from male-oriented to female-oriented images of decolonization," a remark that points us, once again, to the absence of gendered consideration in the works of Nixon and the Vaughans.[103] Through Sycorax, Brathwaite names his African and spiritual origins, his mother tongue; through the video style that he names after her (and after his old computer, also named "Sycorax"), he attempts to put words on the page that visualize sounds in their immediacy. Sycorax is the muse in the machine that wires the poet to originary energies. "It is this spirit in the form of Sycorax, the anti-colonial matrix of creativity, who inspires the machine, the Western computer, to produce Brathwaite's video style, which so markedly brings orality into the written word," Savory summarizes.[104] Brathwaite puts it this way, in conversation with Nathaniel Mackey:

> *Sycorax* being the submerge African and woman and *lwa* of the pla(y), Caliban mother and person who deals with the herbs and the magical sous-reality of the world over which Prospero rules. And therefore I celebrate her in this way—thru

the computer—by saying that she's the spirit/person who creates an(d)/or acts
out of the video-style that I workin with She's the *lwa* who, in fact, allows me the
space and longitude—groundation and inspiration—the little inspiration—that
I'm at the moment permitted[105]

"X/Self's Xth Letter" becomes a letter written by Caliban to his mother,
about the discovery of the computer as a way to curse Prospero "wid im own /
curser" (*X/Self*, 85). This Caliban is not Shakespeare's

> learnin prospero linguage &
> ting
> not fe dem/not fe dem
> de way caliban
> done
>
>   (84–85);

the machine is turned back upon its inventor; techne is mined for energies
that cannot be controlled by the colonial project; X writes "fe we / fe a-we" (85).
This "we" also appears elsewhere in Brathwaite as "mwe," a singular plurality. It aims at negritude as Brathwaite defines it: "[T]here is a black Caliban
Maroon world with its own aesthetics *(sycorax)*" (*X/Self*, 130), Caliban and
Sycorax joined, indeed, Caliban retrieved from colonial inanition by Sycorax,
joined as "mwe," me and we, man and woman.

If these cross-gendered, singular-plural configurations remind us of Cliff,
there are nonetheless worrying limitations in Brathwaite's project, for example, in "Caliban, Ariel, and Unprospero," where Sycorax is translated as
"the obeahman or native preacher" (43), a masculinization that reads entirely contrary to Cliff's moves across gender since it enhances only one gender,
the male. Rohlehr, in "'Black Sycorax, My Mother,'" offers a close reading of
Mother Poem and the function of Sycorax in it, worth pausing over in this respect.[106] Sycorax serves, Rohlehr catalogues, as "Mother Tongue," "archetypal
Mother" (279), "archetypal presence and Muse," and "Mother Earth" (281).
This symbolic maternity is crucial—for her son. Her future possibilities lie in
him; he needs her to find his essence, what Brathwaite calls his "nam." That
spiritual seed is "man" spelled backward:

> ma ma ma: she is tell muh
> ma ma *man:* she is tell muh
>
> ma ma *man:* she is tell muh
>
> say *man:* she is tell muh
> say *man:* she is tell muh
> ("Nametracks," *Mother Poem,* 57)

Edward Brathwaite was renamed Kamau in Africa by his spiritual mother, Ngũgĩ wa Thiong'o's grandmother; Kamau, as he spells the name in *Barabajan Poems* (239–40), when read forward letter by letter, hails him as male, spirit, chief, sun, and universal spirit; read backward, it names him as female, mouth, womb, secrecy, anima. Rohlehr finds the "âme" in "nam," and in this he seems to follow Brathwaite, who absorbs the feminine principle into himself.

Responding to an essay by Bev Brown that had accused Brathwaite of such erasures/incorporations of "woman" into a masculinist plot, Rohlehr insists on the fullness of representation of women in Brathwaite.[107] It is true that black women are amply and sympathetically represented in *Mother Poem* and elsewhere as impoverished, beaten down by labor, or forced into unwanted pregnancies, unhappy marriages, and prostitution.[108] They are, however, always represented in relationship to men (or sometimes to female slaveowners, whose race and position align them with male domination), not in relationship to each other. Their men are in danger of emasculation— by slaveowners, by capitalists, and by their wives, who also have the possibility of redeeming/remasculinizing them. Mothers have sons, it seems, not daughters; their futures and pasts are entirely bounded by relationships with men. In Brathwaite, patriarchal oppression is answered by what Sue Thomas summarizes as a "'pro-family' patriarchal sexual political ideology," a plot that Cliff for one has understood as a continuation of colonialism in the domestic sphere, which Alexander has linked, as we have observed, to the regimes of the neocolonial state.[109] Brathwaite's repudiations of the West and of colonialism stop short of a rethinking of the sex/gender system. Women are tied—and should be, he implies—to the institution of marriage, to the biology of procreation as female destiny.

Rohlehr reads the strong women of *Mother Poem* as "fathering." Brathwaite, however, has referred to Lamming's sentence as "this awful axe/ione that it's the mothers who father us" (*ConVERSations,* 52), and he wishes to heal the split through a reconstituted nuclear family of the kind named in his second trilogy: mother, sun, and an X who may make good on the blighted sunship of the father, filling his place as the (w)holy son (X is Caliban's self-nomination in Aimé Césaire's *Une Tempête*). Rhonda Cobham has read the terror of the awful axiom in a parenthesis in Brathwaite's telling of his renomination as Kamau.[110] The African women spit on him, as they "nam" him, and, in small type, in parentheses, Brathwaite solicits empathy for his situation: "(I was very much alarmed to say the least at first)" (*Barabajan Poems,* 236). Dependence upon and liberation through Sycorax (the mother, the machine) are anxiogenic. Brathwaite has countered it, especially through his latest computer, named Stark, generator of the Sycorax video style and a figure Brathwaite has recently added to his *Tempest* personality types. Stark, the new computer, is also Caliban's sister; she is, moreover, a set of black women writers whom Brathwaite hails as fellow practitioners: Paule Marshall, Alice

Walker, Erna Brodber, Toni Morrison, Maryse Condé, Jamaica Kincaid, Caro-livia Herron, and Cynthia James, most notably. Here is how Brathwaite de-scribes her in *Barabajan Poems:*

> *Stark*/Sister Stark, Caliban's sister, is my own imaginative invention. . . . she did not walk clearly away from me until the October evening 1991 at NYU when I spoke of Paule Marshall's then new book, *Daughters* and recognized Stark in what Marshall was doing—the first time that the Plantation has a black woman w/ firm feet, sensitive/aggressive breasts and a space & plan if not always a room of her own. (316)

Although it is certainly salutary to find Brathwaite including women in *The Tempest* plot and its anticolonial rewriting, the nature of the sexualiza-tion of the scene of the encounter, as the figure in his head greets him with her "sensitive/aggressive breasts," gives pause. As Cobham points out in "K/Ka/Kama/Kamau," Brathwaite embraces women writers in order for them to confirm his vision; they serve as his narcissistic mirrors, she charges. This can be seen most starkly in *ConVERSations,* where Brathwaite cites from the work of Maria Headley, one of his students, who praises him for the circulation of Sycorax in his texts "as a sort of hidden mother": "In Brathwaite's poem/letter from Sycorax. the very form of the letter is telling— she is not able to speak in person. but must articulate some further view-point. must become dissociated from personal contact. The invisible mother is one who can inform from afar and through silence" (191).[111] Headley refers to Brathwaite's "Dream Sycorax Letter," a poem in which Sycorax writes on behalf of her dead/dread son (Caliban Brathwaite) to the publishers who have been unsympathetic to his video style—a lack of sympathy that seems exaggerated even if Brathwaite registers the fact that for him now, as was the case for Lamming in the 1950s, he lacks a sustaining cultural milieu at home.[112] The Sycorax who writes the poem insists that she has "no désir, or wish to become any more visible" (126), no desire to speak in propria persona. She speaks as the text/font; as the immediacy of his dead voice, as his living principle. Sycorax has become text, but her text is his:

> "dreamstorie" "nansesem" "nam-histories &
> herstories" "manscapes" "panyard"
> solar
> "jazz/legba" "tranesong/shango"
> *"the sycorax video-style"* as i say
> name after mwe!
> ("Dream Sycorax Letter," 131)

So far as I know, Brathwaite has referred only once to Michelle Cliff. In his ᵗologies of New World *Tempest* figures in *Barabajan Poems,* she appears

under the rubric "Caliban" but with those "wrought or fraught with DICHOTO-
MOUS sometimes SCHIZOPHRENIC CONFLICTS" (316). A question mark beside her
name shields her a bit from the charge of schizophrenia that Simon Gikandi
has leveled at Clare in *Abeng,* a pathologizing to which Myriam Chancy has
recently replied.[113] Although Chancy does not quite say it, Gikandi's judgment must be linked to his inability to reckon with Clare's relationship to Zoe
and its incipient sexualization. Gikandi's charge parallels Rohlehr's dismissal
of feminist readings in "Brathwaite with a Dash of Brown" as the imposition
of an improper outside on native male-centered creation. Rohlehr repudiates feminism as Western, as brown not black. His position could be aligned
with Wynter's critique, but it is here deployed in the service of Brathwaite's
black male powers. Brathwaite's labeling of Cliff alludes primarily to her
crossed racial positioning. However, as is well documented, race, gender, and
sexuality are often tied together in black nationalist rhetoric that aims at a
determinately male and heterosexual racial revitalization. Brathwaite seems
to have moved beyond his double and divided (schizophrenic?) Caliban to one
that has regained integrity through Sycorax, a claiming of femaleness that
consolidates his gender, race, and sexuality. (This can be appealing to some
of Brathwaite's female admirers, who find their racial and gendered confir-
mation backed by heterosexual positioning.)[114] Nonetheless, there are massive exclusions in these consolidations of black heterosexual subjects. Cliff's
difficult project of attempting to make coherences across differences seems
answered and refused by Brathwaite's project even as it shares many similar components. This need not be the case. As Cobham notes of Brathwaite's
turning Sycorax and Stark into computers, "there is nothing inherently
invidious about this utopian image of woman as supportive cyborg" ("K/Ka/
Kama/Kamau," 307); it could locate "woman" elsewhere. Yet it seems that in
Brathwaite, the cyborg is brought back into male orbit, Sycorax once again
subordinated, as she is in Caliban's account, to her god Setebos.

ALL THE CHARMS / OF SYCORAX

Cliff does not refer to Brathwaite in "Caliban's Daughter," but she does make
significant gestures to Aimé Césaire, which prompts a consideration now of
his rewriting of *The Tempest* as *Une Tempête.* Césaire's deployment of Caliban
has, like Brathwaite's work, been subject to feminist critique as masculinist,
with considerable cogency: Césaire accords Sycorax no speaking part in *Une
Tempête,* something he clearly could have done, since his version of the play
does add characters to the original cast.[115] Nonetheless, it seems fair to assume that Cliff's gestures toward Césaire cannot aim at the consolidation of
a patriarchal/heterosexual masculinism, and they will lead us further to dehomogenize and complicate the scope of feminist interventions. Moreover, her
valuation of Césaire must be put beside a critique offered by Tom Hayes in an
essay on the humanist subject as embodied in Prospero across the history of his

reinscriptions. However incisive *Une Tempête* may be at critiquing Prospero, Hayes avers, Césaire writes with the aim of reinvigorating a native masculinism, as best evidenced by the introduction of "Eshu, a black-devil god," the one character whose addition to Shakespeare's cast list Césaire announces.[116] Eshu appears in the masque scene (at just the moment in the play when Sycorax could have appeared) to "whip you with his dick" (48),[117] scandalizing the goddesses, reinforcing the subordination of women, and thus introducing a black male in the position that Hayes calls the humanist subject, a figure intent on securing a racialized and heterosexual masculinity. Hayes faults Césaire for forgoing the homosexual possibility that can be found in cannibal/Caliban.

I turn to Césaire now, moreover, because he represents an even earlier generation of Caribbean writers than Brathwaite (he was born in Martinique in 1913); his has been a founding voice in Caribbean consciousness throughout the second half of the twentieth century. His *Notebook of a Return to the Native Land,* which first appeared in 1939, and his *Discourse on Colonialism* (the earliest version dates from 1950) are cited again and again. Fanon—who was taught by Césaire in Martinique (as was Glissant)—fetches his initial epigraph in *Black Skin, White Masks* from the *Discourse,* and he cites Césaire frequently throughout his text as he wrestles with questions of black authenticity. Lamming uses lines from the *Notebook* as the epigraph to his chapter on *The Tempest* in *The Pleasures of Exile;* Wynter invokes Césaire repeatedly, for example, ending the essay that fetches its title from Trumper's "different kind of creature" by citing Césaire's project as exemplary in its aim "to resemanticize meaning/being from the perspective of alterity" ("'A Different Kind of Creature,'" 168). *Une Tempête* is, moreover, a rewriting of Shakespeare's play as a play, formally closest to the original of the anticolonial reinscriptions of *The Tempest,* and it is thus an apt site to consider the deeply imbricated relationships between texts that seem denied in a project like Brathwaite's. Although in Nixon's account ("Caribbean and African Appropriations," 572) the play is summed up in the revolutionary gesture signaled by Caliban's first word in the play—*Uhuru,* the Swahili word for "freedom" that was a black revolutionary byword in the 1960s—*liberté* is in fact Caliban's last word in the play. I want to pursue that pathway from this opening:

CALIBAN: Uhuru!

PROSPERO: What did you say?

CALIBAN: I said, Uhuru!

PROSPERO: Mumbling your native language again!

(*A Tempest,* 11)

Prospero's denigrating the African word as "native"—he says *barbare* in the original (24)—points, of course, to the project that engaged Césaire in France in 1930s, the negritude movement (Césaire probably coined the word *négri-*

tude) that importantly insisted on the African origins of Caribbeans against colonial denigration, self-hatred, and alienation of the kind analyzed in *Black Skin, White Masks*. As Césaire indicates in a lecture he delivered at about the same time he was writing *Une Tempête*,

> [I]t must not be forgotten that the word *négritude* was, at first, a riposte. The word *"nègre"* had been thrown at us as an insult, and we picked it up and turned it into a positive concept. . . . We thought that it was an injustice to say that Africa had done nothing, that Africa did not count in the evolution of the world. . . . Our faith in Africa did not result in a sort of philosophy of the ghetto, and this cult of, this respect for, the African past did not lead us to a museum philosophy.[118]

Nonetheless, this "originary" move of African reclamation (for Caliban, in the play; for Césaire, whose trajectory is, in part, represented through the character) is an initial gesture as the play moves from *Uhuru* toward a re-semanticized *liberté*. *Une Tempête* is Césaire's last major publication (his *Oeuvres complètes* appeared in 1976), and it has a strong retrospective cast. It rewrites *The Tempest* in abbreviated form; before the first act is over, Prospero has given up revenge on the Europeans to ally himself with them against Caliban's impending revolt.

Caliban proceeds in the play through a series of self-identifying moves; soon after uttering "Uhuru," he demands that Prospero call him "X": "Call me X. That would be best. Like a man without a name. Or, to be more precise, a man whose name has been stolen. You talk about history . . . well, that's history, and everyone knows it! Every time you summon me it reminds me of a basic fact, the fact that you've stolen everything from me, even my identity! Uhuru!" (15). In this context, the use of "Uhuru" involves a resemanticization of the kind that Wynter applauds, a recourse to Africa as a strategic historical and discursive act. It produces not a name for Caliban but a place for him to reject his name and the charges of brutality and cannibalism lodged in it. Yet *X* marks necessarily a place of crossing, the condition of the subject made in colonialism, functioning even as a sign of minimal literacy within the Western scriptive order. Moreover, *X* also is a name, as Césaire makes clear in a scene that he provides for Caliban and Ariel (act 2, scene 1), who enact a confrontation between Malcolm X and Martin Luther King Jr. In this scene, Caliban affirms, in English, "Freedom now" (21), espousing revolutionary violence against Ariel's more quiescent and conciliatory path that aims at sounding Prospero's conscience. Ariel, pointedly, is a mulatto, and the play seems unequivocally to be on the side of 1960s black nationalism.

However, once sides are drawn—Prospero (one with the European aristocrats) against Caliban (allied to Stephano and Trinculo)—the play comes to an impasse. Caliban realizes that he has made common cause with fools, a move that may parallel one by Césaire, who in the *Discourse* had made interchangeable racial liberation and worker revolution but who by 1956 had resigned from the French Communist Party. Given the opportunity to kill Prospero, Caliban demurs, just as Césaire, from his position as mayor of Fort-de-France (to which he was first elected in 1945; Césaire only retired from elected office in 1993), led the way not to independence for Martinique but to its becoming a French overseas *département* in 1946, a stance he came to regret.[119] The play ends with Caliban and Prospero locked in dialectical struggle, Prospero on the wane, the island overrun with untamed, "unclean" (68) nature, and Caliban offstage chanting "FREEDOM HI-DAY, FREEDOM HI-DAY" (68).[120] This is, in fact, the same line he sang when he joined forces with Stephano and Trinculo (44), an indication that Césaire also seeks to resemanticize the proletariat cause that had foundered by masking its colonialism under republican slogans: Stephano nonetheless would be king of the island; Caliban would be *his*.

Nixon's estimation of the play as a revolutionary manifesto echoes prevailing views of the play as simply a reversal and refusal of the colonialist plot of *The Tempest,* a reading rightly called into question by Joan Dayan. Dayan argues for a much closer relationship between the two texts; for her, both exhibit the resources of ambiguity and irresolution.[121] "Oscillation" in Shakespeare's Caliban is his destiny, she claims (128), sounding much like the Vaughans in this, the dialectic of the play's close the opportunity for Hegelian "reciprocal recognition" (131) that echoes the "labor of reciprocity" (130) that constitutes Césaire's artistic practice. For Dayan, the play is locked into its original just as the neocolonial state is tied to the West, a pernicious system, she insists, but also the way (the only way, she implies) for Césaire to participate in "the western cultural tradition" (141), the only game in town. Cozy couples: Césaire and Shakespeare, Caliban and Prospero. They show the "fertile collision and mutual abiding of these reciprocal worlds" (140).

Between Nixon's view of nativist revolutionary energies mobilized in repudiation and revolt and Dayan's of a mutuality that is, in effect, capitulation, there seems to be no choice politically; yet it seems clear that the play straddles these dichotomies. Hardly "fertile" at the end—except insofar as the island is on the verge between ruin and some possible opening that could rewrite the French revolutionary ethos of freedom—the impetus for this recovery still lies in the initial cry of "Uhuru," which has been displaced but not abandoned. Césaire is recognizing the difficult terrain of the postemancipatory situation; his Caliban finally is more Ariel-like than would have been imagined initially. *Une Tempête* is a play for a black theater, a psychodrama in which the actors don masks. It is in the black skin, white masks of the ongoing colonial situation that the play situates its struggle. Césaire rewrites *The Tempest* past the point where the plot ran out.

Dayan's happy story of reciprocity, with its un-self-reflexive casting of 'is as male-male coupling, endorses a version of what a feminist critic like

Jyotsna Singh, in "Caliban versus Miranda," deplores in Césaire. By having his Caliban repudiate any desire for Miranda, she charges, Césaire, like
Shakespeare before him, imagines women only as objects of homosocial exchange; the revolution is thus "an all-male" enterprise (205). Worse: "[I]n the
absence of a native woman as his sexual reproductive mate" (206), "Césaire's
call for a revolution lacks credibility as he prevents Prospero's former slave
from peopling the isle with Calibans" (207). Singh cites Wynter, but she takes
the installation of a proper racial mate as leading to properly racialized procreation. The woman Singh desires would be in precisely the position that
Brathwaite mandates: coupled, procreative. This, for her, is the "revolutionary" role for women that Césaire denies representation.

Césaire does represent Singh's heterosexual imperative, however, through
his Miranda, who is reduced to a mere outline of Shakespeare's character but
with a few telling changes. Baffled by Prospero's revelation that she is a princess, she affirms a relationship with nature, describing herself as "wild,"[122] if
an aristocrat only "queen of the wildflowers, of the streams and paths, running
barefoot through thorns and flowers, spared by one, caressed by the other" (6).
Her attachment to nature is apparently maintained when she first encounters
Ferdinand: "I hope you'll like it here with us. The island is pretty. I'll show you
the beaches and the forests, I'll tell you the names of fruits and flowers, I'll
introduce you to a whole world of insects, of lizards of every hue, of birds . . .
Oh, you cannot imagine! The birds! . . . " (18). These lines, transposed from
Caliban's offer to Stephano and Trinculo in Shakespeare (2.2.154–58), could
suggest an identification between Miranda and Caliban. However, Miranda's
ties to nature or to Caliban have been broken by her knowledge of her royal
status, and no naivete can be found in her initial exchange with Ferdinand,
which precedes her offer of a tour of the island. She recognizes him instantly as
a flatterer and as royalty, and the revelation in the chess scene, that she is as
much of a power politician as he is, comes as no surprise. In Césaire's stripped-
down version of the character, Miranda passes from a state of innocence to
one of experience almost instantaneously in assuming her role as Ferdinand's
mate. It is possible in this to find a shorthand allusion to Lamming's treatment
of the play in *The Pleasures of Exile,* in which he notes the shared innocence
of Caliban and Miranda, both pawns to Prospero, but goes on to remark the
crucial difference, from Prospero's point of view, that Miranda can be included
in his designs, whereas Caliban must remain outside. From a certain feminist
perspective, one could read Césaire's (mis)treatment of Miranda as parallel
to Shakespeare's masculinism; could find it even further heightened in the
context of some black nationalist calls to unleash violence—including rape—
against white women.[123] From another feminist perspective, it is possible
to say that Césaire's brutal treatment of Miranda may have potential for a
critique alert to the difference that race makes in gendered/sexual formations.

In that respect, rather than taking (heterosexual) offense at Caliban's declaration that he "couldn't care less" (13) about Miranda, one could imagine Césaire doing what Wynter insists, showing that Miranda is not an inevitable object of male desire. Césaire's Caliban happily hands Miranda over to Ferdinand. True, this makes Miranda a pawn not only for her father but also for Caliban; yet it also suggests that Césaire cannot imagine that once Miranda has been conscripted into her father's designs—from the moment she knows her social status—she could be drawn back into the orbit of nature that she has repudiated. Césaire's Caliban equivocates his desire for Miranda, answering Prospero's charge: "Rape! Rape!" he exclaims, "Listen, you old goat, you're the one that put those dirty thoughts in my head" (13). The translator here chooses one possible meaning in Caliban's line: "[T]u me prêtes tes idées libidinouses" (27), which can just as easily mean "you ascribe to me your libidinous ideas." This response answers Lamming's "Lie," adduces Fanon's rereading of the colonial psychology that Mannoni attributes to such incestuous fantasies. If rape were attempted, it would not reveal Caliban's indigenous/racial character or his essential maleness.

If Caliban's handing of Miranda over to Ferdinand makes explicit that her coming-to-consciousness involves her implication within the colonialist adventure and thereby her de-naturing, this highlights Caliban's attachment to nature in the play. Nature is gendered female in *Une Tempête,* an equation of woman and nature that certainly can be suspect, as it is in Brathwaite, and as Singh charges (196) when she wishes for something more than a symbolic Mother Earth in the play. Yet her complaint is prompted by the very lines that Cliff quotes in "Caliban's Daughter" (46), as Caliban defends Sycorax against Prospero's denigrations:

> [S]he was my mother, and I won't deny her! Anyhow, you only think she's dead because you think the earth itself is dead ... It's so much simpler that way! Dead, you can walk on it, pollute it, you can tread upon it with the steps of a conqueror. I respect the earth, because I know that it's alive, and I know Sycorax is alive. (12)[124]

Cliff can value his words as not merely symbolic because she insists on the difficulty of recovering this primordial attachment even as something to be known and valued, let alone as the basis for a reordered future that might break with the depredations of colonialism. Caliban's insistence on an unbroken tie with Sycorax, and his recognition elsewhere in the play that Prospero's arsenal of weapons involves the misuse of a nature that might be marshaled against him, are not merely symbolic uses of nature—or of the feminine—but indications of a difficult impasse in the recovery toward which Cliff aims. For Cliff, Caliban's invocation of his mother is most significant for its relocation of his being on this natural/maternal terrain. Feminine identification cannot assure him normative masculinity. Césaire's Caliban's gesture, as Cliff prompts us to read it, is not incorporative and erasing; it is, rather, gender transforming (and potentially, therefore, nonheterosexualizing as well). The Caliban with whom Cliff identifies as Caliban's daughter is in fact Césaire's Caliban.

Before a Sycorax can be represented as a real possibility, there must be the kind of voicing and desiring and identification that Caliban articulates. Cliff takes Caliban's lines as her own, as she does too when she cites a passage in Césaire's *Notebook of a Return to the Native Land* in "Caliban's Daughter" (39), a passage describing a schoolboy, a "sleepy little nigger" whose teacher cannot pry a word from him, "for his voice gets lost in the swamp of hunger" (37).[125] Cliff overrides Césaire's masculine identification with a "sleepy little nigger" by way of racial identification, perhaps too along the route of "his voice," "sa voix," a plot that is gendered grammatically in French ("voix" is a feminine noun), not biologically naturalized.

The identifications that Cliff makes—with Caliban, with Césaire—cross and complicate gender but remain in the service of an affirmation of the primordial (and silenced) black woman whose realization would be a new subject position necessarily differentiated from the normative (and colonialist) heterosexuality instanced by Césaire's Miranda and Ferdinand. Singh's deployment of Wynter is tilted in the direction of the feminism against which Wynter cautions, one that forgets race and mandates heterosexuality as the way for a woman to be a woman. Césaire's interrogation of "nature" denaturalizes as colonial the imperative of heterosexual coupling. The recovery of nature is the recovery (from the colonial perspective) of the unnatural.

As Singh notes, Césaire's play ends with Caliban and Prospero locked in a Hegelian dialectic. She terms it a "curious, almost natural bond" ("Caliban versus Miranda," 205), the muted (but unmistakable) implication being that this male couple embodies a masculinist misogyny tantamount to homosexuality. Tom Hayes offers a similar critique, except for him such masculinist bonding cannot be a sign of a sexual link since he believes that male homosexuality per se must be politically progressive. As M. Jacqui Alexander has demonstrated, however, there is now a flourishing white gay male travel industry in the Caribbean indistinguishable from the mainstream industry that has been such a support for a nationalist/heterosexualization project that guarantees the immiseration of women.[126] Cliff's point that native homosexuality ought not be seen as a form of colonialist imposition and degradation does not deny that there has been colonialist/homosexual imposition (in prostitution, in imposing Western-style sexualities as normative truths about sexuality); her point is just that such plots do not exhaust the possibilities of explaining or regulating "native" sexuality. Césaire sees this too when, following the scene of the student in *Notebook,* the "exacerbated stench of corruption" is laid at the door of "the monstrous sodomies of the host and the sacrificing priest, . . . the prostitutions, the lubricities, the treasons, the lies" (37). The question in such a formulation must be whether Césaire has foreclosed the possibility of nonheterosexual forms of "native" sexuality as inevitably the result of the tainted scene of sodomizing the native, a question raised too by similarly lurid descriptions of European decadence in Césaire's *Discourse,* or by the fact that male mutilation in the *Notebook* is named explicitly as castration (61).

Nonetheless, in the face of desires to disidentify with the "nigger" made by colonialism, the gesture in the *Notebook* is to say "I accept," to affirm oneself as Caliban/cannibal, to embrace and reclaim through the term "negritude" a territory of shame and abjection:

> I accept . . : negritude . . . measured by the compass of suffering
> and the Negro every day more base, more cowardly, more sterile, less profound,
>   more spilled out of himself, more separated from himself, more wily with
>   himself, less immediate to himself,
> I accept, I accept it all. (77)[127]

Although the speaker of the *Notebook* is undoubtedly male, he aims to unleash monsters, buried energies of the land that can be symbolized by its "fat tits" or "orgasmic" waters (39) or figured, as in the opening lines, as the face of a woman telling lies or occupied in her lyric cadence, a flow that may be the same as that of a peasant woman urinating or, elsewhere in the poem, of his mother pedaling for life at her Singer sewing machine (41). Certainly this is a poem in which the speaker reiterates his "virile prayer" (69, 73) and wishes for germination, for the awakening of voice and activity. Yet the plot of the poem is not so gender exclusive as to preclude the kinds of identifications Cliff makes. Indeed, as the poem moves to imagine futurity, it crosses gender and complicates what at first seems like a heterosexualized coupling:

> [L]et the ovaries of the water come where the future stirs its testicles
> let the wolves come who feed in the untamed openings of the body at the hour
>   when my moon and your sun meet at the ecliptic inn. (67)[128]

The union of the speaker and his people in this poem may be imagined as a sexual embrace, but these lines exceed literal heterosexual figuration for this. Although "fraternity" is one insistent name for this "male thirst and the desire stubborn" (45), this male-male embrace includes a feminized earth and the "feminization" at times of a male speaker characterized by "untamed *[sauvages]* openings."

This body is far more determinate in its racialization than it is in its gender, and its race begins, as it does for Cliff, in the grandmother's bed (*Notebook,* 43). So if we return to the moment in *A Tempest* that has been taken to mark the limits of Césaire for feminist or queer reading, the insistent phallicism of ⸍e Yoruba god Eshu whom Césaire introduces into the play, we might first

note that the trickster/metamorphic figure could be based in the abject equation of black man and phallus that Fanon details in *Black Skin, White Masks*.
There are many risks here, not least—as Lee Edelman's "Part for the (W)hole"
persuasively argues[129]—that the very attempt to secure heterosexual masculinity may involve a display of the penis tantamount to an announcement of
castration (and, within this logic, homosexuality). The entanglement of race
and sexuality here, as in Fanon, crosses the line between homophobic masculinism and homosexual display. Eshu's main effect is to scandalize the goddesses. His song takes shots at queens and brides, sending the queen naked
into the streets and the bride into the bed of another man. Whether this
misogyny marks him as hetero- or homosexual is not so easy to tell. Eshu
proclaims an erotics aimed at the anerotics of the original wedding masque,
a disruptive force that makes Prospero wonder whether he is losing his grip.
The god reveals the male-male tie in which it is always the racial Other who
is the exemplar of sexual potency. "Power! Power!" Prospero intones, "what is
power, if I cannot calm my own fears?" (49).

   In these impasses of indeterminate, projected sexualities, having and
being the phallus—which is to say, being male or female as much as being
hetero- or homosexual—is thrown into question precisely because of the racialized difference Eshu embodies. But Eshu also offers another set of terms
to understand his sexuality in the lines he speaks when he appears:

> How about something to drink? . . . Your liquour's not bad. However, I must say
> I prefer dogs! *(Looking at Iris)* I see that shocks the little lady, but to each his
> own. Some prefer chickens, others prefer goats. I'm not too fond of chickens, my-
> self. But if you're talking about a black dog . . . think of poor Eshu! (47)

Eshu's slide along the registers of appetite allows for an embrace of bestiality. Eshu, overwhelmingly male, Myriam Chancy reminds us (by way of
Henry Louis Gates Jr.'s deployment of the god in *The Signifying Monkey* as
the embodiment of multiple meaning), was "originally believed to be a bi-
sexual God, both feminine and masculine."[130] His declaration of alternative
appetites/sexualities finds its parallel when Ariel resists Prospero's claim to
have "delivered" him from his tree prison by expressing a desire to have remained there: "After all, I might have turned into a real tree in the end" (10).
As the editors of Césaire's poetry remark, this tree-desire is often expressed
in his poetry; it suggests a rootedness in a nature whose capacity for meta-
morphosis and transformation remains the hoped-for source of energy to resist the deformations of colonial domination.[131] When Prospero frees Ariel, he
promises "a very unsettling agenda," to be the voice in the wind and the earth
making "the most forgetful slaves" yearn for freedom (60).

   In this context of strange desires, one can register the force of the "sodomies" invoked in the *Notebook* and place them beside a scene that Césaire
adds to his *Tempest* (by way of Ernest Renan's rewriting of *The Tempest*, which

Césaire also is recasting), a friar's accusation that Prospero professes "heretical perversion" (7).[132] Here, as in the *Notebook,* the perversity would seem to be an ascription by the very institution (the church) that Césaire explicitly names in the *Discourse* as the site of the ideological production of a justification for colonial greed and rapacity. The friar's condemnation of Prospero in the play is not taken to be naming a fact about him; rather, the accusation is exposing the church's mendacity. This leaves open a space for perversion, as when the speaker of the *Notebook* affirms his obscene apostasy (51–53). The so-called friar who appears in *Une Tempête* (his title in scare quotes in the original French) is a travesty of the scandalous fraternity that Césaire affirms, an identification with abjected people and place that the church might call "sodomy" but that is recoded as nature. Hence, the scene between Ariel and Caliban that Césaire added to Shakespeare (on the model of Renan, in fact) ends with Ariel and Caliban exchanging the name of "brother" despite their fundamental differences (23). Here, as in the final scene between Caliban and Prospero, fraternity is a male-male relationship. Yet, as *X* suggested earlier, it is still a place of crossing, potentially available beyond gender determination.

If *Une Tempête* offers no brief for full-scale revolution, it is because such an overturning merely reverses the dialectic. This explains the long exchange between Caliban and Prospero at the end of *Une Tempête.* As Césaire has claimed elsewhere, in remarks that guide later comments in describing the play by way of Hegel, the play reveals that "the slave is always more important than his master—for it is the slave who makes history."[133] In the closing dialogue, Caliban and Prospero throw back at each other the sentence, "I hate you." Nonetheless they end locked in a relationship: "And now, Caliban, it's you and me!" (67). The play closes with them as the sole inhabitants of the island, and just before Caliban shouts his cry of "Freedom," Prospero, withered and diminished, recognizes again that "it's just us two now . . . you-me . . . me-you" (68).[134]

This odd coupling takes place in a scene that Cliff names through the Jamaican word "ruination": "the reclamation of land, the disruption of cultivation, civilization, by the uncontrolled, uncontrollable forest" ("Caliban's Daughter," 40). Prospero looks about him to find the landscape overrun with opossums, animals he had imagined erecting themselves on their tails (*A Tempest,* 67). Seeing only "dirty nature" (68), he sees the Sycorax he had claimed was dead. Caliban calls Prospero "the Anti-Nature" (52) as he assembles his rebel forces—nature spirits—flinging the charge of perversion, of the unnatural, back where it belongs. In the final stagnation and stalemate with which the play ends, like the inanition of the *Notebook,* the island awaits the charge of a new life seized in the old word "freedom," a resemanticization of the old categories of abuse and old divisions. The new demonic monstrous ground for change is Caliban—and Sycorax.

In Césaire, the "unnatural" in Caliban lies precisely in his affirmations of nature, for this is nature without civilization (civilization being, of course, the misnomer for conquest and exploitation), nature opposed to the patriarchal, aristocratic, white male imperial design. Caliban's "nature" is the tie to his mother that cannot be broken; this is how he has access to himself. No wonder, then, that Cliff cites Caliban's defense of Sycorax, for these lines represent the play's counterplot that lodges a hope for futurity. Not cited by Cliff, but central to this project of risked identifications, are the lines that Caliban speaks immediately after his invocation, in which he reports that Sycorax haunts his dreams, even appearing to him when he "was lying by the stream on my belly lapping at the muddy water" (13). His/her reflection warns him of the approach of "the Beast" in which he might see in the waters the figure that Prospero would have him see as his identity, and with which he would destroy Caliban.

> you lied to me so much,
> about the world, about myself,
> that you ended up by imposing on me
> an image of myself:
> underdeveloped, in your words, undercompetent
> that's how you made me see myself!
> And I hate that image . . . and it's false!
>
> (64)

When the monster speaks French, the lines of difference can no longer be maintained. "There is no reason why André Breton should say of Césaire, 'Here is a black man who handles the French language as no white man today can'" (Fanon, *Black Skin, White Masks*, 39).

DO YOU LOVE ME, MASTER?

If Cliff's estimation of Césaire (or Wynter's, for that matter) can be seen from the vantage point of a certain feminism to constitute a violation of gendered solidarity, it is nonetheless a move toward racial alterity that invites, from a standpoint that still could be called feminist, a rethinking of sexuality and gendered proprieties. These debates within feminism could be resituated further through the complex terrains in "the long crisis of modern sexual definition" succinctly mapped by Eve Kosofsky Sedgwick's *Epistemology of the Closet*. Sedgwick notes how sexual definition has been fractured by minoritizing impulses (which assume homosexuality as the identity of a discrete subgroup) and universalizing impulses (which assume a spectrum of sexual identities). These definitions intersect with formulations about gender: sexual identity as a matter of consolidating gender (where male homosexuality would be continuous with masculinism, for example) or sexual identity as a matter of cross-gender identification (where male homosexuality would testify to a "woman" within or be revealed in "effeminate" behavior).[135] These alignments can crisscross in surprising ways in the indicatively European and U.S. contexts for male identity that Sedgwick explores. They gain further complexity when to sex and gender one adds a consideration of their embodiment in racialized subject positions.

In *Abeng,* as Clare ponders the scene in which she fired a gun at the male intruder who interrupted her intimacy with Zoe, she wonders whether fear or shame had motivated her, and she thinks about her uncle (and godfather) Robert, labeled "funny" by her family: "Robert had caused some disturbance when he brought a dark man home from Montego Bay and introduced him to his mother as 'my dearest friend'" (125). Robert's parents recoil at the indiscretion of his statement but also at the friend, a U.S. Black, who, they assume, "led him into all this foolishness" (125). Clare asks her parents' maid Dorothy to explain what makes Robert "funny" and is told he is a "battyman—him want fe lay down wit' only other men" (125). "Explanations" for Robert's homosexuality (his being a battyman, a buttman) multiply: that he is crazy, uncontrolled, or the product of inbreeding or cross-breeding or of oversolicitous maternal care. Clare responds aversively to Robert even as his case seems to parallel her own, something she cannot quite see although he has come to mind as she thinks about her desire for Zoe, whose "fault" she understands to be congruent with what she has been taught is wrong about "loving someone darker than herself" (127), an "error" that has been presented to her in terms of heterosexual choice and gendered propriety.

The "explanations" about Robert are, as usual in the novel, evasions and complications around the twinned unspeakabilities of sexuality and race. Robert's desire for a darker black man—and an American to boot—divides race by color and nation. In that context, the American can function as a Westerner subverting native desire from its straight path. But Robert's desire, insofar as it is innate, also follows along the tracks of an account of race that Clare has been taught: that to be black is to be deficient, to be made to suffer, to be tied to the indignities of a body whose dangerous eruptions must be tamed or borne. Robert's "condition" is allied to bad blood or bad upbringing, much as Clare has been removed from a maternal line of race identification into the nonetheless maternal line of middle-class femininity. Yet Clare also wonders whether the term "battyman" can be applied to her, whether Robert's failed masculinity is equivalent to her unfeminine desires. Indeed, there also is presented to her the possibility that her desire for darkness represents not so much a deficit of femininity as its excess.

These tangles complicate Timothy Chin's claim in "'Bullers' and 'Battymen'" that Cliff sees Clare's incipient lesbianism as parallel to Robert's homosexuality. It is notable, for instance, that in "battyman" *Abeng* has a "native" word for male-male sex, whereas it lacks one for female-female relations, which suggests, at the least, a certain visibility and legibility for Robert's desire that cannot produce gender equivalence. *Abeng* thus asks whether male homosexuality and lesbianism can be equated, even as it suggests their congruence. How and when does Robert's "funny" nature become visible as disturbance? Does the label "battyman" simply mean homosexual, or does it mean a desire that is multiply transgressive: for another man, for an American, for someone darker? The last thing Clare is told about Robert is that "the disease was the fault of Robert's mother," that Robert was "spoiled" by maternal love (126). Is the incipient charge of gendered failure (on his mother's part, on his) the same as the charge brought against Clare, of wanting to be a boy, a charge leveled at her identification with her light-skinned father, rather than with her mother, which may yet be a feminine identification with the line of Nanny?

Robert is not the only "battyman" in *Abeng;* the term is also applied to Clinton, a man who has returned from the United States and moved back in with his mother, showing no interest in women. Taunted by neighbors as a battyman, Clinton is left to drown, his body unburied. His mother, once thought of as a powerful obeah-woman, is reseen as Mad Hannah, as she worries that her son's spirit will never be at rest. "Where they used to poke fun at Clinton, they now poked fun at his mother" (63). Through its disdain for Hannah, the community disavows its ties to African belief systems of obeah, Sycoraxian magic, and knowledge of nature; it refuses to see that its rejection of Clinton is allied to this racial refusal. Clare is drawn to Hannah; her questioning of normative regimes could land her in the "mad" position of Hannah because she recoils at the limits of a prescribed femininity or in the position of Clinton, who drowns in the mockeries of community refusal. Uncle Robert also drowns.

Cliff's representation through Clare of the possibility of drawing male-male desire into the orbit of female-female desire—along with her linking of both of them to the Calibanic project of reclaiming Sycorax and through her both Africa and the Caribbean landscape as sites of new possibilities—is significant not only in its own terms but also insofar as it points to the fact that nonphobic representations of male homosexuality in Caribbean literature are almost exclusively to be found in the work of women writers and theorists. Patricia Powell's *Pagoda,* for instance, has as its central character Lowe, a Chinese immigrant to Jamaica in the late nineteenth century, a woman who cross-dresses as a man both to escape forced marriage in China and to enable her immigration. Lowe is protected by the white man who raped her and provided her with a wife so that Lowe can continue her disguise and bring up their child in a seemingly ordinary family. The villagers suspect the two "men" of a "nasty" cross-racial/sexual relationship, of being "devil workers" (15). They do not suspect what the novel gradually reveals, that Lowe and her wife are lesbian partners (Lowe, in fact, is not her wife's only female lover). The novel suggests that female-female relationships are commonplace (in the rum shop women complain about their husbands and children and talk about "the women they loved on the side" [57]). The lability of female desire provides a route for Powell to represent the complexities of relationships that may appear to be heterosexual or homosexual but that are, at root, female-female. The difficult project that the novel imagines for its hero(ine) is the revelation to her daughter that her father was her mother, that the woman she took to be her mother, and who indeed mothered her, was not. This plot resonates with *Me Dying Trial* in its extensions of female community and in the centrality of a fraught mother-daughter relationship (here, the mother rather than the daughter is "lesbian"). It draws these into cross-gendered plots that begin to implicate male same-sex coupling, a feature even more in evidence in *Me Dying Trial,* where the proto-lesbian Peppy has a particularly close relationship with her proto-gay brother Rudi. It is in fact his coming out that drives a wedge in the family, leading to maternal repudiation. And the most painful point of this is that earlier in the novel, as Gwennie, the mother, attempts independence, she is guided by her friendship with a man who is involved with another man; this man becomes a model for Rudi. Powell's point in these novels is to suggest a range of enabling extrafamilial relationships that need to be valued rather than excoriated.

To the extent that male homosexuality is understood in Caribbean cultures on a cross-gender model, it is not surprising that it is rarely represented in work by male writers or that when it is, it is denigrated. The battyman represented by Guyanese writer Roy A. K. Heath in *The Murderer* (1978) is a sinister character: a police informant who lives with his alcoholic prostitute mother who wonders "where he pick up the germ from"; the novel suggests that it was from her.[136] Recall Jeremy from Lamming's *Water with Berries,* also politically suspect, and the parallel Miranda figure Randa, who betrayed her marital vows. Consider Brathwaite's only reference to male homosexuality of which I am aware: In *Barabajan Poems,* he laments the destruction of a street in Barbados by developers who have no respect for the past and who seek to make the island a tourist paradise. In highly ambiguous remarks, Brathwaite recalls Bajan lore about Sandylane, that it had been a pickup site for wealthy Europeans to entice "poor/needy/ambitious? young Bajan males into homosexual service" (309). It is difficult exactly to locate Brathwaite's nostalgia for a street in which, he claims, Bajans were made "aliens" by a sexual experience that he clearly understands as parallel to recent exploitative developments— difficult, moreover, since he applies the terms "bullers" and "battymen" to these Bajans, that is, uses indigenous terms for men who are supposedly made alien by having sex with men. A slight pause of identification does occur in his telling—"we were the ALIENS," he affirms—but on the whole the story of Sandylane battymen is told as some kind of joke. ("Battyman," "buller," and "auntie man," the most common terms used in the Caribbean, are slangy, pejorative, and derisive in usage.)[137] Does Brathwaite defend against the truth that Hilton Als blithely announces in *The Women,* as he describes his mother's lack of surprise that a friend of hers is an "auntie man": "[A]untie men were not mysterious beings to her; in Barbados, most ostensibly straight men had sex with them, which was good, since that left women alone for a while."[138] Als himself identifies as an auntie man, an identity formed through his identification with his mother as a "Negress."

In her work on mati workers in Suriname, Wekker mentions in passing that the term can refer not only to women's relations but to those between men as well ("One Finger," 331), a parallel that may be attributed to the separation of male and female homosocial cultures. Mati may have derived from a term for shipmate ("Mati-ism," 149), a derivation parallel to a male-male lexicon among Indo-Caribbeans, or so Sean Lokaisingh-Meighoo argues in an essay on the lability of the language for male-male camaraderie that arises from the term *jahaji bhai,* "ship brother."[139] This term can be applied by either gender to each other but also extends, he argues, to male homosocial relations that also are sexual. The map of sexuality provided by these examples is complex: It may involve the separation of gender as a social fact or a commonality marked by a shared term; it may describe same-sex sexuality as a matter of cross-gender identification or as the consolidation of same-sex social relationships.

These provide sites of possibility written across diasporic existence, as Stuart Hall, for one, has argued.[140] The multiplicities of these social/sexual arrangements for new kinds of persons are the antidote to the lethal binarisms that pit groups against each other, clinging to older paradigms of exclusive identity. But precisely for that reason, as groups attempt to consolidate power, same-sex relations are the sites of severe stigma, scarcely represented at all in Caribbean literature beyond the examples I have been gathering on these pages. When Cliff jokingly calls up "Trinidadian" as a possible name for lesbian relations, she does so because the term "Jamaican" seems unavailable. In 1992, when a gay march took place in Jamaica, it was met with violence; in 1997, when the state proposed distributing condoms in prisons to decrease the rate of HIV infection, the move was regarded as tantamount to promoting homosexuality, a position the government then insisted it certainly did not seek to take.[141] One need not go to the Caribbean, of course, to witness state-sponsored homophobia. Responses to the possibility of making same-sex relationships visible echo those to be found in the United Kingdom or the United States. Nor is the legendary homophobia of Jamaica unique; Alexander's work on failed attempts in the early 1990s to liberalize sexual laws offers overwhelming evidence of the assumptions of ignorance on the part of state managers in the Bahamas and Trinidad, their display of the privileges of unknowing that Sedgwick so tellingly explores in *Epistemology of the Closet.* Nonetheless, the point here is that both the homophobia displayed and the attempts to organize sexual life in terms of the homosexual/heterosexual distinction constitute refusals of Caribbean sociality and sexual organization. AIDS, of course, may quickly dissolve any such distinction, though not the difference of how the disease is lived in the Caribbean. In *My Brother,* Jamaica Kincaid's powerful account of the 1996 death of her brother Devon, his only chance to stay alive comes from her bringing him AZT. The drug is not otherwise available in Antigua; AIDS is an imminent death sentence. In Powell's *A Small Gathering of Bones,* a novel about AIDS in Jamaica in the late 1970s, HIV infection, as Aparajita Sagar argues in an essay on the novel, is not simply to be understood as a sexual infection; it is a disease spread by the particularly virulent response that homosexuality evokes.[142]

That virulence, as both Kincaid and Powell suggest, is the product of the colonial experience that has promoted the disunity and disintegration of Caribbean life that so many commentators, from Césaire, Fanon, and Goveia on, have detailed. "Antiguans are not particularly homophobic," Kincaid writes in *My Brother;* their homophobia parallels the fact that "they are quick to disparage anyone or anything that is different from whom or what they think of as normal."[143] This matches their lack of sympathy for those in pain or in trouble, and the reason for this, Kincaid explains, as so many before her have done, lies in the history of "subjugation, leaving in its wake humiliation and inferiority; to see someone in straits worse than your own is to feel at first pity for them and soon better than them" (186).

The valuing of homosexual existence against such deeply ingrained colonialist legacies of feeling and behavior is a central point in *Spirits in the Dark* (1993) by H. Nigel Thomas (born in St. Vincent, now located at Laval University, Quebec). Thomas's novel is virtually the sole Caribbean novel written from a gay male perspective.[144] It is, in many respects, a familiar story about a young man passing through the colonial education system, recognizing its limits and its aim to divide islanders as a way to further and reinforce neocolonial regimes. In the novel, the world of Isabella is black, but anti-African, and although texts by Fanon, Lamming, and Malcolm X are available, Thomas portrays little organized political resistance. His hero, Jerome Quashee, differs from many protagonists of Caribbean novels, however, insofar as the divisions and alienation that lead to his mental breakdown are compounded by his homoerotic desires. From the vantage of an unspeakable difference, he sees the intolerance of difference in his milieu, linking its racial divisions (black against white, black against Carib) and sexual antagonisms (men against women) to homophobia. The novel proposes a utopic solution through an Afro-religious group whose democratic/socialist sociality recalls Césaire's descriptions in his *Discourse* of precolonial Africa or Lamming's fantasies about the original Tribe Boys. In this community, Jerome can hope to find acceptance for his same-sex desires. Nonetheless, the best that Jerome's spiritual counselor can propose is that he share this knowledge about himself sparingly, that he suffer his trials and tribulations, for most members of the community are not yet ready to receive it: "Is true that people is always growing, some faster, some slower. But most o' the brethren ain't grown enough fo' understand why you is how yo' is and fo' accept yo' as yo' is" (212–13).

Timothy Chin devotes several fine pages to *Spirits in the Dark:* "[A]t the same time that it exposes the complicity of the community, Thomas's text, like Cliff's, demonstrates an acute sensitivity to the ambiguous and sometimes contradictory spaces that inevitably exist in any culture" ("'Bullers' and 'Battymen,'" 139). It is, he continues, "within the context of concrete affiliative social relations that the potential for negotiating these contradictions can exist" (140). *Spirits in the Dark* represents Jerome and a few other men with homosexual desires as a distinct minority; none of the brethren presumably feel such desires or have homosexual sex. The sites of possibility that Chin describes are valuable ones, and they are notable for their cross-gendered potential: a marketwoman, for example, who is, in fact, a man and yet is fully accepted by the other marketwomen. Moreover, Jerome's initiation into the brotherhood involves a symbolic death and rebirth in which he descends into a cave, a womb, to be reborn from Mother Earth and to derive from her *and from his mother* the strength to endure: "There followed another silence, during which he struggled with his memory. He told himself he wouldn't get out of the cave whole without it. Suddenly it was as if his body chose to relax and he heard within himself an echo of his mother's voice. 'Some things yo' can't hurry, no. Yo' just have fo' let them finish in their own time. Meekly wait and murmur not.' . . . *I will endure*" (193).

What Jerome achieves at this moment parallels Césaire's Caliban's invocations of his mother. The difficulty of this reclamation—so central to Cliff—is also key to the novels of Patricia Powell, as we have seen in *Me Dying Trial.* Fraught relations with mothers are the focus in her *Small Gathering of Bones* as well. The character in the novel who is dying of AIDS is literally killed by his mother, Miss Kaysen, who throws him down the stairs; when she found out about his illness, she repudiated him: "I am not your mother" (*Small Gathering of Bones,* 21). At the novel's close, the novel's protagonist, Dale Singleton, also faces Miss Kaysen, and perhaps a similar demise (he also is HIV positive, although he has not yet recognized that). Dale is strongly identified with his mother; his relationship with Nevin, his former lover, with whom he continues to live, in fact parallels his mother's relationship with his father. Both men are unfaithful. Dale had attempted to tell his mother about his sexuality, but she had refused to hear him; now she is dead. Early in the novel, we see Dale at his desk. Over it are "faded etchings of: 'Jesus Saves', 'Batty-man', and 'One Love Jamaica'" (14). All betray him in the course of the novel. He leaves his church (in which he had learned the lesson that he should silently suffer his difference), and although there is a network of gay men and of locales in which to socialize, Dale plunges into unprotected anonymous sex. Jamaica is the villain in the novel, and the country is embodied in the figure of the rejecting mother.

Beside the murderous Miss Kaysen, there is Mrs. Morgan, Nevin's mother. She has maimed her husband (fathers are basically absent in the novel). She holds her son close. They work together, live in houses that back each other. Mrs. Morgan knows about her son's sexuality and uses her knowledge to blackmail Dale when he will not help her break up the affair her daughter is having with a Rastafarian. Mrs. Morgan resembles no one more than the mother in Kincaid's *My Brother*. There, too, the sons live in a house right behind the mother's. One brother no longer speaks to his mother; the other broke her neck "by throwing her onto the ground in the process of trying to stop her from throwing stones at him because she disapproved of him bringing a girlfriend, or any woman with whom he had a sexual relationship, into the structure where he—they all—lived" (*My Brother,* 188).

Kincaid's mother wishes her children dead, the telos of the kinds of divisions that characterize Antigua in Kincaid's scathing *A Small Place*. In *My Brother,* Kincaid writes about the brother who did die, not of the two who have survived in these violent repudiations that parallel Kincaid's own ferocious writing, filled with loving hatred of her mother. When Devon fell ill, Kincaid assumed heterosexual sex was responsible. "If he had had homosexual sex, he would not have advertised it" (40). Abandoned by everyone when he is hospitalized, except his mother—who relishes his suffering (when he recovers enough to leave the hospital, he shares a bed with her)—she apparently does not know what Kincaid discovers only after her brother's death, when she meets a woman at a reading who introduces herself as a lesbian who kept her home open as a place for gay men to meet. Devon had been among them. This life of Devon's remains opaque for Kincaid. Looking at his corpse, she reports, "[W]e did not and cannot know what he looked like as the seducer of men" (181). His sexual life apparently left no traces. Yet it was lived under his mother's eye.

> [H]e had died without ever understanding or knowing, or being able to let the world in which he lived know, who he really was—not a single sense of identity but all the complexities of who he was—he could not express fully: his fear of being laughed at, his fear of meeting with the scorn of the people he knew best were overwhelming and he could not live with it openly. His homosexuality is one thing, and my being a writer is another altogether, but this truth is not lost on me: I could not have become a writer while living among the people I knew best, I could not have become myself while living among the people I knew best— and I only knew them best because I was from them, of them, and so often felt I was them—and they were—are—the people who ought to have loved me best in the whole world. (*My Brother,* 162)

The painful silence in Kincaid's account, like the stigma and silence around same-sex relations in most Caribbean novels, keeps suggesting what Als claims to be true, that the highly occluded representation of same-sex behavior exists side by side with the ordinariness of its occurrence in mother-dominated societies, where the mother is herself positioned by self-division. Stuart Hall is fond of saying that he left the Caribbean because he needed to get away from his mother. He has also pointed to the utter hopelessness of Fanon's claim that the Oedipus complex is unknown in the Antilles, a region Hall characterizes by "deeply troubled and assertively heterosexual and often homophobic black masculinities."[145] As Als puts it: "'[M]aleness' is not a viable construct in colored life. Colored life is matriarchal" (*The Women,* 40), and he virulently faults black power movements for their mesmerizing relationship to what he regards as the utterly spurious figure of the black male and his empowerment. The identity he claims—as Negress—is, he implies, closer to the truth about black men. The pleasure he takes in seducing black men lies in his making them see their vulnerability. *The Women* thus draws us back into the orbit of cross-gendered identification and, within the typologies we have been exploring, back to the relationship of Caliban to Sycorax that Cliff reclaims.

The "women" in *The Women* are Als and his mother, as well as Dorothy Dean and Owen Dodson, the figures to whom he devotes eulogistic chapters. These "women" are, themselves, divided in various ways, and not merely by gender (only two of them are female). Dean was a fag hag, living in a world surrounded by privileged gay white men: "I am a white faggot trapped in a black woman's body" (73), s/he says of herself. Dodson is the opposite, a male Negress: "He competed with women sexually for what he desired: a man—which he did not consider himself to be" (135). When Als has sex with Dodson, he becomes a man; Dodson "was my first woman" (132). These identifications across race and gender are not sites of comfort in *The Women.* For necessarily they are also sites of disidentification with whom one is or is supposed to be. These are black men and women who desire whiteness in various ways, culturally and physically. It is part of Als's point to expose that unspeakable cultural desire as rooted in various forms of black consciousness, both in the Harlem Renaissance, which, Als claims, denatured Dodson's genius in its search for a middle-class respectability, and also in the black power movement, about which Als is particularly cruel, exposing the poetry of Nikki Giovanni, for example, for its vaunting of black male heterosexual privilege and power and tearing into Malcolm X's autobiography for its failure to represent his mother. Als goes so far as to claim that Malcolm's desire for male power was his desire to be the white man who had raped his grandmother. Als dismisses the "dreary marginal issues of race, or class, or gender" (19) for the complexity of the identification he claims (from his mother) as Negress: "It is difficult to be Negress-identified, since the Negress rarely identifies with herself" (44). Negress-identification is necessarily disidentification. It is to locate oneself and one's desire as "a disgrace to the race" (73), as a "Bad Nigger" (83). Als thus refuses identity for the sake of the kinds of wrong identifications that Cliff entertains.

When Cliff resumes the story of Clare Savage in *No Telephone to Heaven,* she tells it from the vantage point of Clare's final decision to return to Jamaica, to claim it, rather than England (where she has been studying art history) as her mother country. She returns, moreover, to join with Jamaican revolutionaries united under "the name of Nanny" (*No Telephone to Heaven,* 5); to them she gives her maternal grandmother's ruinate land (Miss Mattie is long dead) as a base for their operations. Clare dies at the end of the novel, burned into the ruinate forest by government forces that decimate the rebel band. This return joins together Clare's desires: for mother, grandmother, Jamaica, Africa, the past, the land, another voice—a desire that one might call "lesbian" (even though Clare has no sexual relationship with a woman in the novel) in the extended sense by which the term might describe the networks of an alternative sociality that might revolutionize society and in the sense, too, that Als claims himself as a Negress or that Thomas's Jerome finds himself through his mother's voice.

That desire positions Clare as Césaire's Caliban, as the novel makes explicit in a moment recognizable from "Caliban's Daughter," when Clare, lonely in her London flat, reads *Jane Eyre* and repudiates the identity her father would wish for her: "No, she could not be Jane. Small and pale. English." Rather, Clare sees, Bertha is "closer to the mark. Captive. Ragout. Mixture. Confused. Jamaican. Caliban. Carib. Cannibal. Cimarron. All Bertha. All Clare" (116).[146] Mixed, confused, colonial, Clare entertains an identity simultaneously an entirety ("All Bertha. All Clare") and yet made up of the incommensurate terms paratactically listed, but not easily parallel, crossing gender for the sake of racial nomination.

These mixtures of different and nonidentical forms of nonwhiteness are only further complicated by the fact that these names also have oppressive meanings associated with them. The burdens associated with this can be seen, for instance, in a stunning moment when Clare voices resistance to her father and affirms herself through her mother. Kitty and Boy had emigrated to the United States, where, faced with the kind of blatant racism that Lamming's *Trumper* reports, Kitty experienced intense dislocation. Working in a laundry, she writes subversive messages decrying American racism on the flyers included with the clothes laundered by a fictional company spokesperson, "Mrs. White." Ultimately, Kitty comes out as Mrs. Black and announces she has killed Mrs. White. Soon after, she leaves Boy and returns to Jamaica, where she dies. In her orphaned state, and after the massacre of girls her own age in a church in Birmingham, Clare lashes out at her father's pursuit of whiteness and refusal to make common cause with American Blacks. "My mother was a nigger," she says. "And so am I" (104). Through the virulent term of racial denigration, Clare allies Caribbean and African American identity, against her father's and her culture's mode of thinking. Clare at this moment fulfills Trumper's discovery.[147]

Clare nonetheless leaves the United States for England. Her return to Jamaica is facilitated by the letters she receives from her friend Harry/Harriet, calling her home. Clare and Harry/Harriet are bonded in the novel from their first appearance together, when she gags after having had sex with one of the boys at a party and Harry/Harriet opines that "cock-juice don't mix with champagne, sweetheart" (88), something he undoubtedly knows firsthand as an openly effeminate battyman. The return to claim a despised identity is prepared for in an acidly comic scene in a Kingston bar (Clare home on a visit) in which Clare and her friend rename themselves for some Western tourists through terms of denigration that include the charge of African cannibalism. Clare's list is not as startling as the words that she and Harry/Harriet fling up, but their juxtapositions are just as telling. "I am Prince Badnigga, and this is my consort Princess Cunnilinga," Harry/Harriet tells the tourist, adding that his eye shadow is an ancient mark used by his African tribesmen to distinguish them from the enemies they ate (125).

Harry/Harriet sounds more than a bit like Hilton Als here. S/he is the central political figure of the novel. Her cross-gender status (ultimately resolved in the decision to "be" Harriet) parallels Clare's as she finally embraces herself as a black woman. As Judith Raiskin notes about this symmetrical moment, race and gender choices are moved "beyond the biological determinations of these positions" (*Snow on the Cane Fields,* 191). It is also crucial that this mirroring preserves differences between Clare's racial assumption and Harriet's gender.

> "Girlfriend, tell me something. Do you find me strange?"
>
> Clare looked into her friend's eyes. Mascara and eye shadow washed away by the salt water, the eyes stood out, deep brown. Her own eyes naked, green as the cane behind them. She thought, Of course I find you strange; how could I not? You are a new person to me. At the same time I feel drawn to you. At home with you.
>
> "No, I don't find you strange. No stranger . . . no stranger than I find myself. For we are neither one thing nor the other." (131)

Harry/Harriet has a past similar to Clare's, or to Caliban's. His mother was a dark-skinned maid forced to submit to her light-skinned employer; he has been brought up in the master's house, tolerated as a cross-dressing battyman, repudiated the moment he chooses to take his homosexual identity seriously. If Clare yearns for a relationship with a woman, she has it, in a sense, with Harry/Harriet, not least because he identifies so completely as a woman, and precisely through the stunning moment from his past that he tells Clare about, when he was raped by a white policeman: "Ten years old and guilty that a big man in a khaki uniform, braided and bemedaled, in the garrison of Her Majesty, did to me what he did. What else to expect but guilt . . . or shame . . . whiteman, Black bwai" (128).

Harry/Harriet acknowledges how seductive it would be to treat this rape as a symbol of colonialism: "Darling, I know how hard it is to listen to all of this; it is hard to tell. I have been tempted in my life to think *symbol*—that what he did to me is but a symbol for what they did to all of us, always bearing in mind that some of us, many of us, also do it to each other" (129). Yet he insists upon its literality, only extending its meaning to embrace his mother's experience: "I only suffered what my mother suffered—no more, no less" (129). That is, he grants it symbolic value precisely in terms of his mother's actual experience. He refuses, moreover, to read the rape as an explanation of his homosexuality: "And no, girlfriend, before you ask, if you intended to ask, or assume, that did not make me the way I am. No, darling, I was born this way, that I know. Not just sun, but sun and moon" (128). Cliff's point here is to affirm Harry's homosexuality rather than to treat it as simply a sign of colonial decadence, the forced imposition of a Western form of sexuality unknown in the Caribbean. Césaire's Caliban is thus also a model for Harry/Harriet's "lesbianism" in his attachment to and identification with his mother, playing out a sexual potential for Caliban that Belinda Edmondson notes in *Making Men:* the "masculine" revolutionary force also symbolizes colonized, feminized territory (60–61).

When Harry/Harriet chooses to *be* Harriet rather than to play the part, when she chooses to be a revolutionary, she does so in the face of the hatred he would incur if her fellow revolutionaries knew there was a penis under her dress. Harry/Harriet is the novel's privileged political spokesman because of the sexual position s/he inhabits. Those politics are therefore sexual politics, a gender politics that can be called black lesbian feminist, and whose challenge to those identity labels comes from the fact that Harry/Harriet—a biological male—is its embodiment.

As the "new person" made possible by the colonial past, Harry/Harriet's debt to the script of *The Tempest* is as unstraightforward as her relationship to the terms of identity politics; insofar as the play—and its history of revisionary rewritings—lies behind Cliff's writing, the positions occupied by her characters arise not only from the unspoken, repressed, and unrepresented but also from the unspeakable and monstrous in the play. Caliban/Bertha is one way Cliff names the position as Clare moves to reclaim an identity she has been taught to despise.

The Tempest's male Sycorax, Césaire's female-identified Caliban, the blue-eyed hag and her sodomite son stand behind Clare and Harry/Harriet, as well as behind the third central character of the novel, the impoverished black

Christopher, who is intent upon giving proper burial to his grandmother. Christopher kills his light-skinned employers, desecrating their genitals. He also brutally murders the dark maid who sides with them, slashing her body beyond recognition. He hears his grandmother's voice as he performs these acts. As Edmondson comments, linking Christopher to Clare, "that these *other,* black, maternal bodies have been dead but not buried reminds us of the invisibility of black women in the narration of West Indian revolutionary discourse, as embodied by Caliban's mother, the absent Sycorax, who represents Caliban's past heritage of might and agency" (*Making Men,* 130). Christopher is the novel's most violent representation of the forces unleashed by unresolved mourning for the dead grandmother, the unreclaimable, unburied, and unburiable past. Christopher plunges into madness (like another Caliban figure in the novel, Clare's sometime lover Bobby, incurably wounded by the Agent Orange he administered in Vietnam). He too is consumed in the conflagration that ends the novel. The revolutionaries have targeted a U.S. movie company filming a travesty romance version of the Maroon history of Nanny and Cudjoe. Christopher—inarticulate, crazed—has been conscripted to play the part of an African god. "Howl! Howl! . . . Try to wake the dead. Remember, you're not human" (*No Telephone to Heaven,* 207), the film director tells him as he utters the cry with which he unwittingly triggers the government fire that brings down the revolutionaries.

The revolutionaries' violence had been directed at the false representations of the filmmakers. As in the passage in which Harry/Harriet describes his rape, the symbolic and the real are inextricably tied together, and *No Telephone to Heaven* stages its possibility more in its chances of rewriting than in the actuality of social transformation. Although there is good warrant to privilege Clare in an analysis of the novel, Harry/Harriet, Clare, and Christopher are tied together: in versions of revolutionary struggle and in attachment to the (grand)mother and the land, ruinate and stagnant (Christopher lives in a garbage heap), dead and yet—like Sycorax in Césaire's *Tempête*—alive. Moreover, in their varied relationships to class and color positions, to gender and to sexuality, they form a kind of composite figure, one not to be reduced to some singularity but to be seen instead as a matrix of transformations, always strange and yet close. The ways Cliff's characters occupy various positions on the grids of intelligibility can only be negotiated through the recognition that no singular figure emerges from the template they provide. In this, the characters are—at once—utterly singular in their actions and histories even as they come to make up a kind of symbolic picture of the colonial and neocolonial dilemma. As the character who continually struggles toward and fails to consolidate an identity that gives its due to all its conflicting elements, Clare is most representative both of the personal dilemma that Cliff traces and of the larger cultural field in which she operates.

And it is in watching Clare grope to bring together what can never finally be brought together that the novel offers its sobering vision of possible futures.

These are limited by all the forces that continue colonialism under new forms of economic domination, forces not simply outside but inside as well, as Harry/Harriet insists in his reading of the rape as something done not only by whites to blacks but also by empowered blacks to those who live in poverty (the revolutionary band is betrayed by one of its own members) and by forces that not only operate at the economic level but are lived in the stigma attached to everything that is thought not to be normal. One sign of how contingent and difficult such attempts at wholeness and recovery must be is the fact that the closest the novel comes to representing the "lesbianism" that would consolidate Clare's identity is, as Cliff remarks in an interview, the figure of Harry/Harriet.[148] The representation of homosexuality as a liminal gender position only partly explains this cross-identification. For Harry/Harriet's identification as a woman has everything to do with his identification with his mother, with her underclass condition, with the fact of her rape, and with all the ways these facts also are symbolic of the colonial motherland. "Woman" is therefore incapable of being read only as a term of gender since it is so inflected with these further meanings and histories. The limit represented by Clare's failure to achieve lesbian identity is overcome through this extended sense of what "lesbian" would mean in the Caribbean context.

In this extended sense of the term, Clare's decisions to return to her grandmother's ruinate farm, to hand the land over to the revolutionaries, and to fight with them can be called lesbian choices. They are summed up in the figure celebrated in the briefest chapter of the novel, section 7, "Magnanimous Warrior!" a two-page invocation to the figure so named. The section ends by asking, "Can you remember how to love her?" (164), and sentence after sentence addresses her as "Magnanimous Warrior," as "Mother" and "Warrior" in alternating sentences. M/W: Cliff has in mind the Fon deity Mawu-Lisa, female and male creation god(dess). But "warrior" also names a conventionally male role, and in a word that alliterates with "woman," while "m" and "w" cross genders. This primordial female figure—call her Nanny, call her Sycorax—is also Harry/Harriet. "One old woman, one who kenned Harriet's history, called her Mawu-Lisa, moon and sun, female-male deity of some of their ancestors" (171). "I was born this way," Harry/Harriet had affirmed, we recall: "Not just sun, but sun and moon" (128). This primordial ground of femininity is at the same time a ground of male femininity. As Timothy Chin tellingly remarks, "sites of ambiguity and contradiction—which often reflect how 'differences' are actually lived and negotiated—are, paradoxically perhaps, the ones that can potentially enable new forms of social and cultural relations."[149]

Miranda's Meanings

MIRANDA'S MEANINGS

HUMANE CARE

"Remember, you're not human": The film director's words to Christopher in *No Telephone to Heaven* point us, once again, to the demonic ground of difference upon which Cliff operates, the terrain claimed by Wynter through the category of "nigger"/"native" as the "ultimate Conceptual Other" to the human as the "technological master of nature and ostensibly supracultural, autonomous 'Man' of the Western bourgeoisie," the character embodied in Césaire's Prospero. Can any valuable sense of the human remain after the depredations of colonialism and neocolonialism?[1]

In *Abeng*, in a stunning moment recalled but uncomprehended by Clare, an old, obviously poor, black woman approaches two of her darker-skinned classmates, asking the time. The other girls rebuff her, but Clare gives her the time "and the threepence busfare she begged," lashing out at her classmates, "How could you be so inhuman?"[2] The narrator takes up an analysis of the scene, explaining, first, why the woman had approached the other girls, assuming sympathy and identification, and then, why they had refused her: "[T]hey hoped to pass or were being trained to pass beyond the suffering and the expectation of their oneness with this state of being and to make a separation for themselves" (78), a separation—beyond their color—they believe to be theirs, thanks to their schooling. Clare's supposedly humane act of charity also is based on separation and is not offered as a sign of human identification, certainly not of racial identification. Her charity, as much as denigration, is a colonialist act of the sort that Shakespeare's Prospero claims for himself when he says he showed "humane care" for a Caliban that he names in the very same line as essential filth—"filth as thou art" (1.2.346)—Caliban to whom he had earlier accorded a "human shape" (1.2.284) in lines whose ambiguity we have already had occasion to remark.

The narrator's analysis moves Clare's inhuman/human lashing out at her classmates along the colonial route carved out in the belief that "the sufferer was not expected to be human" (78). Therefore, suffering unleashed upon those made to suffer needs no justification; no justification was needed to feed the "sufferers" to the colonizer's dogs, as was done regularly, most spectacularly when a group of so-called Panamanian sodomites met this end at Balboa's hands. "All monsters. All inhuman" (*Abeng,* 78). The European imagination had populated the New World with forms of animal mixture, cannibals, monstrous "Men / Whose heads stood in their breasts" (*The Tempest,* 3.3.46–47), as Gonzalo, the humanist, recalls his Mandeville and the images of "natives" that fill Renaissance travel books like Sir Walter Ralegh's on Guiana. The true heart of darkness, Cliff's narrator maintains, is a core connecting the extermination of natives, the enslavement of Africans, the Jewish Holocaust. "Inhuman" is the foundation of Clare's classmates' unforgivable but understandable act, as they distance themselves from themselves and identify with the forces of "civilization"/extermination. But it is also the root of Clare's kindness to the old woman.

The regimes of "man" and of the "human" seem inadequate to remedy the situation created by the divisions in this scene, to suspend the proliferation of invidious differences that Wynter's work unveils, or to ameliorate the post-Enlightenment situation underscored in the conversation G has with Trumper in *In the Castle of My Skin,* wherein Trumper, we recall, notes the U.S. habit of racial denigration that says "nigger" rather than "nigger man," as in Barbados. In the latter term, the word "man" preserves the illusion of a commonality in the human. "One single word make a tremendous difference. . . . I'm a nigger or a Negro an' all o' us put together is niggers or Negroes. There ain't no 'man' an' there ain't no 'people.'"[3] Hence the "Rights of Man" is an empty slogan. "If the rights o' Man an' the rights o' the Negro wus the same said thing, 'twould be different, but there ain't 'cause we're a different kind o' creature" (297). Has the "different" future arrived, one in which "man" and "Negro" are identical, which Trumper glimpses and forecloses, one in which "different" is the human same? Or is such an overcoming of difference inevitably a triumph for the Eurosame? Could "human" name the new kind of person whose existence Wynter summons in "Caliban's 'Woman'" and that Cliff configures in Harry/Harriet? Is not the supposed universalism of "human" and "Man" inevitably the mark of privilege denied variously to those said to be too close to nature to be thought of as cultured and human, to those called unnatural and thereby outside human nature, to those relegated to live in shit, as Césaire insisted, as Cliff remembers, citing this passage as an epigraph to a chapter of *No Telephone to Heaven:*

And this land screamed for centuries that we are bestial brutes; that the human pulse stops at the gates of the slave compound; that we are walking compost hideously promising tender cane and silky cotton and they would brand us with red-hot irons and we would sleep in our excrement and they would sell us on the town square and an ell of English cloth and salted meat from Ireland cost less than we did, and this land was calm, tranquil, repeating that the spirit of the Lord was in its acts.[4]

In *Une Tempête,* Gonzalo and his confreres have come to the island to expropriate guano; it is the colonizer who trades in excrement.

Prospero's declaration of his "humane care" is followed by lines in which Miranda reviles Caliban, a speech eleven lines long, the only words she addresses to him in the course of Shakespeare's *Tempest.* Prospero's justification of his enslavement of Caliban for his alleged attempted rape, Caliban's assertion,

> Would't had been done!
> Thou didst prevent me—I had peopled else
> This isle with Calibans
> (1.2.348–50),

prompts Miranda to speak:

> Abhorred slave,
> Which any print of goodness wilt not take,
> Being capable of all ill! I pitied thee,
> Took pains to make thee speak, taught thee each hour
> One thing or other. When thou didst not, savage,
> Know thine own meaning, but wouldst gabble like
> A thing most brutish, I endowed thy purposes
> With words that made them known. But thy vile race—
> Though thou didst learn—had that in't which good natures
> Could not abide to be with; therefore wast thou
> Deservedly confined into this rock,
> Who hadst deserved more than a prison.
> (1.2.350–61)

These lines embody "Miranda's Meanings" for Wynter, and provide the basis for her analysis of the seismic displacement that allowed "Woman" to join the regimes of "Man," as "a co-participant, if to a lesser *derived* extent." They also serve as a kind of textual crux in *The Tempest:* "From Dryden to Kittredge," Orgel notes in his Oxford edition of the play, "this speech was almost always reassigned to Prospero." In the introduction to their Arden edition, the Vaughans credit this, along with the "wife"/"wise" dilemma, as the only real textual cruxes in the play, deciding that the lines rightly belong to Miranda.

Her anger, they opine, "is timely and appropriate," befitting "her character, which is more forceful and sexually aware than early editors seemed to pre-fer."[5] Wynter's argument that the ascendency of "race" "now enables the par-tial liberation of Miranda's hitherto stifled speech" (BMM, 361) would seem to obviate this textual problem. No need, therefore, to worry the question whether the speech is "properly" Miranda's and "may be taken," in Orgel's phrasing of the problem in his gloss to lines 350–61, as indicative of "an important aspect of her nature." It would reveal, rather, in Gayatri Spivak's phrasing, "the mesmerizing focus of the 'subject-constitution' of the female individualist," an individual who nonetheless speaks for the group that calls itself "human."[6]

What does need to be asked, following the impetus of Wynter's critique, and still on the basis of textual prompting, is whether Miranda's use of the word "race" in these lines (a usage that seems to refer not simply to some-thing located within Caliban's character but to an identity that might link him to others) can legitimately be brought into the scope of the racial plot that Wynter reads out from the lines.[7] Miranda's usage is close enough to a modern notion of "race" that it seems important to ask whether such a usage is indeed possible in an early modern text. I have all along been supposing this possibility. To support it, I will turn to the meanings of "race" to be found in Shakespeare and then broaden the inquiry along paths laid down by Wynter (and by Lamming), to explore the regimes of the human. In Miranda's lines there is a tension between, on the one hand, a belief that those characteris-tics that would secure humanity and the essential freedoms attendant upon it may be acquired by any subject through a system of deliberate and struc-tured pedagogy and, on the other, a belief that some beings may be nomi-nally human but nonetheless incapable of this achievement of full humanity.[8] These tensions, mobilized in the service of securing categorical demarcations, are the ways in which "race" in Miranda's lines anticipates the racialized dis-courses of Enlightenment philosophy and political discourse that ramify into the ideological support of liberalism and colonialism.

. . . THY VILE RACE

Shakespeare's plays make use of the word "race" some dozen times, where it most often designates a notion of birth and lineage that confers a specific so-cial rank.[9] We find "the Nevils noble race," for example, in *2 Henry VI* (3.2.215) and a "happy race of kings" in *Richard III* (5.3.152), and Marina's pupils in *Pericles* are of "noble race" (5 Chorus 9). Such usages could be said to form the antithesis to Caliban's "vile race," thereby nudging Miranda's phrasing in the direction of lineage. Indeed, in *Timon of Athens,* Timon divides the world, which he refers to as "the whole race of mankind," into "high and low" (4.1.40). In these usages, race is naturalized as a rank conferred by birth. Such natu-ralization of social status is echoed in the other frequent usage of "race": to

designate a stock of animals or the cultivation of plants. "Race" attaches itself
to animal breeds (horses, both in an analogy that Lorenzo draws for Jessica
in *Merchant of Venice* [5.1.72] and in a comment marking how preternaturally
Duncan's horses, "the minions of their race," devoured each other at his death
[*Macbeth*, 2.4.15]), and *The Winter's Tale* famously represents grafting as the
joining of the "bark of baser kind, by bud of nobler race" (4.4.95).

It is in passages where such mixtures are regarded as threateningly
destabilizing that Miranda's usage of "race" finds its closest parallels. When
Antony disdains the blandishments of Cleopatra that have stood in the way
of "the getting of lawful race" with Octavia, that "gem of women" (*Antony
and Cleopatra*, 3.13.107), his meaning seems close to Miranda's insofar as
illegitimate sexual union (in his case, adultery rather than rape) is seen as
productive of an adulterated kind. Shakespearean usages of "race" frequently
worry the question of mixture (whether of plants or of people), and they pose
the possibility of adulteration, even within a noble strain (Duncan's horses
are the best example of this). Many of these usages suggest that untoward
union (of Lorenzo the Christian and Jessica the Jew; of Antony the Roman
and Cleopatra the Egyptian) may be the matrix of "race." Even the allusion
to the "race" of the Nevils arises in a context of crossbreeding and political
contention.[10]

Orgel glosses Miranda's usage with a line from *Measure for Measure*,
Angelo's declaration, "Now I give my sensual race the rein" (2.4.160). This
might seem rather obliquely related to the usage of "race" in *The Tempest*,
but it is pertinent insofar as Angelo's unleashing of the horses of his passion
might relate to the charge against Caliban if only because the indication of his
"race" lies in his attempt at rape.[11] That Angelo has hitherto controlled the
reins he now drops points, however, to his marked difference from Caliban,
whose "race" has something uncontrollable in it—an otherwise unnamable
"that in't"—that leads him to rape. When Miranda's lines point to something
"in" Caliban's "vile race" that makes him unassimilable to European stan-
dards of moral behavior, they indicate that his sexual desire signifies an
unnatural attempt at "unlawful" mixture showing he has failed to recognize
the unbreachable difference between "kinds." That failure, it might be said,
suggests that Caliban is virtually outside the pale of the human—a category
constituted precisely by the ability to recognize high and low status distinctions, as Timon's previously cited lines imply. In these ways, Caliban appears
more animal than human. Miranda's lines recoil at sexual violence. They
voice disgust at a repellent mixture and, even more, at someone incapable
of understanding fundamental social distinctions. "Race" in Miranda's lines
pushes in the direction of modern racism as it ontologizes the divide between
human and savage. Caliban's wish for a progeny of "Calibans" is in line with
this as well, for it posits the reproduction of a separable kind.

In *Racist Culture*, David Theo Goldberg cites Miranda's lines to illuminate early modern usages of "race" that equivocate between its "natural and social" meanings, that is, between its usage as a category of animal or plant and its application to groups of people. As Goldberg puts it, "the conflation of natural with the social kinds . . . were already well rooted nearly two hundred years prior to the Enlightenment!"[12] Although it is not his point to suggest that the early modern term is identical to its post-Enlightenment incarnations, he argues persuasively that early modern attachments of "race" to lineage cannot simply be assumed to have nothing in common with later usages. What makes Goldberg's Enlightenment connection even more plausible is the fact that Miranda's lines invoke the high/low distinction within a moral framework akin to typical Enlightenment usages. If Caliban's "race" is "vile," that term both indicates a status distinction and makes a moral judgment, a slippage even more evident in Miranda's self-nomination and inclusion in the group she characterizes as "good natures." Something of the trajectory of such status terms can be noted in the historical transformation of "noble," which endures in modern English to suggest moral qualities rather than aristocratic blood. Given the radically reduced cast of characters in *The Tempest*, Miranda's lines equivocate this moral positioning even further. Whether the "race" exemplified by Caliban is simply a sign of his personal moral failure or whether it is a shared characteristic cannot be determined. At the time that Miranda utters these lines, the only others she has seen on the island are her father and Caliban; hence any statement she makes about "good" or "vile" natures can be only literally singular but is potentially generalizable precisely in the direction of those Enlightenment discourses on "race" that assumed the innate moral superiority of Europeans.

Goldberg argues that modern ideas of "race" find their earliest articulation in the sixteenth century in the context of colonialism, a point of undeniable pertinence to *The Tempest* and especially to Caliban, whose name was made possible by the ascription of cannibalism to Native Americans. It is because of such ascriptions that I have been guided throughout this study by the work of modern writers from the Caribbean like Lamming, who refuses to treat Shakespeare with respectful philosophical distance, knowing all too well the work that so historically remote a text as *The Tempest* has been made to do. Nonetheless, the discourse mobilized by Miranda does not so much depend upon New World associations as indicate how the mobilization of incipiently modern racial distinctions to describe Native Americans or black Africans depended upon the discourses of difference within—and beyond—the human in Miranda's lines. Assuming that when Europeans saw "others" they immediately saw them as *racially* Other too easily naturalizes racial difference. I would suggest, rather, that the language Miranda uses, of unbreachable social distinction, and the prevarication between social and natural mixing are necessary preconditions for the application of racial difference to foreigners, and I would further suggest that "race" in such instances is not grounded in physiognomy.[13]

In making this point, I follow the argument that Foucault offered in a series of lectures delivered under the title "Il faut défendre la société" ("Society Must Be Defended") at the Collège de France in 1976.[14] Against the ruse of a political theory that posits sovereignty as a transcendental model located above the social fray, a contract in which members of a society delegate powers to a ruling apparatus, Foucault sees the sovereign as, rather, an instance of accumulated power, the outcome of struggle within a divided social terrain. In Foucault's model, the social is a state of war that is insurmountable, a war, moreover, that conceptualizes itself as racialized struggle, "la guerre des races" (51). In a stunning example, Foucault adduces the mobilization by revolutionary forces in mid-seventeenth-century England of the Norman yoke in order to claim for themselves a true Englishness, pointing thereby to the foreign origin of the sovereign and claiming native status for themselves (61). In this example, the king was seen not merely as a foreigner but also as an enslaver. A revolutionary insurgent history making claims for those normally excluded was voiced in the racialized terms of lineage and origin. At more or less the same time, Foucault argues, similar arguments were launched in France, but this time by aristocratic opponents to the king. In that instance, a rearguard politics battened on racialized difference. From these early modern instances, Foucault proposes that the ongoing history of state formation entails a continuous battle in which social differences are fought as racial differences. "Race" is less invented in colonialism than deployed to others, at least at a certain moment in the history of the West.

The supreme modern instance of race for Foucault is Nazism (a conjunction reiterated in Paul Gilroy's *Against Race*),[15] and he details how notions of race mobilized in the seventeenth century against the sovereign came to be attached to the modern state as the supreme instance of the "good natures" devoted to the extirpation of "vile races," enemies within. Along the way, he suggests ways this trajectory intersects with the formation of other kinds of modern differences and other modern categories, notably those of class and sexuality. Foucault's lectures at the Collège were coincident with the publication of the introductory volume of his *History of Sexuality*. Its final section, on the politicization of biology as the culminating point in a history of sexuality coincident with the apparatuses that seek to further "life" by deciding whose lives are worth preserving, is also the terminus for "race." Wynter picks up on these arguments in "The Ceremony Must Be Found," claiming that the creation of the "natural community" is a potentially lethal formation of ontologized racist difference.[16] Foucault's argument suggests, in short, that the early modern invention of "race" is extraordinarily consequential, ramifying indeed beyond the domain signified by the term "race" in modernity. Miranda's lines can be read along these pathways of "race." In their description of a failed pedagogic project, they begin the work of justifying the unequal distribution of cultural capital. They do so in a register drawn from the world of print.

. . . ANY PRINT OF GOODNESS

Miranda ends her speech to Caliban by reiterating her father's claim, that Caliban deserves slavery—confinement—or worse for his attempted rape. Her conclusion follows and rewrites Prospero's narration in which his "humane care" (1.2.346) has been answered by Caliban's filthy, abhorrent act. As Miranda tells it, her attempts at care took the form of a pedagogy that failed to work its effects. This, too, reinscribes Prospero's script. He has been her schoolmaster, and now she repeats the lessons learned for Caliban's supposed benefit, but to little avail: The "print of goodness wilt not take" (1.2.351). Miranda casts Caliban's language lesson—her giving him language and thus the means to make his meanings known—as a particular form of language giving. She writes pedagogy as inscription, as if he were the slate to be inscribed, printed. "Goodness," what she would write on him, is also, as "good natures" indicates, what she claims for herself. The attempt to form Caliban as proper pedagogic object is also one that aims to make him a form of Miranda, as she herself, taught by her father, was informed by him. Pedagogy here is thereby a means for reproduction, cultural reproduction that nonetheless, in its very metaphorics of printing, suggests sexual reproduction as well.[17] The metaphorics of printing and the pedagogic project of literacy seem to assume that Caliban, like Miranda before him, is capable of a fully unproblematic grafting of the kind represented in *The Winter's Tale*. This time, however, there is no saving revelation of royal blood. The humanitarian project reaches its racial limit.

In its imagining of education as inscription, Miranda's metaphor is not unusual. In *The Schoolmaster* (1570), Roger Ascham stresses the importance of beginning education early, as the time most apt for "men . . . to receive goodness." "For the pure clean wit of a sweet young babe is," he continues, "like the newest wax, most able to receive the best and fairest printing and, like a new bright silver dish never occupied, to receive and keep clean any good thing put into it."[18] Ascham's images tally with Miranda's, and he also employs metaphors of grafting in drawing his "similitude" of the schoolhouse. Whereas it might seem that Ascham's image of the purity of the uncorrupted mind, capable of receiving goodness, fails to imagine the situation that Miranda describes—in which Caliban, "capable of all ill," has some unnamed "it" within that points to his limited capacity for inscription—it must be remarked that Ascham's project does not even imagine a Caliban as a possible pupil. Ascham's innocent and pure mind is not some tabula rasa assumed as the condition of *any* pedagogic subject; rather, the goodness that Ascham would inscribe is directed at a good subject—a gentleman, in short.

Even if the pedagogic project in *The Tempest* seems to extend humanistic education to a subject clearly not a gentleman, it does so under the conditions that Richard Halpern has described in *The Poetics of Primitive Accumulation*. Although education did promote social mobility, enlisting thereby new kinds of people into higher echelons of society, it also had what Halpern describes as a "demonstrative" purpose, through which educational failure was taken to indicate those incapable of education. Rather than recognizing that the sorting mechanism of education distributes the prestige of learning unevenly, the mechanism itself was thought to reveal the limits in those it solicited.[19] Halpern refers to this as a discourse of "capacities," and Miranda describes Caliban as "capable of all ill," and therefore only in a very limited way able to receive what she offered.

This difference can be contextualized by recourse to "race," and it is implicit in the social distinction that underlies a book like Ascham's. If one turns to a pedagogic text that is aimed not solely at a gentle audience but also at a wider one, the project of naturalizing "capacity" is further evident. Richard Mulcaster's *First Part of the Elementary*, for example, insists upon the importance of education as a humanistic—indeed, a humanizing—project. It aims to move its subjects from an existence that Mulcaster calls "mere being" to one that he names "well being."[20] This movement—as the distinction between "mere" and "well" suggests—is not simply hierarchical but implicitly social. Pedagogy aims to print goodness, to produce "well being," on subjects that are not innately good.

Whereas Ascham would seize the gentle youth before he has had the chance to be misprinted, Mulcaster imagines the originary situation of the pedagogic subject as an existence in a state of nature that is, at best, neutral. "Mere being" is a situation of "first humanitie" (*Elementary*, 31), in which life is merely sustained, while "well being" is equivalent to what he calls "best humanitie." Mulcaster thereby divides human being into two states, and only the latter is completely human. To live in the state of "mere being" is, he says, to be "but half a beast," whereas "well being" makes man "likest him, of whom he hath his being, and most sociable" (31). The similitudes here—in which "well being" makes the subject at once godlike and sociable—mark the social thereby as a stratum of the elite constituted by the pedagogic apparatus. Were education not to work, those solicited but not remarked by the apparatus would remain in their quasi-bestial condition. "Well being" involves the exercise of reason, for it is reason that indicates "our difference in comparison with beasts" (34), but, it would appear, it also indicates our difference from ourselves before we attain to "well being." Guided by reason, we are trained and thereby taught a series of restraints so that we are no longer devoted merely to perpetuating our existence, no longer driven by appetite and desire. Full humanity marks the difference between "he that liveth, fedeth, multiplieth" and he who exercises judgment, taking, in Mulcaster's example, "food with moderation, encrease with continence" (34). The division within the human—the division that institutes the properly human—is one that retroactively marks those who fail to be reformed as less than or other than fully human.

"The beginning of everie thing," Mulcaster writes, translating Plato, "is of most moment, chefelie to him, that is young and tender, bycause the stamp is then best fashioned, and entreth deepest wherewith ye mean to mark him, and the sequele will be such, as the foretrain shall lead, whether soever you march, bycause naturallie the like still draweth on the like" (23). This march of mechanical reproduction, of like upon like—the printing of goodness—is an interrupted trajectory, and one that can always fail. For Mulcaster's "sequele," the sequence from "mere being" to "well being," is not simply a natural telos. The graft may not take on those capable only of ill.

Caliban is one of those, for the particular failure that he represents is ascribed to a defect rooted in him; "good natures" cannot be received by those that have that unnamable something within that so debilitates them. Miranda's lines subscribe to Mulcaster's thesis, that Caliban is all but reduced to "mere being," that what is innate in him—and, by extension, in all those who are not rehabilitated and made fully human by the pedagogic project—is a matter lodged in his "race."

Miranda's humanist pedagogy underwrites the program of colonialist education. It also anticipates Enlightenment distinctions between those who have and those who lack reason. As in those later texts, the question of human being is fully equivocated. In her *Critique of Postcolonial Reason,* Spivak takes up Kant's Third Critique in order to show that his philosophical project, so often taken to be in the service of a universalism, is founded on a radical exclusion. Answering those like Frances Ferguson, who embrace Kant as proposing through the analytic of the sublime "the absolute equality of all persons in relation to the transcendental schemata,"[21] Spivak insists that the egalitarianism of the Kantian project is not universally available. Rather, a divide within the human is opened that runs along the fault lines of what she calls "the axiomatics of imperialism" (27). Spivak zeros in on "the raw man of the Analytic of the Sublime—stuck in the *Abgrund*-affect without subreptitiously shuffling over to *Grund*" (26).

The "raw man" here is Spivak's literal translation of a figure who appears in James Creed Meredith's translation of *The Critique of Judgement* as "the untutored man."[22] A pedagogy is at stake, and in this instance, as in the case of Caliban, it involves a movement from "mere being" to "well being," to recall Mulcaster's categories. "Without the development of moral ideas, that which, thanks to preparatory culture, we call sublime, merely strikes the untutored man as terrifying" (*Critique of Judgement,* 115). For anyone, Kant claims, the experience of the sublime is at first discomfiting; one passes from the state of being overwhelmed through a necessary self-reflexiveness that constitutes a rising above the immediacy of perception and sensation to the secondary state of transcendental consciousness. It takes training, it appears, to do this, even to recognize the sublime. It takes a cultural inculcation, and some are incapable of it. As Spivak suggests, some remain caught in the abyss, in the entirely negative experience of the sublime, and lack the capacity for the turn that transforms the abyss into a foundational moment. Spivak, translating exactly, calls this subreption, for the moment is one of discontinuity and the ground of the ground is without ground. Or, rather, in order for the transcendentalizing moment to occur, its ground must be cast off to an elsewhere, to someone incapable of this transformation, someone caught in the primordial abyss, a being without morality, however human; a being not yet and never quite capable of being fully human.

Spivak picks a difficult but indeed foundational moment in Kant's schema to notice that an exclusion is being performed. Wary of overly anthropologizing or incorrectly materializing the trope of the "raw man," and thereby of committing the very sort of faux pas that Kant disallows, Spivak teases from this figuration the unnamed excluded Other as the "native," collating this passage with one in *The Critique of Teleological Judgement* in which Kant wonders aloud whether humans need to exist at all—a question for him made obvious by recourse to the example of "New Hollanders or Fuegians."[23] In choosing to search in a text whose transcendentalizing gives so little immediate evidence of the exclusions that its supposedly universal system operates, Spivak eschews the notorious passage in Kant's early, precritical (as it is called) *Observations on the Feeling of the Beautiful and Sublime,* in which Kant momentarily entertains a proposition voiced by a black man only to dismiss it summarily: "[T]his fellow was quite black from head to foot, a clear proof that what he said was stupid."[24]

Race is not a topic much considered by Kantians, most of whom would probably demur from Robert Bernasconi's claim that the modern "concept of race bears Kant's signature."[25] The remark just cited is taken as typical of Enlightenment racism by African American scholars like Henry Louis Gates Jr. or Ronald A. T. Judy, as well as by David Theo Goldberg, whereas most Kantians would be likely to dismiss it as an early crude remark not worthy of the mature Kant and not to be read as in any way connected to his later thought.[26] Spivak's difficult reading thus makes possible a connection most Kantians would eschew. As Judy has argued, even if the thinking of the later Kant seemingly rules out his earlier statement, Kant nonetheless has a "Negro problem," as he puts it, one most manifest precisely in the complicity between Kantian transcendentalizing and an order of exclusionary inscription.[27] Most forcefully, Emmanuel Chukwudi Eze has reminded Kantians that Kant's lifelong teaching on geography and anthropology deploys invidious racial distinctions that cannot be sheltered from—but are, rather, fully consistent with—his final three critiques. The sentence in the *Observations* may be early and precritical, but the texts on geography and anthropology are lifelong projects.[28]

As Eze demonstrates, the Kantian "project of overcoming 'raw' nature" ("Color of Reason," 212), as announced, for example, at the opening of *Anthropology from a Pragmatic Point of View,* is barred to those who remain in the state of nature: non-Europeans incapable of the self-reflexiveness necessary to make that desired self-transformation and self-perfecting that Kant thinks is the work of becoming human. Kant notes, "it does not depend on what Nature makes of man, but what man makes of himself."[29] The non-European, especially a black man, remains for Kant someone unable rationally "to 'elevate' (or educate) oneself into humanity" (Eze, "Color of Reason," 215). "For Kant," Eze concludes on the basis of his reading in texts on geography and anthropology for the most part available only to those who read Kant in German, "European humanity is *the* humanity par excellence" ("Color of Reason," 221). The supposed universalizing process of humanization by which "man" rises out of nature is only realized by whites. "Physiological knowledge of man aims at the investigation of what Nature makes of man, whereas pragmatic knowledge of man aims at what man makes, can, or should make of himself as a freely acting being" (Kant, *Anthropology,* 3). But some men are incapable of that move, and that incapacity is marked physiologically—as the outrageous sentence in the *Observations* affirms of those who are "quite black." In the light of Eze's arguments, Spivak's "suspect" anthropologizing is hardly that; it suggests, rather, the need to bring together parts of Kant's corpus usually kept apart. As Paul Gilroy comments, "however beautiful they appear to their benefactors, Kant's democratic hopes and dreams simply could not encompass black humanity" (*Against Race,* 60).

In his 1775 essay "On the Different Races of Man," as well as in the notes drawn from his lectures on geography, Kant promotes the superiority of European—indeed, of Germanic—peoples. Although he thinks all people are human, he also insists that natural differences are racial differences, and innately so. Much as Miranda points to an unnamable "it" within Caliban's "race" that renders him incapable, Kant points to the "appropriate developments" of racially/geographically different peoples as suggesting innate differences that cannot be explained by any visible circumstances or geography: "Even there, where nothing answering the purpose is manifest, the mere capacity to reproduce its particular assumed trait is proof enough that a particular germ or natural disposition was to be found in the organic creation. For external things can be causes of an occasion, but not evocative causes."[30]

Geography and climate, in other words, do not explain differences in peoples. Rather, some "germ or natural disposition" is to be assumed, even if Kant cannot exactly provide an account of what this reproductive principle might be. This structure of thinking is identical to the one that Kant describes in the analytic of the sublime, positing a break from the physical to the transcendent. On the verge of the suspect biologism that will clinch racial difference, Kant also harkens back to the reproductive schema that underlies Miranda's lines, one that can be found as early as the theory of race propounded by George Best in 1553.[31] Best too does not think that climate explains the difference between whites and blacks. Impressed by the example of "an Ethiopian as blacke as a cole brought into England, who taking a faire English woman to wife, begat a sonne in all respects as blacke as the father was" (180), Best proposes a myth of origins in the familiar biblical account of the sons of Noah, one of whom was cursed with slavery and black skin.[32] In Best's account, Cham is punished not for spying his father naked but for failing to abstain from sex on the ark. From this sexual immoderation sprang an "infection in the blood" (182) passed down to future generations. "Blacknes preceedeth . . . of some natural infection" (180) is Best's guiding presupposition. Just as Miranda can do no more than point to something unnamable—innate—in Caliban's nature, instanced in his attempted rape, that dooms him to failure, so too Kant locates something within, a reproductive insistence, tainted (as in Best), that supplies the irremediable difference of race.

This connection—of something innate, something tied to sexuality—is only furthered when we restore the context for Kant's statement in *Observations on the Feeling of the Beautiful and Sublime*:

> Father Labat reports that a negro carpenter, whom he reproached for haughty treatment toward his wives, answered: "You whites are indeed fools, for first you make great concessions to your wives, and afterward you complain that they drive you mad." And it might be that there was something in this which perhaps deserved to be considered; but in short, this fellow was quite black from head to foot, a clear proof that what he said was stupid. (113)

Although neither Eze nor Judy pauses over this, Kant actually momentarily entertains the black man's thought, and he does so because of the opinion the man expresses about relations between men and women, husbands and wives. In fact, Kant only pretends to quote Labat here; he has supplied the black carpenter's speech. In Labat, the discussion is about why black men have their wives and children serve their meals rather than sitting with them, as the white governor in Guadeloupe does. The carpenter replies that "the governor is not wiser in that respect; although he well believed that whites had their reasons, blacks also had theirs; and that if one wished to consider how proud and disobedient to their husbands white wives were, one would affirm that the Negroes, who keep theirs in a state of respect and submission, are wiser and more practical than whites in this regard."[33]

Kant's willingness to entertain a black man's opinion about managing wives highlights the point for which Isabel Hull is a valuable guide, that Kant's thinking about gender is fraught, congruent with (although not fully parallel to) his thinking about race, I would argue.[34] As Hull shows, Kant equivocates between a universalizing view of humanity and a definition of the human as citizen. The exclusionary force of citizenship bars "children, the mentally impaired, the poor or economically dependent, and women" (301; Hull's list might well include nonwhites). When Kant writes *Mensch* he really means *Mann* (305). Although there may be nothing theoretically within Kant's thought that would necessitate these distinctions, women and blacks are thought and positioned similarly in Kant's work: Men and women constitute "two sorts of human being" (*Observations,* 77), and women—like blacks (for the generalization about men and women is tacitly about whites)—are closer to nature.

It is striking that in Kant's *Observations,* the beautiful and the sublime are gendered, the former female, the latter male, and that there, as in his *Anthropology,* Kant believes that women should not be educated in masculine, abstract subjects, that they are made by nature to be reproductive machines. Part of what they do is to reproduce the species, but they also reproduce culture by limiting male sexual drive, which, as Hull argues, is also the drive toward freedom, which is a male prerogative. Women solve for men the problem of sexuality, and for Kant it *is* a problem, since it represents for him a sheer and mere appetitiveness capable, as he puts it in the *Anthropology,* of enslaving a man (capable, in *The Tempest,* therefore, of warranting Caliban's enslavement). He writes, "Passion . . . no man wishes for himself. Who wants to have himself put in chains when he can be free?" (*Anthropology,* 157). The problem is that the solution to being enslaved by passion is enslavement to a woman: "The woman becomes free by marriage; whereas the man loses his freedom thereby" (223). A woman is free when she fulfills her task, entrapping a man. Kant worries the question of sexual domination, the question of who rules in marriage. He nominally hands over the domestic sphere to women as properly theirs, but he also makes clear that their power there is balanced by their disempowerment in the public and civic spheres. Domestic "power" is therefore a ruse, since women are denied the full humanity of the citizen. "The woman should reign and the man should rule" (224); "he loves domestic peace and gladly submits to her rule, so that he does not find himself hindered in his own affairs" (217). No wonder Kant almost finds the black man worth listening to as he criticizes European marital arrangements that threaten domestic confinement. Just as *Observations* moves from a generalized discussion of the beautiful and the sublime to their embodiment in gendered difference and then in national difference, so too *Anthropology from a Pragmatic Point of View* moves from its considerations of "human" faculties of thought and desire to their embodiment in gendered and national/racialized differentiations.

Kant worries that the sexual relationship may constitute a form of slavery, and he solves this problem by imagining marriage to be the only possible egalitarian arrangement. Kant's view, most clearly seen in his *Lectures on Ethics,* is that sexual desire is problematic precisely because it is natural; it is nothing but appetite.[35] It seeks another person not as a person but as sexual object. For Kant, this is irremediable, and the solution is the monogamous couple, each of whom gives over the totality of being to the other. They are equally subject and object in this exchange and thereby avoid becoming merely objects for each other. Marriage is the social institution that solves the problem of overcoming human nature, the sexual drive as mere appetitiveness.

Hull reads this as expressive of the fact that Kant's desiring subject is male, and she finds this version of "mutual objectification" to be a model that "portrays two solipsistic egoists using each other; it is the model of cold property exchange; it is a model of masturbation" (308). Her point, simply, is that there is no woman there. The model accommodates what is for her a quintessentially male point of view, disallowing, for instance, the possibility that women might fulfill themselves in some other way than by becoming wives, might have some cultural task or natural drive other than luring men to them. Other feminist critics—for example, Robin Schott—have made a similar case, stressing that the objectifying view connects Kant forcibly to capitalist modes of exchange and especially to that form of objectification that can be called reification.[36] This "ideal" egalitarian model is a reduction of persons to things, a reduction that is market driven.

Moreover, as Eric Clarke argues, Kant's idealizing paradigm of marriage assumes not only that the universal subject is a property-owning white male but also that he cannot be a man who desires other men (similarly, Kant cannot countenance the possibility of a woman desiring another woman).[37] Humanity and citizenship are once again conflated. Kant says that homosexual desire is not natural; it is one of the crimes against nature. (Kant uncritically invokes the phrase that had prevailed from medieval canon law through early modernity.) In that respect, the paradigm of self-making should not exclude those who desire same-sex partners, since animals, Kant claims, do not exhibit same-sex desire. Unnatural desire is human. But for Kant, this only makes it more abhorrent: "These vices make us ashamed that we are human beings, and therefore capable of them" (*Lectures on Ethics,* 171). "All *crimina carnis contra naturam* degrade human nature to a level below that of animal nature and make man unworthy of his humanity. He no longer deserves to be a person" (170).

Racial, gendered, and sexual nonpersonage—all are tied to a reproductive imperative: Race taints reproduction; women exist to reproduce; homosexuals fail to reproduce. The norm of reproduction secures white male privilege. The universalizing project of Kantian enlightened, self-conscious self-making can produce a vision of nondifferentiated equal subjects only after entire groups of nonpersons have been excluded.

Caliban assumes that had his rape attempt succeeded, he would have produced Calibans. Miranda assumes that had her pedagogy succeeded, she would have reproduced herself as her father had reproduced himself in her. Mixture is, either way, impossible; good cannot be grafted onto ill. The abyss cannot be breached or filled, for it is already full of difference. Faced with a Caliban, there is no possibility of moving from the abyss to the foundation. He is fundamentally incapable of the movement that is foundationally human. Miranda's last words, supporting the logic of Caliban's enslavement as fit punishment for his rape attempt, come as an afterthought, for his attempt has proved that he never was capable of anything but evil, that his being was unreclaimable. The deed points to his nature, to his all-but-utter alterity.

A THING MOST BRUTISH

In her retrodetermination of Caliban as "savage," "a thing most brutish," Miranda ascribes to his nature—his "race"—something that had first been the matter of a single act, his attempted rape. The failure of education to stick, to change what is deeply within him and totally determinative of his behavior, reinscribes the pedagogic project as an anthropology. Miranda had offered a language lesson, and Caliban's lack of language, his originary "gabble" is remarked. The attention to language is overdetermined, and not just a question of the distribution of cultural capital by the pedagogic apparatus. For, as Anthony Pagden remarks in *The Fall of Natural Man,* a book that traces the fortunes of the Aristotelian notion of the natural slave, the slave-by-nature, in sixteenth-century Spanish debates about the nature of Native American populations, a primary aspect of the concept follows from the assumption that Native Americans have no language. Miranda's lines mark Caliban as the Aristotelian slave-by-nature. As Pagden points out, "barbarian" means "babbler"; for the Greeks, someone who did not speak Greek, who thus lacked the language of civilization, was marked thereby as barely human.[38] In some sixteenth-century thought, it was doubted whether the inhabitants of the New World were human. Miranda's "gabble" seems to translate barbarian "babble" insofar as both terms are thought of as imitative of the nonsensical sequence of sounds made by those without true language.

Miranda assumes that Caliban's native sounds did not convey meaning, that they were mere noise. Here, as in the texts Pagden examines, the definition of having a language and of lacking one depends upon the notion that some forms of language are transparently rational, that they convey inner intention in outer utterance. To lack language is to lack other qualities, especially the deliberative ability to form political associations. Thus, when Aristotle opens his *Politics* by pondering the history of political formations and offers an analysis of those who are forever barred from such forms, he points to the barbarians, who are incapable, as he puts it, of realizing the end of political formation, which starts as "a means of securing life itself" and culminates by securing the "good life."[39] Aristotle's terms are echoed by Mulcaster and, in turn, by Miranda's invocation of unbridgeable racial difference. Man may be definitionally a political animal, but those who do not live in the *polis* are at best subhuman. Lacking reason, they can scarcely be differentiated from animals; lacking morality, they are incapable of state formation. It is such people who, Aristotle claims, are born slaves—"some things are so divided right from birth, some to rule, some to be ruled" (32)—and this division in kinds of people is also a division that makes those born to be enslaved more like beasts than like people. Their bestiality is indicated by the fact that they merely live, without self-control, irrationally driven by their appetites.[40] The division between kinds of people thereby replicates a division within all people, between mind and body. Slaves are little more than their bodies, and as such, they are the property of others whose self-control over their own appetites endows them with the right to possess those who are nothing more than bodies.

Caliban's attempted rape thus offers evidence that he is Aristotle's natural slave. The bare admission to humanity suggested by the parenthetical observation that Caliban did learn something, although not what it took for him to master himself, indicates only that he learned enough to be mastered by others. This is precisely the point that Aristotle makes. "The 'slave by nature,'" he writes, "is he that can and therefore does belong to another, and he that participates in the reasoning faculty so far as to understand but not so as to possess it" (34). As Pagden phrases this, the natural slave—the Native American—is "an imperfect human being" (*Fall of Natural Man*, 24). Pagden claims that the debates about natural slavery stumbled over the problem that in giving even this bit of reason to the native, the path was open to a reformation project. The possibility of "perfecting" the imperfect native through education means, for Pagden, that the outsider was now brought in, recognized as a kind of human (105). If so, this Enlightenment project was strongly belied by the institutionalization of slavery in the course of the seventeenth and eighteenth centuries. It was belied, moreover, by the ways the humanistic project of producing those incapable of learning developed as an exclusionary process. Wynter, contemplating those 1550 debates in Valladolid between Ginés de Sepúlveda and Bartolomé de Las Casas, concludes that the natural slave is a racializing device used to produce the *"non-homogeneity of the human species."*[41] Miranda says it exactly: The aim is to produce someone who has learned only so much; someone who has learned, in other words, to recognize the unbreachable gap between teacher and student, civilized being and savage being; someone who has learned to embrace the condition of natural slave.

Césaire, who transfers the language lesson to Prospero in *Une Tempête*, allows his Caliban to refuse the point: "You didn't teach me a thing! Except to jabber in your own language so that I could understand your orders: chop the wood, wash the dishes, fish for food, plant vegetables, all because you're too lazy to do it for yourself." "Jabber" is *baragouiner* in the original: Caliban's word refuses the colonist's supposition about a native lack of speech through the creolization of New World language, illustrating Glissant's point that "no people has been spared the cross-cultural process." "The idea of creolization," he continues, "demonstrates that henceforth it is no longer valid to glorify 'unique' origins that the race safeguards and prolongs."[42]

"Abhorred slave," Miranda addresses Caliban. What is most abhorrent is not the act of attempted rape but the inability to move out of the barely human condition. Aristotle worries the question of whether slavery is inherently wrong, and he concludes that in relation to those who are all but inhuman, it is right. The affect produced by Miranda is directed at Caliban as a being incapable of passing over into full humanity. In formulations that emerge later in the seventeenth century, the term "slave" invokes the figure of the person who cannot recognize the conditions of freedom and liberty, those, for instance, tied in slavery to the despot-king.[43] Miranda's abhorrence is thus a political gesture, one that will be theorized by Locke, for example, when he justifies slavery in the second *Treatise* for those defeated in a just war.[44] Just wars appear to arise and to be justified when property and liberty are violated, plunging people into a state of being that Locke cannot imagine even to be within the state of nature. "He who makes an attempt to enslave me, thereby puts himself into a state of war with me" (125; ch. 3, paragraph 17). The just outcome of such an attempt on "my" liberty is the deprivation of the liberty of the other; those who emerge from the just war provoked by an attempted infringement on "my" liberty remain, according to Locke, forever barred from civil society, forever in the state of war that marked their condition when they assaulted "me." Since, in his formulations, no man can surrender his liberty, for to do so would be to fail to inhabit the minimal conditions of humanity, the person justifiably enslaved cannot be a person, cannot have been a person in plunging "me" into the state of war. The slave—the person who does not recognize my liberty—is abhorrent, deserving to be put to death. Because he is not a person, he cannot be harmed by slavery. If the slave finds social death intolerable, he can always rebel and be killed, Locke suggests: "For, whenever he finds the hardship of his slavery outweigh the value of his life, it is in his power, by resisting the will of his master, to draw on himself the death he desires" (128; ch. 4, paragraph 23). Miranda, too, avers that Caliban deserves something worse than enslavement.

"Caliban may become Man; but he is entirely outside the orbit of Human."[45] This is how Lamming phrases his understanding of Miranda's lines in *The Pleasures of Exile,* "the cantankerous assertion, spoken by Miranda, but obviously the thought and vocabulary of her father" (109). "Caliban can learn so much and no more," Lamming comments; the limits to the possibility of his becoming human are marked by the language lesson that Miranda provides. "Language itself, by Caliban's whole relation to it, will not allow his expansion beyond a certain point" (110); this is the belief upon which colonialism (and colonialist education) depends.

Lamming is paraphrasing Miranda's speech, reading it not by way of Aristotle or Kant, which he could have done. "The *race* of Negroes," Kant avers, "can be educated but only as servants (slaves), that is, if they allow themselves to be trained."[46] Lamming reads the lines through the lens provided by Hegel. "Caliban is not a child of anything except Nature," Lamming states (*Pleasures,* 110), and his remark resonates with a passage from the introduction to Hegel's *Philosophy of History* that Lamming cites elsewhere in his book: "What we properly understand by Africa, is the Unhistorical, Undeveloped Spirit, still involved in the *conditions of mere nature* and which had to be presented here only as on the threshold of the World's history" (*Pleasures,* 32, citing Hegel).[47] "To be a child of Nature," Lamming comments, continuing his analysis of the representation of Caliban, "is to be situated in Nature, to be identified with Nature, to be eternally without the seed of a dialectic which makes possible some *emergence* from Nature" (111). Lamming is not accepting Hegel—or Shakespeare—as offering the truth about Caliban. A child may be in a state of nature, he suggests, "but a slave is not a child. Nor is a slave in a state of Nature" (*Pleasures,* 15). Lamming is, however, pointing to a claim made about Caliban—about the Caliban made through this claim—that aligns Hegel's claim about the African with Kant's figure of the raw, untutored man, incapable of the self-reflection that constitutes the human. In Hegelian terms, Caliban remains within a state of "mere nature," which is resolutely not the basis for any futurity.

Hegel refuses the Lockean state of nature, refuses Locke's notion that the state develops from a primordial human condition in which property relations are already present and recognized as being in need of a formalization that will guarantee them and that will allow for the state of liberty for all members of the community. For Hegel, nature is mere being, a rawness of predation. It is the state of war that Locke placed outside the state of nature. History for Hegel is not something that simply continues life; rather, but even more extremely than in Mulcaster's schema of "mere being" and "well being," there is a fundamental break between the rawness of nature and the true beginning of history. For Hegel, it is only through reason, and with it the formation of the state, that the conditions for historical possibility and freedom arise. In Hegel's schema, the only geographical areas that participate in this movement are the temperate zones. The frozen North has no history, and Hegel does not even discuss it as an area. The South, for Hegel, is Africa, and after a few pages describing how the African can never achieve the minimal rationality and self-reflection necessary to constitute the state, to constitute the human, and thus to be on the path of the Universal Spirit, which is the path of history, he leaves Africa behind, "not to mention it again" in *The Philosophy of History* (99). Lamming collates these rankling remarks on racial exclusion with the representation of Caliban, and writes back—to Shakespeare, to Hegel—not merely to indicate his understanding of the scheme from which he has been summarily dismissed but, even more, to suggest that the gift of language, meant as a tool of enslavement, has instead allowed Caliban a being that was thought to be impossible, the impossible being that also necessarily constitutes him as a different kind of creature.[48]

Lamming's Hegelian reading of Miranda's speech realizes that the elements there are the materials from which a more fully recognizable racialized schema emerges in modernity. But it is just as important to note that in preserving the notion of the Aristotelian "natural slave" lacking in the self-control that indicates self-reflexiveness and rationality, in locating in Africa the states of tyranny, cannibalism, and sexual promiscuity that Aristotle had found in "barbarians," Hegel is himself indebted to the very sources that also lie behind Miranda's words.[49] And although he denies Locke's state of nature, he also thinks that slavery is proper to the African, who is impressionable only in that mode to the forces of the West and of history. "Educable," for Hegel, means that they can be colonized, not that there is any cultural or spiritual force in the African.[50] Hegel is not alone here; Kant too imagines that the only way to educate the "Negro" is by lashing him with a bamboo cane; even a whip, he avers, will not penetrate the skin sufficiently.[51] "Beating is the only language you really understand," Césaire's Prospero tells Caliban (A Tempest, 14). Such scenes of instruction realize a possibility in the metaphorics that dominate Miranda's speech, with its image of imprinting, for branding also is imprinting; to be literate can mean to have been so marked. The slave as text marks precisely the historico-anthropological divide that Hegel manipulates: the difference between those without and those with language. Language, in this mode, as it is implicitly in Miranda's metaphorics of inscription, is writing. The writing out of the racialized Other is the very plot of writing.

Miranda speaks these lines because the attempted rape would have produced damaged goods. She would never have been available for Prospero's marriage plot were she not a virgin. As Prospero's property, she speaks to the slave that is his and hers. In Miranda's lines, the fetish speaks, and what remains unvoiced is the alternative ostensibly outside the text, the absent figure that Wynter names "Caliban's 'woman,'" for example, but whose existence, whose figurations as the outside, we have traced in moments of textual trouble in Shakespeare's Tempest: the swirling negativities that surround the sodomite and the witch. A sentence of Wynter's cited earlier deserves reinscription here: "Caliban, as an incarnation of a new category of the human, that of the subordinated 'irrational' and 'savage' native is now constituted as the lack of the 'rational' Prospero, and the now capable-of-rationality Miranda, by the Otherness of his/its physiognomic 'monster' difference, a difference which now takes the coding role of sexual-anatomical difference" (BMM, 358).

Whereas Caliban is structurally racialized through the various positions offered by Miranda's lines—as pedagogic, anthropological, philosophical, and historical (non)subject—Wynter's dense formulation suggests that his embodiment cannot be that of "man." Caliban's racial positioning places him as a site that exceeds and displaces the masculinity he might otherwise share with Ferdinand and that exceeds it precisely in the failure of the rationality he is assumed to lack. That position is marked by the unnamable in Miranda's lines. What is the "it" in Caliban that motivates him and that seems to constitute the core of his impossibility? What makes him more "a thing" than a man? The lines constitute this nonhuman being in the abhorrent figure of the slave. Elsewhere, and insistently, as Wynter telegraphs, Caliban is marked as monstrous. His monstrosity, insofar as it is to be explained—and constituted—is derived from his origin. "Hag-seed" (1.2.364), Shakespeare's Prospero calls Caliban in the lines immediately following Miranda's. "Got by the devil" (1.2.319), Prospero says just before. Demonic paternity, horrific maternity; the "foul witch" (1.2.258) Sycorax was as deserving of death as her son, but "for one thing she did / They would not take her life" (1.2.266–67). The unnamable in these moments hovers around "things" and "its." It looks askance at sexual possibilities that are far from the norm or that are unspeakably coincident with it: cross-racial sex, sex with Prospero, as Lamming imagined. Mixture as the matrix of race. Might this explain why the one specific thing we know about Sycorax is that she had blue eyes?[52]

The rape of Caliban raises the possibility of an unremovable taint; it provokes the kinds of questions that obsess Prospero about the series of events that constitute the parallel to the rape. Just as Caliban wished to take something not rightfully given him, so too did Antonio. "Tell me / If this might be a brother," Prospero asks (1.2.117–18); "unnatural though thou art" is how Prospero finally barely accepts Antonio (5.1.79). This worry about origin is one found in Enlightenment taxonomies of categorical difference, as if the answer to the nature of the racialized Other only could be answered there (rather than in what has been made by the discourses of Othering to which we have been attending). The particularly charged sexual landscape of Caliban's origin and of his attempted rape suggest, however, a further resonance within the history of "race." For as Foucault suggests, the divided terrains of the social fasten in modernity on the figure of the enemy within that must be purged in order for society to be defended. "What is racism?" Foucault asks, answering,

> It is primarily a way of introducing a break *[une coupure]* into the domain of life that is under power's control: the break between what must live and what must die. The appearance within the biological continuum of the human race of races, the distinction among races, the hierarchy of races, the fact that certain races are described as good and that others in contrast, are described as inferior: all this is a way of fragmenting the field of the biological that power controls.[53]

The recognizable racial Other that emerges in this configuration cannot but recall the various breaks constituted by the discourses that shape Miranda's lines. This division, Foucault argues, also describes the racialization of the classed Other. And, crucially for Foucault, this is also the map that locates the modern sexualized subject. In the nexus between the elimination of races in the service of apparatuses bent on reproducing the socially normative and the elimination of those whose sexuality stands as a refusal of the norm, or as the monstrous means of a reproduction outside the norm, the modern sexualized and racialized subject emerges: Caliban . . . or, as Wynter would insist, "Caliban's 'woman.'" Her name is legion. Call her, for example, Harry/Harriet. The racialization of this "woman" indicates that "Caliban's 'woman'" necessarily displaces the woman who speaks Miranda's lines, and the normative desires she represents and articulates.

ONE THING OR OTHER

Caliban's language lesson is not a unique event in the play. Throughout, Prospero assumes the part of severe pedagogue: with Ariel, with Miranda, with the court party, and with Ferdinand, whom he casts in the role of Caliban. These pedagogies imagine the possibility of transformation denied to Caliban: freedom (perhaps) for Ariel, marriage for Miranda and Ferdinand, the reordering and relegitimation of sociopolitical relations between Naples and Milan (in this, even Antonio and Sebastian are included, however grudgingly). Caliban remains at most mere appetitive life, more a thing than a person: Taught "one thing or other," he is for that "a thing most brutish," a "thing," finally, "of darkness," acknowledged as Prospero's own (5.1.275–76).

In these ways, Caliban can be linked to that condition of "bare life" that Giorgio Agamben has identified in *Homo Sacer,* his elaboration of the Foucauldian concept of biopower (those who have a right to live, those who ought to die) that underwrites the theory of race offered in Foucault's 1976 lectures and in the theory of sexuality developed in the final chapter of the introductory volume of his *History of Sexuality.*[54] As that which establishes a principle of exclusion from the political that is nonetheless an included exclusion, bare life for Agamben can be located as early in the history of modernity as those places in Aristotle's *Ethics* and *Politics* that mark mere being off from true existence, distinguishing life from the good life. The divide is political but also ontological. It is indicated by the passage from speech into language that Miranda's pedagogy engages precisely by metaphorizing one as the other. Such metaphoricity suggests transformation into the human. Agamben makes this point from a passage in the *Politics* in which the human is defined by language (as opposed to voice, which humans share with animals): "Politics therefore appears as the truly fundamental structure of Western metaphysics insofar as it occupies the threshold on which the relation between the living being and the *logos* is realized. In the 'politicization' of bare life—the metaphysical task *par excellence*—the humanity of living man is decided" (*Homo Sacer*, 8).

In *The Tempest*, Caliban's status as bare life and his/its included/excluded status are indicated by a kind of reverse pedagogy: It is Caliban who knows the sounds of the island, the places where food can be gathered. The log-bearer is requisite for life, even if his life has no value—or the same value whether dead or alive, as Trinculo opines: "Were I in England now, as once I was, and had but this fish painted, not a holiday-fool there but would give a piece of silver. There would this monster make a man—any strange beast there makes a man. When they will not give a doit to relieve a lame beggar, they will lay out ten to see a dead Indian" (2.2.27–31; these are, we recall, the only lines from *The Tempest* cited in Lamming's *Water with Berries*). At first seemingly exchanging his knowledge of "fresh springs, brine pits, barren place and fertile" (*The Tempest*, 1.2.338) in order to be taught "how / To name the bigger light and how the less" (1.2.334–35), Miranda's teaching would seem to have added to Prospero's pedagogy only Caliban's ability to countenance Stephano's claim to have arrived from the moon: "I was the man i' th' moon when time was." "I have seen thee in her," Caliban replies, "and I do adore thee. My mistress showed me thee, and thy dog and thy bush" (2.2.132–35). Thus, while the education Stephano proffers—"kiss the book," he repeats, as he offers the "language" in his bottle—might appear to parody the "humane" attempts of father and daughter, it merely transfers (in an ideological ruse that Paul Brown identified) the business of colonial education to a site (the lower-class clown) where the desire to "recover," "tame," and sell Caliban can be enunciated.[55]

Miranda's offer to Caliban to make his purposes known, which fleetingly suggests an aim to grant him the consciousness of a "good," human nature, must seem dubious in this context: first, because it assumes that as bare life, without language, Caliban has no access to his purposes; second, because it supposes that the only route to them must be by way of this pedagogy. Although there are moments, precisely around their having language, when Caliban and Miranda, as supposed natives of the island, are structurally parallel—Stephano's "where the devil should he learn our language" (2.2.64) elaborates Ferdinand's exclamations, "My language! Heavens!" (1.2.429)—these flickering identifications are undermined by the claim that Caliban's purposes are irremediably bestial. As Lamming, who builds on these similarities to their ultimate difference, notes, Miranda may become "Man," but Caliban always "is 'Man' and 'other than Man'" (*Pleasures*, 15).

"Whoever says *rape*, says *Negro*":[56] Fanon's startling sentence in *Black Skin, White Masks* underwrites an argument like Ania Loomba's, that whether or not Caliban "is" black, "Caliban's *political* colour is clearly *black*" (*Gender, Race*, 143). Non(human) being, the Negro is an "object in the midst of other objects" (in Fanon's analysis [109]), assuming "the role of thing, excluded, devoid of language," as Lamming puts the condition named Caliban (*Plea-sures,* 166). For Fanon, this "thing" is also, at the same time, the biological (the penis). Rewriting the Lacanian mirror stage to account for racialized difference, which provides a decisive break across any universalizing psycho-analysis, Fanon shows how the black man is posited as the Other for the white man, in whom there is no possibility for recognition: "[F]or the white man The Other is perceived on the level of the body image, absolutely as the not-self—that is, the unidentifiable, the unassimilable" (161 n. 25). The unassimilable could be linked genealogically to that Kantian thinking of the sexual as a merely natural appetitiveness whose inhuman aim is the Other as object. But what this also means, as Fanon argues, is that the Hegelian rela-tionship of recognition, and with it, any ontology, are unavailable to the black man. The master, he comments—and by this he means not only the slave master but the white man after slavery has been abrogated (and continued by other means)—"differs basically from the master described by Hegel. For Hegel there is reciprocity; here the master laughs at the consciousness of the slave. What he wants from the slave is not recognition but work" (220 n. 8).

"My turn to state an equation: colonization = 'thingification.'" The sentence is Césaire's, from the *Discourse on Colonialism* cited frequently by Fanon.[57] Although Césaire seeks mainly to ally the cause of the racially oppressed with that of the proletariat, his text is filled with images of sadism, brutality, rapes, and heads cut off, which intensely sexualize the scenario of Western degradation that he paints under the false surmise that "civilizing" is iden-tical to colonizing: "I look around and wherever there are colonizers and colonized face to face, I see force, brutality, cruelty, sadism, conflict, and, in a parody of education, the hasty manufacture of a few thousand subordinate functionaries, 'boys,' artisans, office clerks, and interpreters necessary for the smooth operation of business" (21).

This complex of sexuality, race, and nonpersonhood could be brought into the orbit of biopolitical analysis, perhaps with this caveat: Whereas for Agamben and for Foucault, the "end" of biopower (the fullest manifestation of what Agamben designates as the "'Nomos' of the Modern" [*Homo Sacer,* 166]) is Nazism, Césaire (who, like Fanon and Cliff, thinks the questions of race alongside the ovens) would remind us that Nazism, insofar as it is called *"the crime against man . . .* is not *the humiliation of man as such,* it is the crime against the white man" (*Discourse on Colonialism,* 14). A logic within the West, and exercised as politics in the West, is the matrix for "race." The lethal energies of biopower were first manifest not in the camps but in the centuries-long systematic destruction of black lives across the Middle Passage, and be-yond. These produced a camp mentality, or so Paul Gilroy argues in *Against Race,* long before the Nazi regime, and that mentality is not yet overcome.

"The Negro of the Antilles will be proportionately whiter—that is, he will come closer to being a real human being—in direct ratio to his mastery of the

French language" (*Black Skin, White Masks,* 18)—closer, but never there, as with Caliban (even the Caliban that humanistic critics hail for his humanity). Fanon may end *Black Skin, White Masks* hoping for a future of shared humanity, but the conditions for such a future cannot come from the West, not even from the Enlightenment traditions that seem to hold out the promise of equality. For that equality is offered on unacceptable terms. Fanon can even look askance at slave revolts (presumably, above all others, the Haitian example, in which the revolutionary principles of liberty, equality, and fraternity were demanded): "[T]he Negro knows nothing of the cost of freedom, for he has not fought for it. From time to time he has fought for Liberty and Justice, but these were always white liberty and white justice; that is, values secreted by his masters" (*Black Skin, White Masks,* 221). Freedom on other terms, in other bodies, would involve a reordering of "life" beyond the Enlightenment project.

. . . MY ENDING IS DESPAIR

Inspired by the closing pages of *Black Skin, White Masks,* as well as by Fanon's call at the end of *The Wretched of the Earth* for a "new man," Paul Gilroy proposes, in *Against Race,* a new humanism to replace race thinking. In Gilroy's view, race has taken two equally unacceptable paths, both of which he connects to Nazism: on the one hand, an atavistic drive toward purity exemplified by the Nation of Islam; on the other, the selling of buffed black bodies in the global marketplace. He decries "the homophobia, misogyny, anti-semitism, and fundamentalist nationalisms currently being affirmed in black political cultures" (198); he mourns "the disappearance of the pursuit of Freedom as an element in black vernacular culture" (184), an element lost in the race for profit. Gilroy's argument has some prompting in Fanon, to be sure, yet Fanon's texts are not so easily mobilized for a humanistic argument. For one thing, although Fanon seeks to end the alienation of the white-masked black man and is wary about accepting a version of negritude that would solidify black identity in the beat of the drum, the new regime of "man" that he affirms is marked by the very misogyny and homophobia that worry Gilroy. Moreover, Fanon can imagine this new emergence only as genuinely new, a future that necessarily—violently—disrupts the past. "The explosion will not happen today. It is too soon . . . or too late" (*Black Skin, White Masks,* 7). "Explosion" is the first word of the book. It names an agenda.

Gilroy acknowledges the intellectual aspect of this agenda when he distances the humanism he advocates from an Enlightenment heritage:

> [T]he alternative version of humanism that is cautiously being proposed here
> simply cannot be reached via any retreat into the lofty habits and unamended
> assumptions of liberal thinking, particularly about juridical rights and sovereign
> entitlements. This is because these very resources have been tainted by a history

in which they were not able to withstand the biopolitical power of race-thinking that compromised their boldest and best ambitions. Their resulting failures, silences, lapses, and evasions must become central. They can be reinterpreted as symptoms of struggle over the boundaries of humanity. (*Against Race,* 30)

Gilroy seeks, in fact, to widen "the boundaries of humanity" to a level of "banal human sameness" (29) that he locates as genetic—bare life—and that he attempts to tie to diasporic black cultures by means of an etymological link: The "spore" in "diaspora," he claims, offers a version of supposedly asexual reproduction. "Could that alternative, gender-free linkage complicate the notion that diaspora is inscribed as a masculinist trope and cannot be liberated from the quagmire of androcentrism?" he asks (126).

Gilroy's book is an ill-named project. It is against race-thinking and racism, but claims (dangerously, I believe) to be against race, even as it attempts to marshal the resources of a black diasporic tradition—exemplified for Gilroy in music like that produced by Bob Marley, with its call for freedom that was heard around the globe—as the only resource for the future. Although Gilroy gestures several times to a dehomogenization of black culture that would recognize the divisions caused by class, gender, and sexuality, he barely mentions any form of cultural production except that produced by men. His degendered project is in danger of reinstating the masculinism he deplores. What he clings to, valuably, is the possibility of cultural production that cannot be reduced to the workings of capital: "The cultural life of recorded sound was not reducible to the simple economic relations in which it was enmeshed. Indeed, a whole tradition grew up around the idea that this music had a value beyond money" (273).

Like David Scott in *Refashioning Futures,* Gilroy looks to such cultural production because he knows, with Fanon, that the solution to the problems caused by colonialism, world wars, and race-thinking cannot be found in the states that have arisen as supposedly independent decolonized regimes. Fanon's predictions about the forms that the newly independent states would take have been more than confirmed. Neocolonial economic dependence marks the Caribbean and other formerly colonized regions of the globe, and those states deemed successful are the ones most enmeshed in international capital, which ensures all the stratifications of colonial society. Those stratifications are embodied in forms of democracy that belie the aspirations Gilroy names as the best in liberal thought, which he too hopefully continues to believe might be rescued from its entanglements with slavery and colonialism. "Have you ever wondered to yourself," Jamaica Kincaid asks,

why it is that all people like me seem to have learned from you is how to imprison and murder each other, how to govern badly, and how to take the wealth of our country and place it in Swiss bank accounts? Have you ever wondered why it is that all we seem to have learned from you is how to corrupt our societies and how to be tyrants? . . . you leave, and from afar you watch as we do to ourselves the very things you used to do to us. And you might feel that there was more to you than that, you might feel that you had understood the meaning of the Age of Enlightenment (though, as far as I can see, it had done you very little good).[58]

The history of failed revolutions—in Grenada, Guyana—the capitulation of the Manley regime in Jamaica, the sad spectacle of tyranny in Haiti that followed almost immediately upon the revolution that C. L. R. James had celebrated in *The Black Jacobins* and from which Fanon distances himself: These, too, are cause for despair. Cuba remains perhaps a hopeful question mark.

Possibility, Scott and Gilroy argue, must come from "popular" culture produced by those who continue to suffer the effects of "independence," from those who register their disenfranchisement and continue to imagine alternatives to it. In *Refashioning Futures,* Scott proposes, against "a decline of the middle-class nationalist-modern, a reduction in the purchase of the ethos that sustained it, an enfeebling of the ethical-political languages through which its vision was articulated, and a contracting of the very social space it occupies in the public sphere"—a litany that echoes against Cliff's novels and the forces against which Clare Savage struggles—a possibility for a future that Scott describes as "Fanon avec Foucault." It lies in "an increasing moral, social, and economic autonomy of the popular classes, an expansion of their ability to insert themselves into the global economy in ways (whether legal or illegal) that circumvent or bypass the middle class–controlled state and the capitalist-controlled economy."[59] Looking to dance-hall culture, to Rasta, to the figure of the "ruud bwai" as practices of freedom that might lead to "unsettling the settled settlements of this very postcolonial sovereignty itself" (*Refashioning Futures,* 205) and toward ongoing acts of refashioning that would refuse normativities, he conjures this future:

> On the one hand, I want to imagine a diverse field composed of multiple public realms, constituencies, or ensembles that constitute in effect different ways of being-in-common, different ways of being citizens or women or black or whatever, and in which, therefore, different but mutually recognized modalities of collective identity are voiced and practiced. And on the other hand, I want to imagine an ethos, or perhaps even a *habitus,* of critical responsiveness to the tendency of such identities to harden into patterns of exclusion that seek to repel or abnormalize emergent or subaltern difference. (217)

For such a future to emerge from the sites Scott envisages, their own limits would need to be overcome: masculinism and homophobia above all, which some commentators, celebrating the popular, do not take seriously as social facts. Carolyn Cooper, for example, positively delights in the way in which "homosexuality is gloriously vilified" in Jamaican dance halls, supposedly for the benefit of women.[60] Gilroy sees the costs to women in such celebrations of their sexuality: that ultimately it is male sexuality and male irresponsibility for unwanted children, abandoned women, that is promoted, often insidiously in the name of patriarchal privilege.

Cultural production may indeed be a site for imagining new beginnings, continual self-making, diasporic flows and their "unanticipated destinations" (Gilroy, *Against Race,* 251). It is nonetheless the case that much that is produced in the region is not available elsewhere, that the conditions that prompt Kincaid in *My Brother* to link Antiguan homophobia to her need to escape her homeland in order to realize herself as a writer remain prominent. It is for these reasons that, for the most part, it has been diasporic writing that has engaged us in the pages of this book. The image by the Trinidadian artist Christopher Cozier that serves as its frontispiece certainly indicates that there are those who operate in the region who are asking the kinds of searching questions that need to be asked about "independent" regimes that foster homophobia and racism and mislead citizens into believing that an exercise of propriety coupled to demeaning work is the proper reward for capitulation to capitalist domination. Nonetheless, it has seemed to many that articulating futures for the Caribbean worth imagining was possible only after they had left the region. Even Fanon, we must recall, did his work in Algeria. Such departures explain why Caribbean literature so often returns again and again to experiences of self-alienation. Much in the educational system remains unchanged; cultural production by writers of Caribbean origin is read anew, it seems, with every generation. Diasporic flows need to move in more than one direction if futurity is not to be rooted to place. The work of writers like Wynter and Cliff and Als, as they suggest, moreover, the labilities of gender and sexuality that belie the dominant views of masculinist and heterosexist cultures, needs to be heard. Work produced in the Caribbean likewise needs to travel. Such work also suggests the resources for possibility that continue to reside in "race," for the danger in Gilroy's "banal" project is the erasure of difference, which is also its goal. Bare life cannot be merely reclaimed. What counts as life is always a contestatory issue. Agamben wrote *Homo Sacer* motivated in part by the devastations that have been the result of the breakup of the USSR, wars fought in eastern Europe (and in Africa as well) in the name of ethnicities, wars conducted as nation-states that were imposed as a result of the world wars of the twentieth century crumble. How shall we think the dislocated future, the energies of diaspora as they might be drawn to these divisive sites or might seek new global conditions bringing together the wretched of the earth in opposition to old impositions? This is the difficult question to be faced; Fanon's espousal of violence is entangled with it.

How shall we think these questions—Fanon's "explosion"—now? At the opening of *Pleasures of Exile,* Lamming proposes, against the sadistic justice of Prospero, the conciliatory "ceremony of the Souls" (9) practiced in Haiti, a Vodun rite in which the dead and the living can be reconciled. It is a ceremony that Lamming also conjures setting his Fola on the path of a revolutionary consciousness, the season of adventure that would make moot the question of paternity in the irresolution of a double father, black and white. It is also the ceremony that Teeton has in mind in *Water with Berries* as he moves to his assignation with Myra on Hampstead Heath, the face of homosexual Jeremy bearing down upon him. Perhaps in this ceremony, in the resources of diasporic culture, the multiple denigrations of race and gender and sexuality can be faced, and something new can come from the negations.

> PROSPERO: What were you hoping for?
>
> CALIBAN: To get back my island and regain my freedom.
>
> PROSPERO: And what would you do all alone here on this island, haunted by the devil, tempest tossed?
>
> CALIBAN: First of all, I'd get rid of you! I'd spit you out, all your works and pomps! Your "white" magic!
>
> PROSPERO: That's a fairly negative program . . .
>
> CALIBAN: You don't understand it . . . I say I'm going to spit you out, and that's very positive . . .
>
> (Césaire, *A Tempest,* 63)

> Rule Brittania / Brittania rules the waves
>
> Britons never, never, never shall be slaves . . .
>
> And we sang and thought the song applied to us. Which it did, by negation.
>
> (Cliff, "Caliban's Daughter," 36)

In *Pleasures of Exile,* the ceremony mutates into a law court, where it turns out that the crucial witness is someone descended both from Caliban and from Prospero: "[H]e sees himself as Caliban while he argues that he is not the Caliban whom Prospero had in mind. This witness claims a double privilege. He thinks he is, in some way, a descendent of Prospero. He knows he is a direct descendent of Caliban" (11). This privileged witness is in the diasporic condition that Gilroy affirms against race, but he is better named, as Lamming suggests, as a subject necessarily divided and doubled. Lamming marks this doubleness as the inevitability that follows from colonialism, the moment in the history of the globe that begins to tie it together on its way to modernity. This double marking must be a preliminary gesture to be complicated by questions of class, gender, and sexuality. For the labilities of incommensurable differences provide the only pathways for connections to others, for possibilities of transformative recognitions that need not be tied to the

violence of difference. As Lamming says, this crucial witness cannot be innocent; indeed, "there are no degrees of innocence" (*Pleasures,* 11):

> Involvement in crime, whether as witness, or an accomplice, makes innocence
> impossible. To be innocent is to be eternally dead. And this trial embraces only
> the living. Some may be corpses, but their evidence is the evidence of a corpse
> who has returned to make the unforgivable apology: "Gentlemen I did not real-
> ize! Although I was there, although I took part, I did not realize! I was not aware!"
> The confession of unawareness is a confession of guilt. This corpse, dead as he
> may be, cannot be allowed to go free; for unawareness is the basic characteristic
> of the slave. Awareness is a minimum condition for attaining freedom. (12)

These are profoundly difficult sentences, but they speak to the condition after
colonialism, after the impositions of new world orders, their explosive repudiations. They speak to the violence of "Enduring Freedom" or the identification
of an axis of evil that needs to be eradicated. Revolutionary consciousness, as
Lamming proposes, throws off the shackles of slavery that bound colonizer
and colonized. It leads to the recognition that we cannot return to the hopes of
the Enlightenment insofar as they are entangled with the misery of invidious
difference fought in the wars of the twentieth century and beyond, all rooted
in colonialist racism, wars that fastened on bare life that could be sacrificed.
"Life" never is innocent.

More than a decade ago, as I was finishing writing *Sodometries,* an ad for
a T-shirt caught my eye: It promised its wearers that "we" would not be
"Saddamized," couching "Desert Storm" in a racist and homophobic image
meant to capture the U.S. masculinist, militaristic imaginary. In a "Shouts
& Murmurs" piece in *The New Yorker* on November 5, 2001, "Doing the CNN
Crawl," a spoof on the absurdities that pass in the ticker on the bottom of
the TV screen, Daniel Menaker fantasizes this item: "Shakespeare scholar
Harold Bloom signs seven-figure book deal for comparative study of Caliban
and Taliban."[61] What's the joke? That Bloom, who has iconic media status,
gets his name attached to just the sort of project he deplores, since his Shakespeare speaks for a humanity that would be beyond such political connections? That Menaker shares this view with Bloom, since he is deriding the
work of literary critics who seek to make political interventions by means of
the cultural objects they study? These are only two examples of a new con-
servatism in the academy and the media, worrisome insofar as they reflect
and contribute to the current political climate. No doubt, the conjunction of
Caliban and Taliban is absurd, an effect of the signifier that fails to signify
meaningfully, and not least because that radical Islamic movement cannot
be imagined to have found a platform of refusal in Shakespeare. But it is not
absurd—or so *Tempest in the Caribbean* has argued—to return to the past and
to some of the most venerated texts in the Western tradition to see that in-

vidious differences are part of the legacy of this canon. It was for that reason that Fanon, in his chapter on national culture in *The Wretched of the Earth,* advocated a complete break with a deplorable past, the explosion advocated in *Black Skin, White Masks.* Against the despair that pits us against them in unstoppable violence (and that Cozier depicts as an elementary-school lesson in the image that serves as the frontispiece to this book), it has been my aim to suggest instead that old sites of denigration can serve as resources for new social imaginings, new social actors, new ways of thinking. A desirable future may be possible if we can recognize and respect alterities and can refrain from imposing false unanimity, even in the name of shared humanity, let alone under the auspices of the so-called free world that Fernández Retamar derides in "Caliban."

NOTES

PREFACE

1. See Paul Gilroy, *The Black Atlantic: Modernity and Double Consciousness* (Cambridge, MA: Harvard University Press, 1993).

2. On the multiple meanings of "the Caribbean" as a locale, see Norman Girvan, "Reinterpreting the Caribbean," in *New Caribbean Thought,* ed. Brian Meeks and Folke Lindahl (Kingston, Jamaica: University Press of the West Indies, 2001), 3–23; see also in that volume, Gordon Rohlehr, "A Scuffling of Islands: The Dream and Reality of Caribbean Unity in Poetry and Song," 265–305, charting artistic responses to the short-lived West Indian Federation of the late 1950s and various subsequent attempts at regional unification (often in the sphere of culture).

3. See Gayatri Chakravorty Spivak, "Three Women's Texts and a Critique of Imperialism," in *"Race," Writing, and Difference,* ed. Henry Louis Gates Jr. (Chicago: University of Chicago Press, 1985, 1986), 264, for her demurral from identification with Caliban, and *A Critique of Postcolonial Reason* (Cambridge, MA: Harvard University Press, 1999), 117–18, for a restatement of the point. For a reading of these reinscriptions that seems enchanted with their being "local versions of the old grand story" that can be deployed toward overcoming colonial depredation, see Edward W. Said, *Culture and Imperialism* (New York: Vintage, 1993), 213.

4. Rob Nixon, "Caribbean and African Appropriations of *The Tempest,*" *Critical Inquiry* 13 (Spring 1987): 557–78.

5. See J. K. Gibson-Graham, *The End of Capitalism (as We Knew It): A Feminist Critique of Political Economy* (Oxford: Blackwell, 1996). Gibson-Graham seek to do for "capitalism" what feminist inquiry has done for "woman" or queer inquiry for the categories of sexual identity: to dismantle a regulatory fiction by showing that capitalism, like all identities, is a temporary fixing, and not one that commands all other forms of economic and social relationships. The aim of the book is to allow for the reality of other forms of economy against the vision of economic determinism that they locate in the arguments of David Harvey, *The Condition of Postmodernity* (Oxford: Blackwell, 1989), among others.

6. Lisa Lowe and David Lloyd, "Introduction," *The Politics of Culture in the Shadow of Capital* (Durham, NC: Duke University Press, 1997), 1, 6.

7. This view of the Enlightenment legacy is by now commonly accepted, as Wendy Brown notes in *Politics out of History* (Princeton: Princeton University Press, 2001): "An understanding of liberal universalism as not simply continuing a history of excluded others but as having a specific normative content—heterosexual and patriarchal families, capital, and 'property in whiteness'—erodes the credibility of its classic story of progressively widening its scope of freedom and equality, extending the goods of enfranchisement and abstract personhood to more and more of the world's populations" (9). In *Free Enterprise* (New York: Dutton, 1993), Cliff offers a densely interwoven account, part fictional, part factual, of the role of women in various New World locales in opposing and ending slavery.

A DIFFERENT KIND OF CREATURE

1. Alden T. Vaughan and Virginia Mason Vaughan, *Shakespeare's Caliban: A Cultural History* (Cambridge: Cambridge University Press, 1991); Rob Nixon, "Caribbean and African Appropriations of *The Tempest*," *Critical Inquiry* 13 (Spring 1987): 557–78; both of these include a comprehensive bibliography, updated in Peter Hulme and William H. Sherman, eds., *"The Tempest" and Its Travels* (London: Reaktion Books, 2000). A recent addition to the field is Chantal Zabus, *Tempests after Shakespeare* (New York: Palgrave, 2002).

2. For some examples, see May Joseph, "The Scream of Sycorax," in *Nomadic Identities* (Minneapolis: University of Minnesota Press, 1999); Coco Fusco, "El Diario de Miranda/Miranda's Diary," in *English Is Broken Here* (New York: New Press, 1995). In their rewritings of *The Tempest,* both Toni Morrison and Gloria Naylor imagine black Mirandas. Morrison's Jadine in *Tar Baby* (New York: Penguin, 1981) is the Europeanized protégé of the Prospero figure, Valerian; she has lost touch with her "ancient [African] properties" (305). Naylor's has not; her *Mama Day* (New York: Vintage, 1988), properly named Miranda, has African/feminine powers that Shakespeare associates with Prospero and excoriates in Sycorax.

3. See Peter Hulme, *Colonial Encounters: Europe and the Native Caribbean, 1492–1797* (London: Methuen, 1986), ch. 3. In an unpublished essay, "The Geography of Disenchantment in *The Tempest*," Kevin Pask continues Hulme's project by arguing for the significance of Atlantic elements in the predominantly Mediterranean environment of the play, a nexus of emergent colonialism in a mercantile context that notably includes the traffic in the bodies of women, both Miranda and Claribel.

4. Virginia Mason Vaughan and Alden T. Vaughan, "Introduction" to their edition of *The Tempest* (Arden Shakespeare, third series; Walton-on-Thames, Surrey: Thomas Nelson, 1999).

5. See Richard Halpern, "'The picture of Nobody': White Cannibalism in *The Tempest*," in *The Production of English Renaissance Culture,* ed. David Lee Miller, Sharon O'Dair, and Harold Weber (Ithaca, NY: Cornell University Press, 1994), 262–92.

6. All citations of *The Tempest,* ed. Stephen Orgel (Oxford: Oxford University Press, 1987), unless otherwise noted.

7. George Lamming, *In the Castle of My Skin* (Ann Arbor: University of Michigan Press, 1991 reprint of 1953 text), 297; hereafter *Castle.*

8. C. L. R. James, "The Making of the Caribbean People," in *Spheres of Existence* (Westport, CT: Lawrence Hill, n.d.), 176; the piece is a transcript of a 1966 lecture.

9. David Scott, *Refashioning Futures: Criticism after Postcoloniality* (Princeton: Princeton University Press, 1999), 204.

10. Roberto Fernández Retamar, *Calibán* (Lleida: University of Lleida, 1995), 24; *Caliban and Other Essays,* trans. Edward Baker (Minneapolis: University of Minnesota Press, 1989), 4.

11. For a stunning schematic mapping of the multiple differences of the colonial condition, see Edouard Glissant, *Discours Antillais* (Paris: Seuil, 1981), 30–31 n. 2; *Caribbean Discourse,* trans. J. Michael Dash (Charlottesville: University Press of Virginia, 1989), 17–19 n. 2.

12. For an important and detailed discussion of the various histories rapidly summarized here, see Robin Blackburn, *The Making of New World Slavery* (London: Verso, 1997).

13. Arguing for the homogeneity of the United States, Fernández Retamar "The white population of the United States (diverse, but of common European origin) exterminated the aboriginal population and thrust the black population aside" ("Caliban," 4), an extraordinary claim on many counts. It ignores the long process of making white of immigrant populations; the survival of Native Americans and a growing Native American movement, exemplified by Vine DeLoria; and the Civil Rights movement. It also ignores the role played by the figure Fernández Retamar advocates in his essay, José Martí, in radical Afro-Cuban populations in the United States; on that point, see Winston James, "From a Class for Itself to a Race on Its Own: The Strange Case of Afro-Cuban Radicalism and Afro-Cubans in Florida, 1870–1940," ch. 8 in *Holding Aloft the Banner of Ethiopia: Caribbean Radicalism in Early Twentieth-Century America* (London: Verso, 1998).

14. Nixon's account of uses of *The Tempest,* unlike Halpern's, never considers how even the masculinist tradition he unfolds engages questions of gender and sexuality. For him, it appears, such issues are women's work and are available only in texts by women. As we shall see in "Caliban's 'Woman,'" there are possibilities for women's engagement with *The Tempest* to which Nixon (like Fernández Retamar) fails to attend. Fernández Retamar has acknowledged his masculinism in "Postdata de Enero de 1993," in *Calibán,* 83, and by including in the list of names that opens the section "Nuestro Símbolo" in "Calibán" (in *Calibán*) several more names of women (39). My thanks to Sara Castro-Klaren for advice about the 1993 postscript, and for confirming its rather perfunctory attention to gender.

15. Ricardo L. Ortiz, "Revolution's Other Histories: The Sexual, Cultural, and Critical Legacies of Roberto Fernández Retamar's 'Caliban,'" *Social Text* 58 (Spring 1999): 33–58. Deploring the homophobic masculinism of "Caliban," Ortiz substitutes a homophilic masculinism.

16. Severo Sarduy, a Cuban associated with the journal *Lunes de Revolucion,* left Cuba for Paris in 1960 and remained there until his AIDS-related death in 1993. There he became associated with Tel Quel and served as the publisher of a number of Cuban writers who could not be published in Cuba, including Lezama Lima. Roland Barthes often cites Sarduy, who wrote several works of fiction as well as theoretical and critical essays. *Mariposa,* "butterfly," is a possible term from the "bestiary" of slang for homosexuals/transvestites; the homophone *maricón* clinches the association. I am grateful to Lawrence LaFountain-Stokes for advice about this lexicon, confirmed by Emilio Bejel in *Gay Cuban Nation* (Chicago: University of Chicago Press, 2001), where he notes, opening his discussion of the Cuban documentary film about a group of transvestites, *Mariposas en el andamio* (*Butterflies on the Scaffold,* dir. Luis Felipe Bernaza and Margaret Gilpin [1996]), "in Cuban culture, as well as in other Hispanic cultures, the word *mariposa* (butterfly) is sometimes used with a homosexual connotation" (196). Sarduy often theorized the transvestite; see, e.g., "Writing/Transvestism," in *Written on a Body,* trans. Carol Maier (New York: Lumen, 1989), 33–37, or *From Cuba with a Song,* trans. Suzanne Jill Levine (Los Angeles: Sun and Moon, 1994), in which the transvestite figures the mixed nature of Cuban culture.

17. Ortiz is indebted, as he notes, to the comprehensive essay by Brad Epps, "Proper Conduct: Reinaldo Arenas, Fidel Castro, and the Politics of Homosexuality," *Journal of the History of Sexuality,* 6, no. 2 (1995): 231–83. It, along with Ortiz's "Revolution's Other

Histories," provides an ample bibliography on the topic of homosexuality in revolutionary Cuba; a subsequent and valuable addition to this literature is José Quiroga, *Tropics of Desire: Interventions from Queer Latino America* (New York: New York University Press, 2000), esp. 118–31.

18. This history, I note in passing, has been all but lost on the present generation of conservative voices, who speak for U.S. gays only by advocating our right to marry and serve openly in the military.

In "Caliban Revisited," his 1986 piece contextualizing the original essay, Fernández Retamar does locate his writing within the context of a seemingly triumphant left that joined "oppressed 'races' and communities, of women, of marginal peoples," immediately distancing himself from the "absurdity" of "hippies and flower power" (*Caliban and Other Essays,* 47–48).

19. All citations from José Enrique Rodó, *Ariel,* trans. Margaret Sayers Peden (Austin: University of Texas Press, 1988). Rodó was a Uruguayan writer; *Ariel* was—and remains—an important cultural manifesto, as Carlos Fuentes attests in his prologue in this edition, which also provides ample bibliographic references.

20. In his riposte to Fernández Retamar, Emir Rodríguez Monegal, in "The Metamorphoses of Caliban," *diacritics* 7 (September 1977): 78–83, makes the counterclaim that Fernández Retamar is influenced by French writers (he means Frantz Fanon and Aimé Césaire; his remark is technically true but erases them as Caribbean writers) and that his (and Che Guevara's) alliances with Blacks are therefore suspect acts of blackface as well. It is unfortunate to find Rodríguez Monegal essentially deploying the same kind of rhetoric against Fernández Retamar as Fernández Retamar uses against him.

21. On this well-recognized point, see, e.g., Oscar Montero, "*Modernismo* and Homophobia: Darío and Rodó," in *Sex and Sexuality in Latin America,* ed. Daniel Balderston and Donna J. Guy (New York: New York University Press, 1997), 101–17.

22. For an acute analysis, see Sylvia Molloy, "Too Wilde for Comfort: Desire and Ideology in Fin-de-Siècle Spanish America," *Social Text* 10, nos. 2–3 (1992): 187–201, which analyzes Martí and Rubén Darío on Oscar Wilde in the context of *modernismo* defenses against and entanglements with homosexual desire.

23. See Sylvia Molloy, "His America, Our America: José Martí Reads Whitman," in *Breaking Bounds: Whitman and American Cultural Studies,* ed. Betsy Erkkila and Jay Grossman (New York: Oxford University Press, 1996), 83–91; in the same volume, Jorge Salessi and José Quiroga, in "Errata sobre la erotica, or, the Elision of Whitman's Body," 123–33, extend the study of "homoerotically repressed scenes of instruction that may be at the root of the Whitman question in Latin America" (124)—in Martí, among others—to Spanish translations of Whitman.

24. Citations from José Martí, "Our America," in *The America of José Martí: Selected Writings,* trans. Juan de Onis (New York: Noonday, 1953), 138–51, quotation at 150. Elsewhere, from the same volume, I cite "Emerson" (216–38), "Whitman" (239–58), and "Simón Bolívar" (152–62).

25. This heady prose seems like a more accurate translation of Martí than the chastened one Peden gives for Rodó, though Fuentes, in a prologue to Peden's translation, praises it precisely for removing the rhetorical swells, which, he confesses with embarrassment, inflamed him as a young reader (*Ariel,* 14). Ortiz notes these remarks by

Fuentes as a sign of the persistence of late-nineteenth-century attitudes ("Revolution's Other Histories," 55–56 n. 12).

26. For one study of this phenomenon, see Jorge Salessi, "The Argentine Dissemination of Homosexuality, 1890–1914," in *Entiendes: Queer Readings, Hispanic Writings,* ed. Emilie L. Bergmann and Paul Julian Smith (Durham, NC: Duke University Press, 1995), 49–91, a study of theoretical texts but also of policing/anthropologizing texts that "uncover" a native homosexual culture in the cities of Latin America even as they insist on a foreign causality.

27. For a very different view from Fernández Retamar's on the relationships between race and nature in Martí and Rodó, see Joseba Gabilondo, "Afterword" to *The Cosmic Race/La raza cosmica,* by José Vasconcelos, trans. Didier T. Jaén (Baltimore, MD: The Johns Hopkins University Press, 1997), 102–3.

28. For an attempt to bring Martí's erotics into the orbit of homosexual desire, see Benigno Sanchez-Eppler, "Call My Son Ismael: Exiled Paternity and Father/Son Eroticism in Reinaldo Arenas and José Martí," *differences* 6, no. 1 (Spring 1994): 69–97. Molloy, "His America, Our America," compares Martí's Ismael with Rodó's Ariel, their shared family romance of fathers and sons without mothers (84).

29. Severo Sarduy, *Written on a Body,* 64. Epps, "Proper Conduct," notes that Sarduy's writing on the body as a site of transvestism and imitation could be brought to bear on the resolute masculinism advocated by the revolution as a necessary front that might still be only that (244), a point congruent to the one I have been making about the homoerotic/homophobic strategies in these various Latin American texts around *The Tempest.*

30. The interview with George Kent first appeared in *Black World* 22, no. 5 (March 1973): 4–14, 88–97. The interview along with numerous other published and unpublished materials are gathered in George Lamming, *Conversations: Essays, Addresses, and Interviews, 1953–1990,* ed. Richard Drayton and Andaiye (London: Karia Press, 1992), 104 for the reference in the Kent interview.

31. The interview originally appeared in Ian Munro and Reinhard Sander, eds., *Kas-Kas: Interview with Three Caribbean Writers in Texas* (occasional publication of the African and Afro-American Research Institute; Austin: University of Texas, 1972; Lamming was a writer in residence in Texas in 1970); republished in Lamming, *Conversations,* cited phrase, 73.

32. For the significance of the "riots" of 1937, see George Lamming, "Caribbean Labor, Culture, and Identity," *Bucknell Review (Caribbean Cultural Identities,* ed. Glyne Griffith) 44, no. 2 (2001): 17–32, esp. 22, a printing of an address delivered in 1994 at the University of the West Indies. Their significance is also explored in David Scott, "The Sovereignty of the Imagination: An Interview with George Lamming," *Small Axe* 12 (September 2002): 72–200; see esp. 75–87. For the role of the "riots" in Lamming, *In the Castle of My Skin* and in cultural-historical context, see Ngũgĩ wa Thiong'o, *Homecoming* (New York: Lawrence Hill, 1972), 110–26, and Supriya Nair, *Caliban's Curse: George Lamming and the Revisioning of History* (Ann Arbor: University of Michigan Press, 1996), ch. 3. For a superb account of congruent events, see Ken Post, *Arise Ye Starvelings: The Jamaican Labour Rebellion of 1938 and Its Aftermath* (The Hague: Martinus Nijhoff, 1978).

33. "Western Education and the Caribbean Individual," one of two pieces gathered

in George Lamming, *Coming Coming Home: Conversations II* (Philipsburg, St. Martin: House of Nehesi Publications, 2000), 25.

34. See George Lamming, "Coming, Coming, Coming Home," in *Coming Coming Home*, 38–39. The problems with this view are detailed by Andaiye in the foreword to Lamming, *Conversations*, 12–14.

35. George Lamming, *The Pleasures of Exile* (Ann Arbor: University of Michigan Press, 1992 reprint of 1960 text); hereafter *Pleasures*.

36. Mannoni was analyzed by Jacques Lacan; see Elisabeth Roudinesco, *Jacques Lacan and Co.*, trans. Jeffrey Mehlman (Chicago: University of Chicago Press, 1990), 234, for a brief account of his analysis, which began in 1947.

37. Lamming, *Pleasures of Exile* (London: Allison and Busby, 1984), 7; the introduction to the 1984 reprint is omitted from the 1992 Michigan reprint.

38. The charge of dependency is also made by Selwyn R. Cudjoe, *Resistance and Caribbean Literature* (Athens: Ohio University Press, 1980).

39. Vera Kutzinski, "The Cult of Caliban: Collaboration and Revisionism in Contemporary Caribbean Narrative," in *A History of Literature in the Caribbean*, ed. A. James Arnold, vol. 3 (Amsterdam: John Benjamins, 1997), 285–302, citation 288. In her *Sugar's Secrets: Race and the Erotics of Cuban Nationalism* (Charlottesville: University Press of Virginia, 1993), Kutzinski has insisted on the heterosexual violence that underwrites tropes of *mestizaje*.

40. Octave Mannoni, *Prospero and Caliban: The Psychology of Colonization*, trans. Pamela Powesland (Ann Arbor: University of Michigan Press, 1990), 76–77.

41. All citations from Frantz Fanon, *Black Skin, White Masks*, trans. Charles Lam Markmann (New York: Grove Press, 1967).

42. Fanon's statement is, of course, an overstatement, since he does devote a chapter to the black woman's desire for the white man. Presumably, as a black man he knows nothing of the black woman. The gendered limits of Fanon's thought have been examined: by Anne McClintock, for example, in *Imperial Leather: Race, Gender, and Sexuality in the Colonial Context* (New York: Routledge, 1995), 360–68; and more capaciously by Rey Chow, "The Politics of Admittance: Female Sexual Agency, Miscegenation, and the Formation of Community in Frantz Fanon," in *Frantz Fanon: Critical Perspectives*, ed. Anthony C. Allessandrini (London: Routledge, 1999), 34–56, and by Lola Young, "Missing Persons: Fantasising Black Women in *Black Skin, White Masks*," in *The Fact of Blackness: Frantz Fanon and Visual Representation*, ed. Alan Read (Seattle, WA: Bay Press, 1996), 86–101, both of whom argue for variously threatening forms of black female agency. More pertinent to the analysis at hand have been attempts to articulate Fanon's views of gender with his views of sexuality, and particularly of male homosexuality; Diana Fuss, for example, in "Interior Colonies: Frantz Fanon and the Politics of Identification," an essay that appeared initially in *diacritics* 24, nos. 2–3 (1994): 20–42, and was reprinted as the final chapter in Fuss, *Identification Papers* (New York: Routledge, 1995), finds not only more lability in Fanon's view of female gender than does McClintock but also connections between his misogyny and his homophobia, including the potentially enabling possibility that a dehomogenized definition of homosexuality might emerge from Fanon's admittedly phobic account. Misogyny and homophobia are also linked in Ann Pellegrini's reading of Fanon in her *Performance Anxieties: Staging Psychoanalysis, Staging Race* (New York: Routledge,

1997); privileging the "blind spot of gender" (93) in her analysis of Fanon, Pellegrini also argues that Fanon's enablement of a vision of the heterosexuality of the black male (and the deflection of homosexuality) occurs through his cross-raced plots, in which the black man possesses the white man's white woman.

43. Henry Louis Gates Jr., in "Critical Fanonism," *Critical Inquiry* 17 (Spring 1991): 457–70, a review of the criticism on Fanon to the time of his writing, fastens on Fanon's figure of the New Man without pausing over why it must be so gendered, or what gender politics and what forms of sexuality Fanon is advocating—or defending against. His summary is nonetheless fairly accurate in terms of the absence of a concern with gender in many of the critics he reviews, including Homi K. Bhabha, Edward Said, and Abdul Jan Mohamed.

44. A stunning discussion of the homophobic logic of Fanon's collapse of white racism into homosexuality can be found in Lee Edelman's "The Part for the (W)hole," ch. 3 of *Homographesis: Essays in Gay Literary and Cultural Theory* (New York: Routledge, 1994). And Kobena Mercer has written equally tellingly on the effects and historical contexts of Fanon's argument for the theorization of gay black sexuality; see "Decolonisation and Disappointment: Reading Fanon's Sexual Politics," in *The Fact of Blackness,* ed. Read, 114–31, and "Busy in the Ruins of a Wretched Phantasia," in *Frantz Fanon,* ed. Allessandrini, 195–218.

45. See Peter Hulme, "Reading from Elsewhere: George Lamming and the Paradox of Exile," in *"The Tempest" and Its Travels,* ed. Hulme and Sherman, 220–35. The significant exception to this generalization would be Ania Loomba, "Seizing the Book," ch. 6 of *Gender, Race, Renaissance Drama* (Manchester: Manchester University Press, 1989). Loomba briefly revisits this material in *Shakespeare, Race, and Colonialism* (Oxford: Oxford University Press, 2002), 5–6, 161–68, and she notes as well that "Lamming and others were far ahead of the Shakespearian scholarship of their day" (164). Pointing to the north-African origins of Sycorax and Caliban, Loomba cautions against a New World model of colonialism that ignores other sites and types of European colonial encounters that contributed to early modern concepts of race.

46. Peter Hulme, "Rewriting the Caribbean Past: Cultural History in the Colonial Context," in *Interpretation and Cultural History,* ed. Joan H. Pittock and Andrew Wear (New York: St. Martin's, 1991), 183.

47. Claribel's north-African marriage is akin to Miranda's alliance with Ferdinand insofar as both are patriarchally arranged aristocratic marriages. Nonetheless, the unspoken but unmistakable racial antipathy reported about the "loathness" (2.1.128) of a "fair soul" (2.1.127) to be married to an African rather than to a European links the King of Tunis to Caliban. Both share a north-African origin. On this topic, see Marjorie Raley, "Claribel's Husband," in *Race, Ethnicity, and Power in the Renaissance,* ed. Joyce Green MacDonald (Madison, NJ: Fairleigh Dickinson University Press, 1997), 95–119.

48. George Lamming, *Season of Adventure* (London: Allison and Busby, 1979), 49.

49. Among the feminist critics would be Nair as well as Belinda Edmondson, whose "Novel of Revolution and the Unrepresentable Black Woman," ch. 5 of *Making Men: Gender, Literary Authority, and Women's Writing in Caribbean Narrative* (Durham, NC: Duke University Press, 1999), follows a trajectory similar to the one I have been tracing.

50. George Lamming, *Of Age and Innocence* (London: Allison and Busby, 1981), 206.

Ngũgĩ, *Homecoming,* 140–42, treats this and related passages in his discussion of the alienating effects of colonialism.

51. For a brief consideration of the occasion and the connections between Lamming's thought and Fanon's, see David Macey, *Frantz Fanon* (New York: Picador, 2000), 165–67.

52. George Lamming, "The Negro Writer and His World," *Présence Africaine* 18/19 (1956): 321; also in *Conversations,* 37–38.

53. Simon Gikandi, *Writing in Limbo: Modernism and Caribbean Literature* (Ithaca, NY: Cornell University Press, 1992), focuses on conditions of language in his discussion of Lamming's *Castle.*

54. D. A. Miller, *The Novel and the Police* (Berkeley and Los Angeles: University of California Press, 1988), ch. 6, "Secret Subjects, Open Secrets," 192–220.

55. Frantz Fanon, *The Wretched of the Earth,* trans. Constance Farrington (Harmondsworth, England: Penguin, 1967), 251; hereafter *Wretched.*

56. Roberto Fernández Retamar, "Caliban Speaks Five Hundred Years Later," in *Dangerous Liaisons: Gender, Nation, and Postcolonial Perspectives,* ed. Anne McClintock, Aamir Mufti, and Ella Shohat (Minneapolis: University of Minnesota Press, 1997), 171.

57. Kent interview, 92; cited from Lamming, *Conversations,* 100. This citation is the starting point for Peter Hulme's analysis of Lamming's final novels and the psychology of (neo)colonialism in "The Profit of Language: George Lamming and the Postcolonial Novel," in *Recasting the World,* ed. Jonathan White (Baltimore, MD: The Johns Hopkins University Press, 1993), 120–36.

58. See Kent interview, 91 (cited from Lamming, *Conversations,* 99–100), as well as the 1979 interview in Daryl Cumber Dance, *New World Adams* (Leeds, England: Peepal Tree Books, 1992), 138.

59. Hulme, "Profit of Language," 120. Lamming's agenda—translating his novels into political allegory—is followed by Sandra Pouchet Paquet, *The Novels of George Lamming* (London: Heinemann, 1982), and by Ambroise Kom, *George Lamming et le destin des Caraibes* (Ville de Salle, Quebec: Didier, 1986).

60. George Lamming, *Water with Berries* (New York: Holt, Rinehart, and Winston, 1971), 12.

61. It is not clear what action the Secret Gathering took; about all we know is that it left behind the corpse of a woman—a white woman—who got her sexual pleasure from kinky sex with one of the revolutionaries and who died having sex. Characteristic of the novel, Lamming moves from this story (45) to have Fola walk into the novel as the sole female member of the revolutionary group (47), attempting to balance the abjection of and violence against women with this sign of gender solidarity.

62. Lamming interprets Jeremy this way in the Kent interview: "He really detests Jeremy. He detests the function which Jeremy performs. Jeremy is a bureaucrat.... There is a part of him which feels that even to be sitting talking to Jeremy is to be involving himself in a pollution which he had put behind" (92; cited from Lamming, *Conversations,* 101).

63. That "Third World" novels should be read as national allegories is the argument of Fredric Jameson, "Third-World Literature in the Era of Multinational Capitalism," *Social Text* 15 (1986): 65–88; the argument is criticized by Aijaz Ahmad, *In Theory: Classes, Nations, Literature* (London: Verso, 1992), ch. 3. Hulme notes this controversy

in "Profit of Language," but he nonetheless reads Lamming's *Water with Berries* as national allegory. On heterosexual romance as a way to code nation building, see Doris Sommer, *Foundational Fictions: The National Romances of Latin America* (Berkeley and Los Angeles: University of California Press, 1991); for a telling critique of the heterosexism of such novels and an opening toward other possibilities, see Rhonda Cobham, "Misgendering the Nation: African Nationalist Fictions and Nuruddin Farah's *Maps,*" in *Nationalisms and Sexualities,* ed. Andrew Parker, Mary Russo, Doris Sommer, and Patricia Yaeger (New York: Routledge, 1992), 42–59, esp. 47, on stigmatization of homosexuality as foreign infection.

64. The fog of the novel is often an alcoholic haze, which may be reflected in its title; it binds the male characters together in the local pub that Roger burns down late in the novel, his act of rebellion after repudiating his wife and their mixed-race child.

65. At the end of Lamming's *Natives of My Person* (Ann Arbor: University of Michigan Press, 1992), a novel in which men and women are entirely separate, the men on their (neo)colonial voyage never arrive at San Cristobal, and the women remain there forever as a future that the men need to discover, a future that might "solve" male-female relations or might dissolve them. As "a future they must learn" (345), men need to renounce masculinity. Although some, including Hulme and Paquet in her foreword to the University of Michigan edition of *Pleasures,* find this conclusion hearteningly feminist in its impulse, it needs to be said that even here, women function for the sake of men.

CALIBAN'S "WOMAN"

1. Significantly, *Othello* is the play with a half-dozen uses of "monstrous." The words are attached to Iago's plot and to the monster in Othello's mind, Desdemona's infidelity, naming thereby the charged site of female sexuality, Othello's racially blackened sexuality, and the terrain shared in his coupling with Iago. It is worth noting that *Othello* is the Shakespeare play that has garnered the most critical attention to questions of race and their entanglements with sexuality. In that regard, Karen Newman's "'And wash the Ethiop white': Femininity and the Monstrous in *Othello,*" ch. 5 in *Fashioning Femininity* (Chicago: University of Chicago Press, 1991), is exemplary. Other important considerations include Patricia Parker, "Fantasies of 'Race' and 'Gender': Africa, *Othello,* and Bringing to Light," and Jyotsna Singh, "Otello's Identity, Postcolonial Theory, and Contemporary African Rewritings of *Othello,*" both in *Women, "Race," and Writing in the Early Modern Period,* ed. Margo Hendricks and Patricia Parker (New York: Routledge, 1994).

2. Jeffrey Jerome Cohen, "Monster Culture (Seven Theses)," in *Monster Theory,* ed. Jeffrey Jerome Cohen (Minneapolis: University of Minnesota Press, 1996), 3–25. In a largely pyschoanalytic vein, Cohen further explores the excess of monstrosity in *Of Giants: Sex, Monsters, and the Middle Ages* (Minneapolis: University of Minnesota Press, 1999). Cohen's stress on the hybridity of an attractive/repulsive body is to be contrasted, I think, with the dynamics of excoriation in *The Tempest* and with the revaluation in modern texts that seize upon devalued difference as a site of alterity.

3. Alden T. Vaughan and Virginia Mason Vaughan, *Shakespeare's Caliban: A Cultural History* (Cambridge: Cambridge University Press, 1991), 10.

4. Ibid., 10. This bibliographic information will, of course, be found in most modern texts of the play, including Stephen Orgel's (Oxford: Oxford University Press, 1987).

5. Peter Hulme, *Colonial Encounters: Europe and the Native Caribbean, 1492–1797* (London: Methuen, 1986), 114.

6. George Lamming, *The Pleasures of Exile* (Ann Arbor: University of Michigan Press, 1992 reprint of 1960 text), 15; hereafter *Pleasures*.

7. Matthew W. Black and Matthias A. Shaaber, *Shakespeare's Seventeenth-Century Editors, 1632–1685* (New York: Modern Language Association, 1937), 95.

8. *The Tempest,* Arden edition, ed. Frank Kermode (London: Methuen, 1954); I cite the lemma to 1.2.282. The original Arden edition, ed. Morton Luce (London: Methuen, 1901), fails to record the *he/she* emendation.

9. The pronoun change to "she" was first made by John Dryden and Sir William Davenant in their rewriting of Shakespeare in *The Tempest, or The Enchanted Island* (1670), as Virginia Mason Vaughan and Alden T. Vaughan record in their 1999 Arden edition (Arden Shakespeare, third series; Walton-on-Thames, Surrey: Thomas Nelson, 1999).

10. See Stephen Orgel, "Introduction" to his edition of *The Tempest,* 18–19, as well as his essay "Prospero's Wife," originally published in *Representations* 8 (Fall 1984): 1–13, and reprinted in *Rewriting the Renaissance,* ed. Margaret Ferguson, Maureen Quilligan, and Nancy Vickers (Chicago: University of Chicago Press, 1985), 54.

11. In this, Prospero would seem to mirror James I, whose misogyny was accompanied by proclamations of his female creative powers as "nourish-father" to the nation, a formulation that makes him at once a nursing mother ("nurse" derives from Middle English "nourrish") and a father; see the discussion of James I's *Basilikon Doron* in Jonathan Goldberg, *James I and the Politics of Literature* (Baltimore, MD: The Johns Hopkins University Press, 1983), 141–43.

12. For a pertinent critique, within the context of historical/critical accounts of witchcraft in the Renaissance, of a dehistoricizing reduction of questions of femininity to questions of the mother in psychoanalytically inflected feminist criticism, see Newman, *Fashioning Femininity,* ch. 4.

13. It is just such a fantasy of male genius that governs Peter Greenaway's film *Prospero's Books* (1991), during which John Gielgud (as Prospero) recites everyone's lines.

14. For an argument congruent with this one, see Ann Rosalind Jones and Peter Stallybrass, "Fetishizing Gender: Constructing the Hermaphrodite in Renaissance Europe," in *Body Guards,* ed. Julia Epstein and Kristina Straub (New York: Routledge, 1991), which concludes that fixing gender on genitals is an eighteenth-century development and that, in the Renaissance, gender could be located elsewhere. Their final examples include other bodily parts, such as the mouth (which will be important for the argument that follows below), or clothing as sites of gender identification. The latter point is developed in their *Renaissance Clothing and the Materials of Memory* (Cambridge: Cambridge University Press, 2000). It is worth remarking here that the character in the play who demonstrates this kind of lability—and subordination—is Ariel, a boy actor who plays female roles every time Prospero assigns him a part: sea nymph, harpy, goddess.

15. In other words, the interchangeability of gender, as it is conceptualized in New Historicist work that depends upon Thomas Laqueur, *Making Sex* (Cambridge, MA:

Harvard University Press, 1990)—for example, Stephen Greenblatt, *Shakespearean Negotiations* (Berkeley and Los Angeles: University of California Press, 1988), ch. 3, or Stephen Orgel, "Nobody's Perfect, or Why Did the English Stage Take Boys for Women?" *SAQ* 88 (1989): 7–29, which is incorporated into Orgel, *Impersonations: The Performance of Gender in Shakespeare's England* (Cambridge: Cambridge University Press, 1996)—does not work in both directions. Moreover, the one-sex model is just that, a model that pertains to anatomical drawing and not to the social meanings of gender that strongly mark male/female difference.

16. *The Tempest,* ed. Arthur Quiller-Couch and John Dover Wilson (Cambridge: Cambridge University Press, 1921).

17. The sentence can be found in the "first letter" ascribed to Hernán Cortés (addressed "to Queen Doña Juana and to the Emperor, Charles V, Her Son") and expresses a sentiment that is ubiquitous in colonialist literature of the period, as I argue in *Sodometries: Renaissance Texts, Modern Sexualities* (Stanford: Stanford University Press, 1992), part 3, examining Latin American and Anglo texts that deploy the figure of the sodomite as the embodied antithesis of colonial order (in Hispanic texts, the figure of the sodomite is attached to the "native" most often, whereas Anglo texts tend to locate sodomy among the laboring class). The illustration I use in *Sodometries,* which shows Balboa feeding "sodomitical" Panamanian natives to his dogs, Hulme uses in his discussion of Caliban (*Colonial Encounters,* 113), referring to Prospero's unleashing of his dogs against him in act 4, scene 1. Hulme does not mention what the scene illustrates, nor does he comment on the pertinence of sodomy to cannibal Caliban.

18. See M. Jacqui Alexander, "Erotic Autonomy as a Politics of Decolonization: An Anatomy of Feminist and State Practice in the Bahamas Tourist Industry," in *Feminist Genealogies, Colonial Legacies, Democratic Futures,* ed. M. Jacqui Alexander and Chandra Talpade Mohanty (New York: Routledge, 1997), 63–100 and n. 12, for the point that the colonial scene underlies the present Bahamian regime, in which "natives" are inducted into the belief that "'native' heterosexuals had more in common with imperial heterosexuals than with 'native' homosexuals" (370); and Alexander, "Redrafting Morality: The Postcolonial State and the Sexual Offences Bill of Trinidad and Tobago," in *Third World Women and the Politics of Feminism,* ed. Chandra Talpade Mohanty, Ann Russo, and Lourdes Torres (Bloomington: Indiana University Press, 1991), 133–52, for arguments about the ideological naturalization of heterosexuality. For an overview of the arguments presented in these two essays, see Alexander, "Not Just (Any) Body Can Be a Citizen: The Politics of Law, Sexuality, and Postcoloniality in Trinidad and Tobago and the Bahamas," *Feminist Review* 48 (1994): 5–23.

19. For a survey of the recent historical literature, see Frances E. Dolan, *Dangerous Familiars: Representations of Domestic Crime in England, 1550–1700* (Ithaca, NY: Cornell University Press, 1994), ch. 5, esp. 171–80, 194–210. Whereas Dolan emphasizes the status of the witch as an "insider," Judith Bennett and Amy Froide, in "A Singular Past," in *Singlewomen in the European Past, 1250–1800,* ed. Judith Bennett and Amy Froide (Philadelphia: University of Pennsylvania Press, 1999), note that "the most likely targets for an accusation of witchcraft were women who lived without men" (14).

20. Alan Bray, "Homosexuality and the Signs of Male Friendship in Elizabethan England," *History Workshop Journal* 29 (1990): 1–19, reprinted in revised form in Jonathan Goldberg, ed., *Queering the Renaissance* (Durham, NC: Duke University Press, 1994).

21. Alan Bray, *Homosexuality in Renaissance England* (London: Gay Men's Press, 1982), 40, 72 cited. On the latter page, Bray also notes as significant that Drago's arrest coincided with an efflorescence of witch trials.

22. See Valerie Traub, "The Psychomorphology of the Clitoris," *GLQ* 2 (1995): 81–113.

23. George Lamming, *In the Castle of My Skin* (Ann Arbor: University of Michigan Press, 1991 reprint of 1953 text), 104, 26.

24. As Gesa Mackenthun puts it in "A Monstrous Race for Possession: Discourses of Monstrosity in *The Tempest* and Early British America," in *Writing and Race,* ed. Tim Youngs (London: Longman, 1997), 52–79, "By having 'littered' a 'puppy-headed' monster, Sycorax is not only marked as a witch but also bears the traces of a monstrous female" (64).

25. The north-African locale for the unspeakable deed may connect Sycorax to a city infamous as a site of white slavery (see Nabil Matar, *Turks, Moors, and Englishmen in the Age of Discovery* [New York: Columbia University Press, 1999] for this significance of Algiers, and Paul Baepler, *White Slaves, African Masters* [Chicago: University of Chicago Press, 1999] for an anthology of texts from the seventeenth to the nineteenth centuries), a site moreover regularly declared a hotbed of male same-sex activity, as Matar notes (as does Bray as well, *Homosexuality,* 75). This plot figures in Cervantes's *Don Quixote* (part 1, chs. 39–41) and in several of his plays, as is demonstrated in Adrienne L. Martín, "Images of Deviance in Cervantes's Algeria," *Cervantes* 15, no. 2 (1995): 5–13. Martín also points to the stigmatization of north-Africans in Diego de Haedo, *Topographiae historia general de Argel* (1612), a text that declares that sodomy was openly practiced in Algiers, a claim taken at face value by Daniel Eisenberg, "Juan Ruiz's Heterosexual 'Good Love,'" in *Queer Iberia,* ed. Josiah Blackmore and Gregory S. Hutchinson (Durham, NC: Duke University Press, 1999), 253. Eisenberg also suspects that the true author of the *Topographiae* was Cervantes. Gregory Hutchinson has argued in "The Sodomitic Moor: Queerness in the Narrative of *Reconquista,*" in *Queering the Middle Ages,* ed. Glenn Burger and Steven F. Kruger (Minneapolis: University of Minnesota Press, 2001), 99–122, that the early modern period is the moment when the sodomitical Moor assumes stereotypical force. And north-Africans were frequently accused of sodomy by the Inquisition, as E. William Monter notes (*Frontiers of Heresy: The Spanish Inquisition from the Basque Lands to Sicily* [Cambridge: Cambridge University Press, 1990], 292). It is further worth mentioning that in William Strachey's account of a shipwreck off Bermuda, a source for *The Tempest,* he compares the New World hurricane to storms "upon the coast of *Barbary* and *Algeere*" (cited in Appendix 1 in the Vaughans' Arden edition, 290). This north-African locale is the charged site of Claribel's marriage as well as the near foundering of Aeneas's imperial ambitions.

26. This interpretation assumes that the lines do simply mean that she was pregnant. According to James C. Oldham, "On Pleading the Belly: A History of the Jury of Matrons," *Criminal Justice History* 6 (1985): 1–64, his study of the records "does not permit a conclusion that a successful pregnancy plea was 'tantamount to a pardon'" (19), as John Beattie has argued in an unpublished essay to which Oldham alludes. Oldham shows that a delay in execution was usual, and that often the death penalty was replaced by imprisonment or by deportation; his evidence is drawn mainly from late-seventeenth- and eighteenth-century cases.

27. On this point, see Jacques Chiffoleau, "Dire l'indicible: Rémarques sur la catégorie du *nefandum* du XIIe au XVe siècles," *Annales* 45 (1990): 289–384.

28. Arthur Evans, *Witchcraft and the Gay Counterculture* (Boston: Fag Rag Books, 1978).

29. Evans depends here on Henry Charles Lea, *Materials toward a History of Witchcraft*, ed. A. C. Howland, 3 vols. (Philadelphia: University of Pennsylvania Press, 1939), 2:485: "[V]os viri cum succubis and *[sic]* vos mulieres cum incubis fornicati estis, Sodomiam veram et nefandissium crimen misere cum illis tactu frigidissimo exercuistis."

30. Jeffrey Richards, *Sex, Dissidence, and Damnation* (London: Routledge, 1991), 143.

31. E. William Monter, *Witchcraft in France and Switzerland: The Borderlands during the Reformation* (Ithaca, NY: Cornell University Press, 1976), 136, 198. A similar view of the relationship between sodomy and witchcraft accusations is offered by Guido Ruggiero, *The Boundaries of Eros: Sex Crime and Sexuality in Renaissance Venice* (New York: Oxford University Press, 1985), 140, which regards the two crimes as parallel instances of the policing of "the normal and the abnormal"; in a note (196 n. 135), he further speculates on the relationship and distribution of these accusations.

32. Cited in Monter, *Frontiers,* 280. Monter details executions for sodomy and for witchcraft in separate chapters of this study but does not draw connections between them.

33. Paul Brown, "'This thing of darkness I acknowledge mine': *The Tempest* and the Discourse of Colonialism," in *Political Shakespeare,* ed. Jonathan Dollimore and Alan Sinfield (Ithaca, NY: Cornell University Press, 1985). Brown's understanding of sexuality is limited to heterosexuality; he also too easily collapses the positions of the native woman (Pocahontas) with Miranda, and although he draws parallels between the gender situation and class antagonism (master/masterless relations, which Dolan argues in *Dangerous Familiars,* 60–71, ignores "insider" servant status), he does not read sexuality in these parallels.

G. R. Quaife, *Godly Zeal and Furious Rage: The Witch in Early Modern Europe* (London: Croom Helm, 1987), 99; Quaife continues by referring to one claim that the devil has a three-pronged penis, thus "permitting him to engage in coitus, sodomy and fellatio simultaneously." In his reviews of previous scholarship, he notes those who have thought of witchcraft prosecutions as policing nonheterosexual relations, whether among women or among men. For further documentation of witchcraft involving anal sex with the devil, see Jeffrey Russell, *Witchcraft in the Middle Ages* (Ithaca, NY: Cornell University Press, 1960), 391. John Boswell, *Christianity, Social Tolerance, and Homosexuality* (Chicago: University of Chicago Press, 1980), 235, has a passing consideration of the witchcraft/sodomy/heresy nexus. Lyndal Roper, *Oedipus and the Devil* (London: Routledge, 1994), also associates the sexual activities of the witches' Sabbath with sodomy (25) but does not pursue the connection further.

34. Retha M. Warnicke, *The Rise and Fall of Anne Boleyn* (Cambridge: Cambridge University Press, 1989), 194.

35. Michael Drayton, "The Moone-Calfe," in *The Works of Michael Drayton,* ed. J. William Hebel, 5 vols. (Oxford: Basil Blackwell, 1932), vol. 3, lines 178, 190.

36. Heinrich Kramer and James Sprenger, *Malleus Maleficarum,* trans. Montague Summers (New York: Dover, 1971 reprint of 1928 text), 30.

37. As Franco Mormando notes in *The Preacher's Demons: Bernardino of Siena and*

the Social Underworld of Early Renaissance Italy (Chicago: University of Chicago Press, 1999), Bernardino is capable of calling both sodomy and witchcraft the worst of sins (122–23), but separately: He is vehemently opposed to both as forms of heresy, but he does not otherwise connect the two except as "the worst."

38. Thomas Weld, cited by Carol F. Karlsen, *The Devil in the Shape of a Woman* (New York: Vintage, 1989), 17–18. As Karlsen comments and goes on to cite Weld further to this point, the monstrous births were seen as the analogues to the monstrous beliefs of Hutchison and her followers. Such accusations against witches are a particular instance of the phenomenon that Marie-Hélène Huet studies in *Monstrous Imagination* (Cambridge, MA: Harvard University Press, 1993), in which the monstrous imagination of the mother is said to be responsible for deformed offspring. This phenomenon is also discussed in Audrey Eccles, *Obstetrics and Gynaecology in Tudor and Stuart England* (Kent, OH: Kent State University Press, 1982); she also notes that sodomy and bestiality were among the supposed causes of deformed offspring (65). A wide-ranging study of monstrosity in early modernity is offered in Lorraine Daston and Katharine Park, *Wonders and the Order of Nature* (New York: Zone Books, 1998), ch. 5.

39. Makeda Silvera, "Man Royals and Sodomites: Some Thoughts on the Invisibility of Afro-Caribbean Lesbians," in *Reclaiming Sodom,* ed. Jonathan Goldberg (New York: Routledge, 1994), 95–105, citations from 96–97.

40. Not that any previous editor has ever noted these implications. David Sundelson, in "So Rare a Wonder'd Father: Prospero's *Tempest,*" in *Representing Shakespeare,* ed. Murray M. Schwartz and Coppélia Kahn (Baltimore, MD: The Johns Hopkins University Press, 1980), does, although the lines are adduced in the context of Prospero's "impotence" in Milan (35). Sundelson does note that once on the island, Prospero assumes paternal and maternal powers.

41. Sundelson, "So Rare a Wonder'd Father," 41. As Sundelson continues to explicate this scene, he reads the greedy mouth as making a female demand and the scene of venting as a parody of childbirth and an expression of female loathing. Although the latter point is not to be denied, I do not think one can simply collapse this scene onto a female body. Nor do I think the relationship between Caliban and Trinculo necessarily needs to be read as a repudiation of relationships with women, as Barbara Bowen seems to suggest in "Writing Caliban: Anticolonial Appropriations of *The Tempest,*" *Current Writing: Text and Reception in Southern Africa* 5, no. 2 (1993): 80–99, when she writes that "the coupling of Trinculo and Caliban, head to tail under the gaberdine, followed immediately by Stephano's song about abandoning 'Kate' in favor of the 'boys' at sea (II.ii.55), clearly suggests an erotic bond" (92).

42. See Jeanne Addison Roberts, "'Wife' or 'Wise': *The Tempest* l. 1786," *Studies in Bibliography* 31 (1978): 203–8. David Bevington prints "wife" in his edition, *The Complete Works of Shakespeare,* 3rd ed. (Glenview, IL: Scott Foresman, 1980); his textual apparatus records "wise" as the F1 reading; he offers no explanation for his emendation.

43. Mark Thornton Burnett, "'Strange and woonderfull syghts': *The Tempest* and the Discourses of Monstrosity," *Shakespeare Survey* 50 (1997): 187–99, 195 cited.

44. Frye, in his Penguin edition, notes at 4.1.123 that "some copies of F read 'wife'" (Baltimore, MD: Penguin, 1959).

45. *The Tempest,* a new variorum editon, ed. Howard Horace Furness (Philadelphia: J. B. Lippincott, 1892).

46. Eve Kosofsky Sedgwick, *Between Men: English Literature and Male Homosocial Desire* (New York: Columbia University Press, 1985).

47. Andrew Marvell, "The Garden," lines 63–64, in *The Poems and Letters of Andrew Marvell,* ed. H. H. Margoliouth, 2 vols. (Oxford: Clarendon Press, 1951), 1:49.

48. Stanley Wells and Gary Taylor, with John Jowett and William Montgomery, *William Shakespeare: A Textual Companion* (Oxford: Clarendon, 1987), 616.

49. See Valerie Wayne, "The Sexual Politics of Textual Transmission," in *Textual Formations and Reformations,* ed. Laurie E. Maguire and Thomas L. Berger (Newark: University of Delaware Press, 1998), 179–210; Wayne discusses the "wife"/"wise" crux on 184–87.

50. One could compare here the note in Luce's 1901 Arden edition, which, as ambivalent as Kermode's, prints "wise" and yet seems in the note to prefer "wife." One of the arguments in the note is that "the rhyme of Paradise with wise is a blemish, and it could hardly have been intentional."

51. Virginia Mason Vaughan and Alden T. Vaughan, "Introduction" to their edition of *The Tempest,* 137–38.

52. Peter W. M. Blayney, "Introduction to the Second Edition," *The Norton Facsimile of the First Folio of Shakespeare* (New York: Norton, 1996), xxi, cited in part by Vaughan and Vaughan, "Introduction," 137. I am grateful to Barbara Mowat for sharing with me her thoughts and further information on this bibliographical dilemma.

53. George Lamming, *Of Age and Innocence* (London: Allison and Busby, 1981), 151; hereafter *Age and Innocence.*

54. For an essay grounded in such principles, see, e.g., Abena Busia, "Silencing Sycorax: On African Colonial Discourse and the Unvoiced Female," *Cultural Critique* 14 (Winter 1989–90): 81–104, an essay indebted in passing to Orgel, "Prospero's Wife"; or May Joseph, "The Scream of Sycorax," *Nomadic Identities* (Minneapolis: University of Minnesota Press, 1999). For a reading of Miranda alert to her difficulties for feminist identification (and which also insists that Caliban's alleged rape attempt makes him a difficult model for the colonial subject), see Laura E. Donaldson, "The Miranda Complex," in *Decolonizing Feminisms: Race, Gender, and Empire-Building* (Chapel Hill: University of North Carolina Press, 1992), which could usefully be juxtaposed to Elaine Showalter, "Miranda's Story," in *Sister's Choices* (Oxford: Clarendon, 1991) (on page 40 of which, Showalter seems to think that Lamming is a conservative Anglo-Canadian writer).

55. Rob Nixon, "Caribbean and African Appropriations of *The Tempest,*" *Critical Inquiry* 13 (Spring 1987): 557–78; quotations at 576, 577.

56. Ironically, the last critic cited by Nixon is Sylvia Wynter (her afterword to Lemuel Johnson's *Highlife for Caliban* [Trenton, NJ: Africa World Press, 1995 reprint of 1973 text]), but this does not prompt Nixon to name her in the text of his essay or to include her in his survey. And although Nixon may be accurate in his roll call of African and Caribbean writers (which, unlike even Fernández Retamar's, includes no women), it is worth noting that Morrison's *Tar Baby,* written by an African American but set in the Caribbean, and self-consciously so, predates Nixon's essay. And it is also worth noting that Paule Marshall, born in the United States to West Indian immigrants, and an author who frequently writes about the West Indies, had, as early as 1961, rewritten *The Tempest* in "Brazil," the concluding story in her collection, *Soul Clap Hands and*

Sing (reissued Washington, DC: Howard University Press, 1988). There, "Caliban" and "Miranda" are nightclub performers. Like the other male-female couples in the stories in this volume, they are examples of people who have lost touch with "native" authenticity, which Marshall plays out in various forms of unsatisfactory sexual relations across differences of age and race (in "Brazil," such mismatching is found even in size; Caliban is called *"O Grande"* but is a midget, and his masculine aggression is undercut). Marshall clearly refuses the kinds of mixing celebrated in Fernández Retamar. In one of the stories, "British Guiana," the man who has lost contact with his genuine origins is also suspected of homosexuality. This plot (of the kind to be found in *Black Skin, White Masks*) is also to be found in Marshall's *The Chosen Place, the Timeless People* (New York: Vintage, 1984 reprint of 1969 text), which centers on a relationship between a "native" and a European woman, as has been noted and deplored by Timothy S. Chin, "'Bullers' and 'Battymen': Contesting Homophobia in Black Popular Culture and Contemporary Caribbean Literature," *Callaloo* 20, no. 1 (1997): 127–41, and by Rhonda Cobham, "Revisioning Our Kumblas: Transforming Feminist and Nationalist Agendas in Three Caribbean Women's Texts," in *Postcolonial Theory and the United States: Race, Ethnicity, and Literature,* ed. Amritjit Singh and Peter Schmidt (Jackson: University Press of Mississippi, 2000). Cobham finds more productive thinking and representing of female-female relations in Marshall's *Praisesong for the Widow* (New York: E. P. Dutton, 1983). These limits are only overcome in Marshall's *Fisher King* (New York: Simon and Schuster, 2000), whose central figures are a single woman and the boy she has raised. *"There're all kinds of family and blood's got nothing to do with it"* (210), Hattie thinks when the boy, Sonny, is claimed by his uncle, and she is validated in her thought: Her claims to the boy reside in her past intimacy with both his grandmother and his grandfather.

57. Sylvia Wynter, "Beyond Miranda's Meanings: Un/Silencing the 'Demonic Ground' of Caliban's 'Woman'"; the essay appears as the afterword in *Out of the Kumbla: Caribbean Women and Literature,* ed. Carole Boyce Davies and Elaine Savory Fido (Trenton, NJ: Africa World Press, 1990); hereafter BMM. Natasha Barnes worries the question of Wynter's opposition to feminism in "Reluctant Matriarch: Sylvia Wynter and the Problematics of Caribbean Feminism," *Small Axe* 5 (March 1999): 34–47, arguing that "Wynter's conclusions lead to a repudiation of feminism as a site of emancipatory imagining" (41). I am grateful to Professor Barnes for some stimulating discussion of this complicated issue, and I discuss below my understanding of Wynter's conflicted relationship to feminism. It is certainly possible to survey Wynter's thought and barely mention gender as a concern, as can be seen in Paget Henry's discussion/evaluation of Wynter in "Sylvia Wynter: Poststructuralism and Postcolonial Thought," in *Caliban's Reason* (New York: Routledge, 2000), 117–43.

58. Sylvia Wynter, "Beyond the Categories of the Master Conception: The Counterdoctrine of the Jamesian Poiesis," in *C. L. R. James's Caribbean,* ed. Paget Henry and Paul Buhle (Durham, NC: Duke University Press, 1992), 63–91. Paget Henry's evaluation of Wynter's work in *Caliban's Reason*—essentially to fault her, in traditional Marxist fashion, for her refusal to heed the economic as the ultimate determinant of the social—must be motivated in part by the critique of Marxism that Wynter makes in this essay.

59. Sylvia Wynter, "On Disenchanting Discourse: 'Minority' Literary Criticism and Beyond," *Cultural Critique* (Fall 1987): 207–44.

60. Sylvia Wynter, "Beyond the Word of Man: Glissant and the New Discourse of the Antilles," *World Literature Today* 63, no. 4 (1989): 637–47, 640 cited.

61. In "On Disenchanting Discourse," Wynter glosses "demonic" by way of an essay in biological theory as "logical representations of reality which exclude a space-time oriented observer" (207 n. 3).

62. David Scott, "The Re-Enchantment of Humanism: An Interview with Sylvia Wynter," *Small Axe* 8 (September 2000): 119–207, 125 cited; my gratitude to Natasha Barnes for providing me with a typescript of this interview before its publication. The interview is invaluable, both for information about the shape of Wynter's life and career and for the exposition of the crucial ideas that she has been developing that Scott's questions provoke; I will refer to it as "Interview" in further citations in my text. For a 1980 interview with Wynter, see Daryl Cumber Dance, *New World Adams* (Leeds, England: Peepal Tree Books, 1992), 276–82.

63. Lamming refers to Wynter alongside C. L. R. James in a 1966 essay ("Caribbean Literature: The Black Rock of Africa," in *Conversations: Essays, Addresses, and Interviews, 1953–1990,* ed. Richard Drayton and Andaiye [London: Karia Press, 1992], 124); Edward Kamau Brathwaite devotes several pages to her in his "The Love Axe (1): Developing a Caribbean Aesthetic, 1962–1974," in *Reading Black: Essays in the Criticism of African, Caribbean, and Black American Literature,* ed. Huston Baker (Ithaca, NY: Cornell University Africana Studies and Research Center Monograph Series, no. 4 [1976]), 20–36, see esp. 25–28. I will not be writing here about Wynter's work before 1970, extraordinary as it is.

64. "Interview," 174. The interview is the best place to start assembling a bibliography of Wynter's writing; it can be extended through Brathwaite, "Love Axe (1)."

65. Wynter, "Beyond the Word," 644; Sylvia Wynter, "'A Different Kind of Creature': Caribbean Literature, the Cyclops Factor, and the Second Poetics of the Propter Nos," *Annals of Scholarship* 12, nos. 1–2 (1997): 153–72, 153 cited. See Edouard Glissant, *Caribbean Discourse,* trans. J. Michael Dash (Charlottesville: University Press of Virginia, 1989), 117–19, for Glissant's mention of the Caliban tradition that encompasses (for him) Fanon, Césaire, Lamming, and Fernández Retamar. In *Poetics of Relation,* trans. Betsy Wing (Ann Arbor: University of Michigan Press, 1997), Glissant associates Caliban with the possibility of community founded in a sense of the fragility of life on earth (54), an alternative form of humanity.

66. See Wynter, "'A Different Kind of Creature,'" 156; the quotation is from Wynter, "1492: A New World View," in *Race, Discourse, and the Origin of the Americas: A New World View,* ed. Vera Lawrence Hyatt and Rex Nettleford (Washington, DC: Smithsonian Institution Press, 1995), 41. On these views, see also Wynter, *"Do Not Call Us Negroes": How "Multicultural" Textbooks Perpetuate Racism* (San Francisco: Aspire Books, 1990).

67. This finds a parallel in W. E. B. Du Bois, "The Development of a People," in *Writings,* ed. Herbert Aptheker (Millwood, NY: Kraus-Thomson Organization, 1982), 1:201–15, in his concise and stunning sentence "The African Slave trade was the child of the Renaissance" (207). My thanks to Nahum D. Chandler for drawing this text to my attention. Unlike Eric Williams, in *Capitalism and Slavery* (London: Andre Deutsch, 1964 reprint of the 1944 text), which established the economic links between emergent capitalism and the slave trade, Wynter's focus is on ideological productions that have

material effects, particularly on the entailments and ramifications of humanism. She elaborates her model of social transformation in "Beyond Miranda's Meanings" in such essays as "'A Different Kind of Creature,'" "1492," and "Columbus, the Ocean Blue, and Fables That Stir the Mind: To Reinvent the Study of Letters," in *Poetics of the Americas: Race, Founding, and Textuality*, ed. Bainard Cowan and Jefferson Humphries (Baton Rouge: Louisiana State University Press, 1997), 141–63.

68. There is scarcely an essay of Wynter's that does not advance this thesis, though it is continually redeveloped and redeployed in relationship to the specific concerns of each of her essays; in addition to those cited already, one could add "The Ceremony Must Be Found: After Humanism," *boundary 2* 12, no. 3, and 13, no. 1 (Spring/Fall 1984): 19–70. "Interview" is perhaps the best place to start; "Beyond Miranda's Meanings" is an extraordinarily compressed and compacted piece of writing. The summary I provide in the text is far too schematic and hardly does justice to the complexities of Wynter's thought.

69. Wynter refers often to Goveia's crucial essay "The Social Framework," *Savacou* 2 (1970): 7–15, in which Goveia lays out patterns of social division in the West Indies as well as the overriding uniting factor of racial division as the legacy of colonialism that must be repudiated.

70. In "Reluctant Matriarch," Barnes worries a congruent issue, that Wynter's early affiliation with nationalist movements may make her work legible through aims that have ignored and delegitimated the concerns of women. "Caribbean feminism is stigmatized as shrill, partisan, generating its rhetoric and modes of analysis from suspicious foreign sources," she notes (35; see 41–42 for development of the point). This issue is also significant for the analysis that M. Jacqui Alexander offers in her essays on sexual regulation.

71. Without overstating this, it is nonetheless a point affirmed, for example, by Barbara Smith in a 1997 essay revisiting those (for her) formative years; see "Where's the Revolution?" in *The Truth That Never Hurts* (New Brunswick, NJ: Rutgers University Press, 1998), e.g., 180, where she remarks that "unlike the early lesbian and gay movement, which had both ideological and practical links to the left, Black activism, and feminism, today's 'queer' politicos seem to operate in a historical and ideological vacuum." For some examples of this imbrication, see the recently reissued 1972 volume *Out of the Closets*, ed. Karla Jay and Allen Young (New York: New York University Press, 1992).

72. In BMM, see also 359 (where "sexual preference" is mentioned twice as a distinction that becomes racialized in modernity) and 360 (on "Caliban's 'woman'" as representing an "alternative sexual-erotic model of desire"). The suspect category of "'natural' erotic preference" (365) is further glossed in a note as well as in other essays by Wynter, including "Columbus," 148, and "1492," 37.

73. Cliff was born in Jamaica in 1946; she spent her first years and her early adolescence in Jamaica, and the period in between in the United States. She did graduate work in London at the Warburg Institute and has worked in publication and in the U.S. academy for the past twenty-five years. She is currently Allan K. Smith Professor of English at Trinity College in Hartford, Connecticut. For further basic biography and critical orientation, see the entry on Cliff by Cora Agatucci in *Contemporary African American Novelists: A Bio-Bibliographical Critical Sourcebook*, ed. Emmanuel S. Nelson

(Westport, CT: Greenwood, 1999), 95–101. For more recent critical literature, see Noraida Agosto, *Michelle Cliff's Novels: Piecing the Tapestry of Memory and History* (New York: Peter Lang, 1999), and Antonia MacDonald-Smythe, *Making Homes in the West Indies: Constructions of Subjectivity in the Writings of Michelle Cliff and Jamaica Kincaid* (New York: Garland, 2001), as well as the essays in *Postcolonialism and Autobiography*, ed. Alfred Hornung and Ernstpeter Ruhe (Amsterdam: Rodopi, 1998), and the chapter on Cliff in Isabel Hoving, *In Praise of New Travelers: Reading Caribbean Migrant Women's Writing* (Stanford: Stanford University Press, 2001).

74. Cliff and Naylor receive consideration (and Marshall a brief mention) in Chantal Zabus, *Tempests after Shakespeare* (New York: Palgrave, 2002).

75. Michelle Cliff, "Caliban's Daughter: The Tempest and the Teapot," *Frontiers* 12, no. 2 (1991): 36–51; all citations are from this version. The essay exists in a number of forms. A bit of it is borrowed from the autobiographical preface, "A Journey into Speech," in Cliff's *The Land of Look Behind* (Ithaca, NY: Firebrand, 1985). An early version is "Clare Savage as a Crossroads Character," in *Caribbean Women Writers,* ed. Selwyn R. Cudjoe (Wellesley/Amherst, MA: Calaloux/University of Massachusetts Press, 1990), 263–68; its most recent recension, "Caliban's Daughter, or Into the Interior," *American Visions / Visiones de las Americas* (1994): 152–59.

76. The identity explicitly claimed in *Claiming an Identity They Taught Me to Despise* (Watertown, MA: Persephone, 1980) is racial; however, the publication of the book by a lesbian feminist press implies gendered and sexual identities as well. Myriam J. A. Chancy, *Searching for Safe Spaces: Afro-Caribbean Women Writers in Exile* (Philadelphia: Temple University Press, 1997), takes "Claiming an Identity" (in *Claiming an Identity,* 43–51) as a key text in her reading of Cliff's entire oeuvre and its racial/gendered/sexual project; see esp. 136–53 (which includes discussion of *Abeng* [New York: Dutton, 1984]), 160–65, 196–200 (on *No Telephone to Heaven* [New York: Dutton, 1987]), 171–84 (on *Free Enterprise* [New York: Penguin Books, 1993]). The un/writing project that entails renaming her scholarly identity as "speechlessness" is captured in Cliff, "Notes on Speechlessness," *Sinister Wisdom* 5 (Winter 1978): 5–9.

77. As Goveia writes in "The Social Framework," "[I]n the lower class, as is well known, marriage is the exception rather than the rule and most children born in the West Indies are illegitimate in the eyes of the law" (9). The 70 percent figure is noted for the Bahamas in Alexander, "Erotic Autonomy," 77, and in Hymie Rubenstein, *Coping with Poverty: Adaptive Strategies in a Caribbean Village* (Boulder, CO: Westview, 1987), 298. These figures, drawn from various locales (Rubenstein studies St. Vincent) over a twenty-year period, suggest that they remain generalizable to the region.

78. In labeling these claims "discursive," I follow David Scott, *Refashioning Futures: Criticism after Postcoloniality* (Princeton: Princeton University Press, 1999), 124, and his important argument that the black community constituted and *produced* around "Africa" and "slavery" arises from the lived condition of racialization but also from the ongoing rewriting of the past toward possible futures. Claiming "Africa" or "slavery" is not so much to name singular origins as it is to mobilize "an always situated argument" (124–25).

79. Faith Smith, "An Interview with Patricia Powell," *Callaloo* 19, no. 2 (1996): 324–29. Powell was born in Jamaica in 1966 and emigrated to the United States in 1982. She has published *Me Dying Trial* (Portsmouth, NH: Heinemann, 1993), *A Small*

Gathering of Bones (Portsmouth, NH: Heinemann, 1994), and *The Pagoda* (New York: Harcourt Brace, 1998).

80. Alexander, "Erotic Autonomy," 69, also takes to task the notion that a Western style of homosexuality (around questions of coming out and identity) is what is needed in the Caribbean.

81. Dionne Brand was born in Trinidad in 1953 and emigrated to Canada in 1970. Cliff cites "hard against the soul" from Brand's sixth book of poems, *No Language Is Neutral* (Toronto: Coach House Press, 1990), the first in which lesbian desire is an explicit theme. Brand writes in this volume, "Perhaps I / always had it in mind simply to be an old woman, / darkening, somewhere with another old woman" (46), expressing an attachment to the primordial woman that Cliff affirms as well. Brand continues to publish poetry; *Land to Light On* (Toronto: McClelland and Stewart, 1997) is a recent volume. She has also recently published two novels. *In Another Place, Not Here* (New York: Grove, 1996) tells the crossing stories of a Caribbean woman "rescued" from forced marriage by the arrival of a Canadian activist, who comes and dies in a revolutionary cause; Elizete, the islander, reverses the route of Verlia, the Canadian, tracking her back to Toronto, to her former lover Abena, whom Verlia abandoned because she "couldn't just live in a personal thing" (102). (In terms of the inquiry we have been pursuing, it is perhaps most notable that Elizete has a sense of herself through a debiologized female genealogy through a woman who sought to rename things by emptying them of their colonized nominations.) *At the Full and Change of the Moon* (New York: Grove, 1999) is a multigenerational novel tracking a genealogical narrative from a slave woman to present scenes of black immiseration. Brand has also made films and written nonfictional accounts of the experiences of black working women in Canada; on the latter, see Chancy, *Searching for Safe Spaces,* 86–95.

82. Audre Lorde, *Zami: A New Spelling of My Name* (Freedom, CA: Crossing, 1982), 255.

83. Makeda Silvera, *Her Head a Village* (Vancouver: Gang Press, 1994), 68–69. Chancy, *Searching for Safe Spaces,* 127–31, comments on Silvera's representation of the difficulty of including lesbian representation for her audience, a theme in the title story of the volume that includes "Baby." "Zammie" is also the term for female friendship in *Basin* (1985), a play by Jacqueline Rudet, an English writer born to Dominican parents who grew up in the Dominican Republic. Joseph, *Nomadic Identities,* cites from the preface to *Basin* as it appears in *Black Plays,* ed. Yvonne Brewster (London: Methuen, 1987), 114: "According to Rudet, '"zammie" is not "lesbian" in patois. The word refers more to the universality of friendship between Black women, no matter what nationality, no matter what class, all Black women have very important things in common. . . . Every Black woman is the "zammie" of every other Black woman,' Rudet continues, 'It's almost an obligatory thing'" (Joseph, *Nomadic Identities,* 121).

84. This is a point in a number of the essays gathered in Audre Lorde, *Sister Outsider* (Trumansburg, NY: Crossing, 1984), and *A Burst of Light* (Ithaca, NY: Firebrand, 1988).

85. The most spectacular (counter)example is provided by the mother represented across Jamaica Kincaid's oeuvre, a woman whose ferocious love is aimed at annihilating her children (particularly her daughter) if they attempt independence.

86. As Rudet puts it in the preface to *Basin:* "Zammie was a word I'd forgotten

about. It was a word my mother would use to describe a close friend, but it had conno-
tations of being more than a friend and, in a strange way, it was a rude word that only
grown-ups could use, as if 'zammie' meant lover" (114). Rudet recalls the word because
one of the characters in her play—a woman who sleeps with other women—invokes
the term to explain her solidarity with and to solicit it from another woman who sleeps
with men (see *Basin*, 132).

87. I will be citing from Gloria Wekker, "Mati-ism and Black Lesbianism: Two Ideal-
typical Expressions of Female Homosexuality in Black Communities of the Diaspora,"
Journal of Homosexuality 24, nos. 3–4 (1993): 145–58; "One Finger Does Not Drink
Okra Soup: Afro-Surinamese Women and Critical Agency," in Alexander and Mohanty,
Feminist Genealogies, 330–52; "'What's Identity Got to Do with It?': Rethinking Identi-
ty in Light of the *Mati* Work in Suriname," in *Female Desires: Same-Sex Relations and
Transgender Practices across Cultures*, ed. Evelyn Blackwood and Saskia E. Wieringa
(New York: Columbia University Press, 1999), 119–35.

88. "Dionne Brand: *No Language Is Neutral*," in *Frontiers of Caribbean Literature*,
ed. Frank Birbalsingh (New York: St. Martin's, 1996), 136, 134 cited.

89. Michelle Cliff, "Object into Subject: Some Thoughts on the Work of Black Women
Artists," in *Making Face, Making Soul / Haciendo Caras: Creative and Critical Perspectives by Feminists of Color,* ed. Gloria Anzaldua (San Francisco: aunt lute books, 1990),
271–90; *Free Enterprise* (New York: Dutton, 1993).

90. For a recent study of the historical and mythic Nanny, see Karla Gottlieb, *The
Mother of Us All: The History of Queen Nanny* (Trenton, NJ: Africa World Press, 2000).
Relying on Edward Kamau Brathwaite's assertions that the story of Nanny's anal
powers was made up by the British, that it is obscene and derisive (75–76), Gottlieb
emphasizes the maternal powers of Nanny: a mother to the nation who herself was
reported to have been childless. It is perhaps symptomatic of the limits of the kind of
recovery practice that this work represents that Gottlieb mentions the existence of a
novel called *Abeng* (46) but declines to name its author. Richard Price demurs from
Brathwaite's views in his preface to the third (1996) edition of *Maroon Societies: Rebel
Slave Communities in the Americas* (Baltimore, MD: The Johns Hopkins University
Press, 1996 edition of the 1976 text), xxii.

91. Chin, "'Bullers' and 'Battymen,'" 137; citations from Cliff, *Abeng*, 35, 77. In his
otherwise acute reading of repressed histories in *Abeng*, Simon Gikandi, *Writing in
Limbo: Modernism and Caribbean Literature* (Ithaca, NY: Cornell University Press,
1992), ch. 7, "Narration at the Postcolonial Moment: History and Representation in
Abeng," barely mentions gender and ignores questions of sexuality that, arguably, are
central to historical recovery in the novel. Gikandi does point usefully to the fact that
the double-meaning abeng—the horn that called slaves to work and that rallied Maroons to revolt—goes back to Africa, where it played no part in slavery and the plantation system but, instead, had another meaning, a point that I would take to suggest
the strategic value of a "recovery" that is also a rewriting of Africa for the purposes of
future solidarity.

It is also likely that Cliff's title recalls the title of a newspaper launched in opposition to the "Independence-in-practically-name-only" (*Abeng*, 5) that came to Jamaica
in 1962, four years after the time frame of the novel. On this, see the essay by one of
the founders of *Abeng*, Rupert Lewis, "Learning to Blow the Abeng: A Critical Look at

Anti-Establishment Movements of the 1960s and 1970s," *Small Axe* 1 (February 1997): 5–17, and Obika Gray, *Radicalism and Social Change in Jamaica, 1960–1972* (Knoxville: University of Tennessee Press, 1991), ch. 8, "The Apogee of Black Power Ideology: The *Abeng* Newspaper Movement."

92. For an examination of linguistic range and polysemy in Cliff, see Françoise Lionnet, "Of Mangoes and Maroons: Language, History, and the Multicultural Subject of Michelle Cliff's *Abeng*," in *De / Colonizing the Subject*, ed. Sidonie Smith and Julia Watson (Minneapolis: University of Minnesota Press, 1992), 321–45.

93. Judith L. Raiskin, "'With the Logic of a Creole': Michelle Cliff," ch. 5 in *Snow on the Cane Fields: Women's Writing and Creole Subjectivity* (Minneapolis: University of Minnesota Press, 1996), 192. Raiskin focuses on *No Telephone to Heaven*, but on 184–85, she offers a useful mapping of the complex crossings in "mixed race" categories that she argues affect representation in *Abeng*. I cite page 149 from Lauren Berlant, "'68, or Something," *Critical Inquiry* 21 (Autumn 1994): 124–55; I cite from Berlant's discussion of Cliff's *No Telephone to Heaven* in relationship to Toni Morrison's *Song of Solomon* (138–53). See also Farah Jasmine Griffith, "Textual Healing: Claiming Black Women's Bodies, the Erotic, and Resistance in Contemporary Novels of Slavery," *Callaloo* 19, no. 2 (1996): 519–36, a study of the ways in which a validation of black female sexuality works to answer the denigration of black women; see 531–36 for her consideration of Cliff.

94. Nixon, "Caribbean and African Appropriations," 574. *Islands* is the third volume of poems in a trilogy that includes *Rights of Passage* (1967) and *Masks* (1968), gathered as *The Arrivants: A New World Trilogy* (Oxford: Oxford University Press, 1973), from which I will be citing. The most thorough reading of the poems can be found in Gordon Rohlehr, *Pathfinder: Black Awakening in "The Arrivants" of Edward Kamau Brathwaite* (Tunapuna, Trinidad: Gordon Rohlehr, 1981, 1992).

95. Scott, in *Refashioning Futures*, 106–18, has respectfully dissented from the Afrocentrism in Brathwaite, finding its nationalist, essentialist historicizing anthropology unnecessary for the nonetheless necessary discursive/political deployment of Africa for New World decolonizing projects. Brathwaite seems to wish to reject the facts that the colonial subject is necessarily mixed, that African "survivals" are necessarily transformations, and that claims to Africa cannot be rooted in some essentialized, prediscursively raced subject.

96. I cite from the reprint of Kamau Brathwaite, *Black + Blues* (New York: New Directions, 1995), 18.

97. Cynthia James, "Caliban in Y2K?—Hypertext and New Pathways," in *For the Geography of a Soul: Emerging Perspectives on Kamau Brathwaite*, ed. Timothy J. Reiss (Trenton, NJ: Africa World Press, 2001), 351–61, I cite 353. This volume contains an extensive bibliography of Brathwaite's writing (435–50) and of criticism of his work (451–66).

98. Edward Kamau Brathwaite, "Caliban, Ariel, and Unprospero in the Conflict of Creolization: A Study of the Slave Revolt in Jamaica, 1831–32," in *Comparative Perspectives on Slavery in New World Plantation Societies, Annals of the New York Academy of Sciences* 292 (June 27, 1977): 41–62, citation on 43. Kamau Brathwaite, *Barabajan Poems* (New York: Savacou North, 1994), 316.

99. Brathwaite's major statement about nation language is "History of the Voice"

(1979–81), reprinted in Kamau Brathwaite, *Roots* (Ann Arbor: University of Michigan Press, 1993 reprint of a 1986 Casa de las Américas publication).

100. Edward Brathwaite, "Timehri," in *Is Massa Day Dead?* ed. Orde Coombs (Garden City, NY: Anchor/Doubleday, 1974). Brathwaite describes himself as "not consciously aware of any other West Indian alternative (though in fact I had been living that alternative). . . . Then, in 1953, George Lamming's *In the Castle of My Skin* appeared and everything was transformed" (32). Trumper's conversation with G is cited on 34. "Timehri" names Native American marks akin to those that Brathwaite commits himself to recording.

101. See Nathaniel Mackey, *Discrepant Engagements: Dissonance, Cross-Culturality, and Experimental Writing* (Cambridge: Cambridge University Press, 1993), 139–61, 271–74, and "Wringing the Word," *World Literature Today* 68, no. 4, a special issue devoted to Brathwaite (Fall 1994): 733–40.

102. Kamau Brathwaite, "X/Self's Xth Letter from the Thirteen Provinces," in *X/Self* (New York: Oxford University Press, 1987). *X/Self* is the third volume in a trilogy that includes *Mother Poem* (New York: Oxford University Press, 1977) and *Sun Poem* (New York: Oxford University Press, 1982). The three volumes were reprinted in revised form as Kamau Brathwaite, *Ancestors* (New York: New Directions, 2001). Kamau Brathwaite, "Letter SycoraX," in *Middle Passages* (New York: New Directions, 1993). *Middle Passages* reprints a number of earlier poems in Sycorax video style.

103. Elaine Savory, "Returning to Sycorax/Prospero's Response: Kamau Brathwaite's Word Journey," in *The Art of Kamau Brathwaite,* ed. Stewart Brown (Bridgend, Mid Glamorgan, Wales: Seren, 1995), 221. In Savory's allegory, "Prospero" stands for publishers who have resisted the new Sycorax video style, an implicitly masculinist refusal of Brathwaite/Caliban's "returning home, linguistically and therefore spiritually, to his mother, Sycorax, the true possessor of the island" (211).

104. Elaine Savory, "Wordsongs and Wordwounds/Homecoming: Kamau Brathwaite's *Barabajan Poems,*" *World Literature Today* 88, no. 4 (Fall 1994): 750–57, 750 cited.

105. Kamau Brathwaite, *ConVERSations with Nathaniel Mackey* (Staten Island, NY: We Press; Minneapolis, MN: Xcp: Cross-Cultural Poetics, 1999), 189.

106. Gordon Rohlehr, "'Black Sycorax, My Mother': Brathwaite's Reconstruction of *The Tempest,*" in *For the Geography of a Soul,* ed. Reiss, 277–95.

107. Bev E. L. Brown, "Mansong and Matrix: A Radical Experiment," in *A Double Colonization: Colonial and Post-Colonial Women's Writing,* ed. Kirsten Holst Petersen and Anna Rutherford (Aarhus, Denmark: Dangaroo, 1986), 68–79. Brown's experiment entails reading Brathwaite against Jean Rhys and Zee Edgell, finding in them a "female homosociality" that is "a source of historicity, with the chief authority being the Great Gran" (74), a move that could be compared to Cliff's "essentialist" and historicist aims. Rohlehr answers in "Brathwaite with a Dash of Brown," in his *The Shape of That Hurt* (Port of Spain, Trinidad and Tobago: Longman, 1992), 209–47.

108. For another positive evaluation of such representations, see Velma Pollard, "Francina and the Turtle and All the Others: Women in EKB," in *For the Geography of a Soul,* ed. Reiss, 43–50.

109. Sue Thomas, "Sexual Politics in Edward Brathwaite's *Mother Poem* and *Sun Poem,*" *Kunapipi* 9, no. 1 (1987): 33–43, cited phrase, 34. Thomas emphasizes the poems' pathos around the emasculated father figure. "Even though Brathwaite is sensitive to

the sufferings of women, he accepts the patriarchal values of those traditions largely uncritically," she concludes (41), a point that could as readily be applied to Rohlehr and to Mackey (who notes that women are placed in a mothering role in Brathwaite without making any critical assessment of that limitation ["Wringing the Word," 734]), as well as to some of Brathwaite's female critics (Savory and Pollard, for example) who embrace the role of mother/daughter in relationship to his work. Zabus, *Tempests after Shakespeare,* has it both ways, agreeing with the feminist critique (61) but also affirming Brathwaite's feminine identification through the Sycorax video style (62–63).

110. Rhonda Cobham, "K/Ka/Kama/Kamau: Brathwaite's Project of Self-Naming in *Barabajan Poems,*" in *For the Geography of a Soul,* ed. Reiss, 297–315.

111. Brathwaite's voicing of the silenced mother has been seen as a project congruent with the work of M. Nourbese Philip, by Mackey, "Wringing the Word"; Joseph, *Nomadic Identities;* and Paul Naylor, *Poetic Investigations* (Evanston, IL: Northwestern University Press, 1999), who follows a chapter on Brathwaite's "tidalectic rhythms" with one titled "M. Nourbese Philip: 'Displacing' Him." Philip has written about her belated discovery in 1991 (when she returned to her native Tobago after an absence of twenty-four years spent in Canada) of Lamming's treatment of *The Tempest* in *The Pleasures of Exile* in her "Piece of Land Surrounded," in *A Genealogy of Resistance* (Toronto: Mercury, 1997). She cites Lamming on the absence of Sycorax and claims locating Sycorax as her project: "To find the true source of authenticity, a more aucthonous lineage and line of descent, it is to Sycorax we must turn" (166), a turn that involves acknowledging that "we are still dumb in the language of Sycorax" (167), which remains to be discovered. A similar point about Lamming can be found in Ngũgĩ wa Thiong'o, "In the Name of the Mother: George Lamming and the Cultural Significance of 'Mother Country' in the Decolonization Process," *Annals of Scholarship* 12, nos. 1–2 (1997): 141–51, which argues for the need to break with the mother country to find the real mother language, that of Sycorax. That "dumbness" in Philip could also be compared to the silence that the Caliban of Brathwaite's first poem of that title needs to hear in the music inspired by African gods. Philip has published a volume of poems, *She Tries Her Tongue, Her Silence Softly Breaks* (Charlottetown, PEI: Ragweed, 1989), that attempts such recovery through exposure of the deformations of language under slavery, and she has published a narrative of such attempts, *Looking for Livingstone: An Odyssey of Silence* (Stratford, Ontario: Mercury, 1991). Philip's project is evaluated by Chancy, *Searching for Safe Spaces,* 99–116; Chancy concludes that one limitation of the project is its refusal to acknowledge the sexualization of the mother-daughter, female-female bonds that Philip poses as an antithesis to a masculinist colonial tradition (see 116, and Chancy's reiteration on page 157, in which Joan Riley, Beryl Gilroy, and Toni Morrison are similarly criticized for creating a homo/heterosexual division that impedes the thinking of race with sexuality). Hoving, *In Praise of New Travelers,* disputes Chancy's claim.

112. Kamau Brathwaite, "The Dream Sycorax Letter," *Black Renaissance / Renaissance Noire* 1, no. 1 (1996): 120–36. Brathwaite left Jamaica after a hurricane damaged the archive of Caribbean writing that he had been gathering and UWI failed to support its retrieval. Cobham stresses this cultural situation of neglect and also links it to a painful document, Kamau Brathwaite's *Zea Mexican Diary* (Madison: University of Wisconsin Press, 1993), composed around the death of Brathwaite's wife, Doris Brathwaite.

The computer Sycorax had, in fact, been hers; when she died, Brathwaite had to learn to access it. Doris Brathwaite had been her husband's prime audience; his tribute to her was the completion of the bibliography of *his* work that she was composing—he was, it seems clear, her work. The Sycorax video style and its desired immediacy would seem related to his ongoing mourning for Doris Brathwaite.

113. Gikandi, *Writing in Limbo,* 249; Chancy, *Searching for Safe Spaces,* 152–53. Chancy, who strongly advocates in her work the need to recognize lesbians as part of a black female community, is herself hesitant in reading the relationship between Clare and Zoe as sexual, perhaps because Clare does not have such a term in her own vocabulary (see, e.g., 151).

114. At least one of these, Pamela Mordeccai—who is represented in *For the Geography of a Soul,* ed. Reiss, by "Images for Creativity and the Art of Writing in *The Arrivants,*" 21–42, and "Three Poems," 269–76—coedited with Betty Wilson the volume *Her True-True Name: An Anthology of Women's Writing from the Caribbean* (Portsmouth, NH: Heinemann, 1989), which included Cliff but went out of its way in the introduction to distance the creole Cliff from authentic black writers. On this unhappy incident, see Lionnet, "Of Mangoes and Maroons," 325–26.

115. All citations will be to Aimé Césaire, *Une Tempête* (Paris: Seuil, 1969), and *A Tempest,* trans. Richard Miller (New York: Ubu, 1992). Feminist critique is best represented by Jyotsna G. Singh, "Caliban versus Miranda: Race and Gender Conflicts in Postcolonial Rewritings of *The Tempest,*" in *Feminist Readings of Early Modern Culture,* ed. Valerie Traub, M. Lindsay Kaplan, and Dympna Callaghan (Cambridge: Cambridge University Press, 1996), 191–209.

116. Tom Hayes, "Cannibalizing the Humanist Subject: A Genealogy of Prospero," in *Genealogy and Literature,* ed. Lee Quinby (Minneapolis: University of Minnesota Press, 1995), 96–115. It must be pointed out that the limit of Hayes's argument is reached when Greenaway's *Prospero's Books* (1991) is praised for its decentering of the humanist subject.

117. "[D]e son penis, il frappe," 70.

118. Aimé Césaire, "Entretien et débat," 1967 talk at the Maison Hélvetique, trans. and cited in Bennetta Jules-Rosette, *Black Paris: The African Writers' Landscape* (Urbana and Chicago: University of Illinois Press, 1998), 34–35. On precedents for Césaire's revaluation of *nègre,* see Brent Hayes Edwards, *The Practice of Diaspora* (Cambridge, MA: Harvard University Press, 2003). Particularly significant would be Lamine Sanghor's 1927 "Le mot 'nègre,'" discussed in ch. 1, and the writing of Paulette Nardal, particularly "L'Eveil de la conscience de race" (1932), discussed in ch. 3. Nardal's essay is available as "The Awakening of Race Consciousness," in *Race,* ed. Robert Bernasconi (Oxford: Blackwell, 2001), 107–11.

119. In her essay on Glissant, Wynter explains this assimilative move through the experience of the French West Indies of German occupation, which moved Antillean consciousness toward an identification with the home country not to be found in the British West Indies. This reading is, in fact, disputed by Glissant in *Caribbean Discourse;* he continues to insist on independence and regards being a *département* of France as threatening an absorptive annihilation of native culture by the metropole. For a superb review of Césaire's career and the argument of his *Discourse on Colonialism,* see the introduction, "A Poetics of Anticolonialism," by Robin D. G. Kelley to

the recent reissue of Aimé Césaire, *Discourse on Colonialism,* trans. Joan Pinkham (New York: Monthly Review Press, 2000), 7–28; see 24 for Césaire's changing views on departmentalization.

120. "[S]ale," 92; "LA LIBERTÉ, OHÉ, LA LIBERTÉ," 92.

121. Joan Dayan, "Playing Caliban: Césaire's *Tempest,"* *Arizona Quarterly* 48, no. 4 (Winter 1992): 125–45.

122. "[S]auvageonne," 19.

123. On this, see Zabus, *Tempests after Shakespeare,* 75, where the rhetoric of El-dridge Cleaver and Amirí Baraka is linked to Lamming's *Water with Berries.*

124. "[C]'est ma mère et je ne la renierai pas! D'ailleurs, tu ne la crois morte que parce que tu crois que la terre est chose morte. . . . C'est tellement plus commode! Morte, alors on la piétine, on la souille, on la foule d'un pied vainqueur! Moi, je la re-specte, car je sais qu'elle vit, et que vit Sycorax" (26).

125. "[C]ar sa voix s'oublie dans la marais de la faim," *Cahier d'un retour au pays natal,* 36. All citations from *Notebook of a Return to the Native Land* and *Cahier* are from the enface edition, Aimé Césaire, *The Collected Poetry,* trans. Clayton Eshleman and Annette Smith (Berkeley and Los Angeles: University of California Press, 1983).

126. See M. Jacqui Alexander, "Imperial Desire/Sexual Utopias: White Gay Capital and Transnational Tourism," in *Talking Visions: Multicultural Feminism in a Trans-national Age,* ed. Ella Shohat (Cambridge: MIT Press, 1998), 281–305. Alexander medi-tates on the painful conjunction of white gay male tourism to the tropics, pointing out the ruses of the embrace of capital to include gays and lesbians who are caught up in furthering the plots of heterosexual domination that her earlier essays have analyzed. She confronts what a critic like Hayes shirks.

127. "[J]e accepte . . . négritude . . . mésurée au compas de la souffrance / et le nègre chaque jour plus bas, plus lâche, plus stérile, moins profond, plus répandu au dehors, plus séparé de soi-même, plus rusé avec soi-même, moins immédiat avec soi-même / j'accepte, j'accepte tout cela" (76).

128. "[V]iennent les ovaires de l'eau où le futur agite ses petites têtes / viennent les loups qui paturent dans les orifices sauvages du corps à l'heure où à l'auberge éclip-tique se recontrent la lune et ton soleil" (66). I am indebted to Christian Nagler for this reading.

129. Lee Edelman, "The Part for the (W)hole," ch. 3 of *Homographesis: Essays in Gay Literary and Cultural Theory* (New York: Routledge, 1994).

130. Chancy, *Searching for Safe Spaces,* 132. On the bigendering of Eshu in Henry Louis Gates Jr., *The Signifying Monkey* (Oxford: Oxford University Press, 1988), see 29–30, a point made in passing in developing a reading of the god as a site of open-ended interpretation.

131. These are among the characteristics of Eshu outlined by Robert Farris Thomp-son, *Flash of the Spirit* (New York: Vintage, 1983), 18–33.

132. Ernest Renan's play *Caliban* (1878) is a crucial intertext for Césaire, since its rewriting of *The Tempest* is well along the lines for which Césaire attacks Renan in the *Discourse,* for a so-called humanism that is antidemocratic and deeply racist. (Césaire claims to see no difference between Renan and Hitler.) Among the ways in which Renan's Shakespeare affects Césaire's are the presentation of Prospero's learning as a form of mastery of nature realized in such inventions as gunpowder and the rallying

call of "fraternity" against him. Césaire reverses Renan's take on each of these claims but goes partway in agreeing with him about the church's opposition to human development, partway because for Renan, "human" means European, not what he explicitly calls "inferior races," which include Blacks. Renan's play is available in English, trans. Eleanor Grant Vickery (New York: The Shakespeare Press, 1896). The most sustained discussion of the three versions of the play is Roger Toumson, *Trois Calibans* (Havana: Casa de las Américas, 1981), a prolix study conducted largely under structuralist protocols. Ruby Cohn, *Modern Shakespeare Offshoots* (Princeton: Princeton University Press, 1976), devotes a chapter to modern *Tempests* in which Renan and Césaire, among others, are discussed; she concludes the chapter with "surprise" at the "polemical note" with which the analysis ends, its humanistic affirmation of blackness (308).

133. S. Belhassen, "Aimé Césaire's *A Tempest*," in *Radical Perspectives in the Arts*, ed. Lee Baxandall (Harmondsworth, England: Penguin, 1972), 176. The citation comes from an interview with Césaire.

134. "Toi et moi! Toi-Moi! Moi-Toi!" (92).

135. Eve Kosofsky Sedgwick, *Epistemology of the Closet* (Berkeley and Los Angeles: University of California Press, 1990), 1; on minoritizing/universalizing and its complex relationships to gender mappings, see esp. 82–90.

136. Roy A. K. Heath, *The Murderer* (London: Allison and Busby, 1978), 92. The murderer in the novel is not the "battyman" but, rather, someone alienated from family life who kills his wife. Barbara Fletchman Smith, *Mental Slavery: Psychoanalytic Studies of Caribbean People* (London: Rebus, 2000), uses Heath's novel as an example of the condition of Caribbean psychic disturbance. She sees such disturbance as rooted in the history of slavery and its disruptive effects on family life, which she thinks needs to be restored along highly heteronormative lines.

137. The point is confirmed in Richard Allsopp, *Dictionary of Caribbean Usage* (Oxford: Oxford University Press, 1996), in the entries on "battyman" as well as those on "zami" and "mattee."

138. Hilton Als, *The Women* (New York: Farrar, Straus, and Giroux, 1996), 29. Als was born in the United States in 1961 to Barbadian immigrants; he spent time in Barbados during his childhood.

139. Sean Lokaisingh-Meighoo, "*Jahaji Bhai*: Notes on the Masculine Subject and Homoerotic Subtext of Indo-Caribbean Identity," *Small Axe* 7 (March 2000): 77–92. The essay builds on the homosocial continuum that Sedgwick examines in *Between Men*.

140. See, e.g., Stuart Hall, "Negotiating Caribbean Identities," *New Left Review* 209 (January/February 1995): 3–14.

141. On these histories, see Smith, "Interview with Patricia Powell," 327; Lawson Williams [pseud.], "Homophobia and Gay Rights Activism in Jamaica," *Small Axe* 7 (March 2000): 106–11; Thomas Glave, "Towards a Nobility of the Imagination: Jamaica's Shame," *Small Axe* 7 (March 2000): 122–26.

142. Aparajita Sagar, "AIDS and the Question of Memory: Patricia Powell's *A Small Gathering of Bones*," *Small Axe* 7 (March 2000): 28–43. "Trauma and dying are what infect and cross from one body to the next, not needing the medium of the human immunodeficiency virus (HIV) but the hatred of the bigot in order to do so" (34).

143. Jamaica Kincaid, *My Brother* (New York: Farrar, Straus, and Giroux, 1997), 40.

144. H. Nigel Thomas, *Spirits in the Dark* (Portsmouth, NH: Heinemann, 1993). In

"Baychester: A Memoir," *Massachusetts Review* 35, nos. 3–4 (Autumn–Winter 1994): 448–62, Thomas Glave similarly asks, "where are the gay Jamaican voices?" (455) and can summon up only Claude McKay, who never directly represents male homosexuality in his poems or novels. On such coded representation, see Rhonda Cobham, "Jekyll and Claude: The Erotics of Patronage in Claude McKay's *Banana Bottom*," in *Queer Diasporas,* ed. Cindy Patton and Benigno Sánchez-Eppler (Durham, NC: Duke University Press, 2000), 122–53. Likewise, A. James Arnold, "The Erotics of Colonialism in Contemporary French West Indian Literary Culture," *Annals of Scholarship* 12, nos. 1–2 (1997): 173–86, deplores the hypermasculinism and antifeminism of *créolité,* finding depictions of homosexuality only in some Hispanic texts from the region (mainly from Puerto Rico); he closes by quickly endorsing Maryse Condé and Simone Schwarz-Bart for writing that is more open, "less dependent on sexual stereotypes" (182) than male *créolistes.* He finds a hint of lesbianism in one of Condé's novels (and also mentions Cliff [as does Glave] as well as the Surinamese Astrid Roemer in this context).

145. Stuart Hall, "Minimal Selves," in *Black British Cultural Studies,* ed. Huston Baker Jr., Manthia Diawara, and Ruth H. Lindeborg (Chicago: University of Chicago Press, 1996): "I really came here to get away from my mother. Isn't that the universal story of life?" (115); and "The After-Life of Frantz Fanon," in *The Fact of Blackness: Frantz Fanon and Visual Representation,* ed. Alan Read (Seattle, WA: Bay Press, 1996), 30.

146. This moment also prompts Thomas Cartelli, "After *The Tempest:* Shakespeare, Postcoloniality, and Michelle Cliff's New, New World Miranda," *Contemporary Literature* 36, no. 1 (1995): 82–102, a study that valuably reads Cliff's novel as a reinscription of *The Tempest.* Although Cartelli thinks Cliff surpasses such models as Lamming and Césaire and frees herself from the hold of the play, his rewriting insists on reading Clare as Miranda, a highly normativized move along gender, and he offers a very schematic reading of the novel as an antipatriarchal brief (racial issues are muted, cross-gendering is considered only by way of Harry/Harriet). Cartelli has also pursued *Tempest* connections in "Prospero in Africa: *The Tempest* as Colonialist Text and Pretext," in *Shakespeare Reproduced,* ed. Jean Howard and Marion O'Connor (London: Methuen, 1987), 99–115, a study with a focus on Ngũgĩ. In slightly revised forms, these essays constitute the chapters in Part 2, "Prospero's Books," of Cartelli's *Repositioning Shakespeare: National Formations, Postcolonial Appropriations* (London: Routledge, 1999). Cliff's rewriting of *The Tempest* is also intermittently the theme of Belinda Edmondson's examination of her work in *Making Men: Gender, Literary Authority, and Women's Writing in Caribbean Narrative* (Durham, NC: Duke University Press, 1999), especially in the section entitled "Black Miranda: The White Creole Woman and the Black Revolutionary Tradition," 126–38.

147. Berlant, "'68, or Something," writes stunningly about Clare's galvanization to racial consciousness during her stay in the United States when she contemplates the murder of four black girls in a church in Birmingham in 1963. A token of the kind of possibility that Berlant wishes to imagine: In the spring of 2000, it seemed possible for the first time that the perpetrators of this crime might actually be brought to justice; in the spring of 2002, one of them actually was sentenced to life imprisonment.

148. Meryl F. Schwartz, "An Interview with Michelle Cliff," *Contemporary Literature* 34, no. 4 (1993): 595–619. "Harry/Harriet is the novel's lesbian in a sense," Cliff says (601) in the context of extricating lesbianism from being regarded as a European

imposition. The figure of Harry/Harriet is also discussed in other interviews; see Opal Palmer Adisa, "Journey into Speech—A Writer between Two Worlds: An Interview with Michelle Cliff," *African American Review* 28, no. 2 (1994): 273–81, where Cliff stresses the completeness of the character as achieved both through struggle and rape, the force of this representation to counter Jamaican homophobia (276); and Judith Raiskin, "The Art of History: An Interview with Michelle Cliff," *Kenyon Review*, n.s., 15, no. 1 (Winter 1993): 52–71, esp. 64–70, where Cliff talks about the overlaps and disjunctions of questions of race, gender, and sexuality.

Bobby, Clare's lover after she leaves England, is also a Caliban figure as well as a kind of "transitional" object for Clare's assumption of a "lesbian" identity modeled on Harry/Harriet; she attempts to heal his incurable wound, anticipating Harriet's role as nurse. Moreover, as a result of sex with the incurable Bobby, Clare is incapable of bearing children. As Cliff insists in the interviews cited above, the form of nonnormative sexual identity she seeks to portray would not preclude loving relations with men. For some acute comments on these queer possibilities, on the opening of alternatives without legislating their forms, see Nada Elia, "'A Man Who Wants to Be a Woman': Queerness as/and Healing in Michelle Cliff's *No Telephone to Heaven*," *Callaloo* 23, no. 1 (2000): 352–65.

149. Chin, "'Bullers' and 'Battymen,'" 139, drawing upon Stuart Hall in reaching this conclusion. Chin has an admirably succinct description of Harry/Harriet: "Constantly transgressing the boundaries that supposedly separate male from female, upper from lower classes, insider from outsider, self from 'other,' 'natural' from 'unnatural' sexuality, Harry/Harriet inhabits an interstitial space—designated by the conjunction 'both/and' rather than 'either/or'" (138). This formation could be contrasted with Paule Marshall's *Daughters* (New York: Athaneum, 1991), the novel Brathwaite praised for its vision of women. Marshall has her own version of Nanny, called Congo Jane, and her partner Will Cudjoe. But the point about this historical/mythical pair is their inseparable coupling: "Jane *and* Will Cudjoe, she quickly adds, reminding herself of the old saying about those two: You can't call her name or his without calling or at least thinking of the other, they were so close" (377).

MIRANDA'S MEANINGS

1. Michelle Cliff, *No Telephone to Heaven* (New York: E. P. Dutton, 1987), 207; Sylvia Wynter, "Columbus, the Ocean Blue, and Fables That Stir the Mind: To Reinvent the Study of Letters," in *Poetics of the Americas: Race, Founding, and Textuality*, ed. Bainard Cowan and Jefferson Humphries (Baton Rouge: Louisiana State University Press, 1997), 153. Although the answer I offer here is "no," within the context of humanist and liberal understandings of the human, it might be that a resemanticization of the concept is possible, as Wynter's work suggests, or as is argued by Jean-Luc Nancy, *Being Singular Plural*, trans. Robert D. Richardson and Anne E. O'Byrne (Stanford: Stanford University Press, 2000), who posits that being is a category of singular plurality and mixture, that identity always involves identification, which makes all subjects hyphenated; or by Judith Butler who, in recent unpublished work, depends upon a shared fragility, mortality, and vulnerability that make the person a necessarily relational category rather than one founded, as "human" usually is, on exclusions.

2. Michelle Cliff, *Abeng* (New York: E. P. Dutton, 1984), 77.

3. George Lamming, *In the Castle of My Skin* (Ann Arbor: University of Michigan Press, 1991 reprint of 1953 text), 297.

4. "Et ce pays cria pendant des siècles que nous sommes des bêtes brutes; que les pulsations de l'humanité s'arrêtent aux portes de la négrerie; que nous sommes un fumier ambulant hideusement prometteur de cannes tendres et de coton soyeux et l'on nous marquait au fer rouge et nous dormions dans nos excréments et l'on nous vendait sur les places et l'aune de drap anglais et la viande salée d'Irlande coûtaient moins cher que nous, et ce pays était calme, tranquille, disant que l'esprit de Dieu était dans ses actes." Citations from *Notebook/Cahier* from Aimé Césaire, *The Collected Poetry,* trans. Clayton Eshelman and Annette Smith (Berkeley and Los Angeles: University of California Press, 1983), 60/61.

5. Sylvia Wynter, "Beyond Miranda's Meanings: Un/Silencing the 'Demonic Ground' of Caliban's 'Woman,'" in *Out of the Kumbla: Caribbean Women and Literature,* ed. Carole Boyce Davies and Elaine Savory Fido (Trenton, NJ: Africa World Press, 1990), 363; Stephen Orgel, "Introduction" to his edition of *The Tempest* (Oxford: Oxford University Press, 1987), 120; Virginia Mason Vaughan and Alden T. Vaughan, "Introduction" to *The Tempest,* Arden Shakespeare, third series (Walton-on-Thames, Surrey: Thomas Nelson, 1999), 135.

6. Gayatri Chakravorty Spivak, *A Critique of Postcolonial Reason* (Cambridge, MA: Harvard University Press, 1999), 117.

7. This is a point explicitly denied in Kwame Anthony Appiah's consideration of the speech in his entry "Race" in *Critical Terms for Literary Study,* ed. Frank Lentricchia and Thomas McLaughlin (Chicago: University of Chicago Press, 1995), 279, and I will proceed to explain why it is possible to take the term to refer to a group to which Caliban belongs.

8. This is the "creaturely" condition that Julia Reinhard Lupton identifies in "Creature Caliban," *Shakespeare Quarterly* 51, no. 1 (2000): 1–23. In Lupton's theological and universalizing account, Caliban is treated as a kind of prehuman anomaly, an exception that points to the rule that all humans are creatures; in this analysis, the kinds of particularity that attach to him and their generalization in terms of questions of sexuality and race are ruled out. The universalism championed in Lupton's essay is resolutely beyond such differences and is therefore on the side of sexual norms as well as against cross-race couplings.

9. All citations from *The Complete Pelican Shakespeare,* ed. Alfred Harbage (Baltimore, MD: Penguin, 1969). Margo Hendricks offers a similar tally in "'Obscured by dreams': Race, Empire, and Shakespeare's *A Midsummer Night's Dream,*" *Shakespeare Quarterly* 47 (1996): 42, but she seems to think that the older genealogical meaning that predominates in Shakespeare is disjunct from more modern uses of the term, which she seems to think depend upon physiognomic difference and are incipient in Shakespeare through images of mixing (in the genealogy of the Indian boy and in Bottom's transformation in the play). Another such tally appears in Ania Loomba, *Shakespeare, Race, and Colonialism* (Oxford: Oxford University Press, 2002), 22, to open a more expansive discussion of the imbrication of "race" with questions of lineage, religion, nation, class, gender, and sexuality. Loomba argues acutely that premodern notions of race, which lack strong ties to questions of skin color and which do not depend on a biological support, are nonetheless capable of the lethal racist energies manifest

in colonialism; that moreover, twentieth-century racism, which no longer calls upon nineteenth-century biological theories, bears more than a passing resemblance to early modern prebiological concepts of race (see esp. 38–39).

10. In her 2001 Duke University dissertation, "Barbarous Play: Race on the Renaissance Stage," Lara Bovilsky argues persuasively for such crossings as one matrix for "race" in early modernity.

11. The line seems overdetermined by the metaphor of a sporting event, in which case "race" would appear to mean something like "race track." Moreover, Angelo's possible control of his libido seems pointedly opposed to Caliban's condition. I am grateful to Kate Losse, both for her suggestion that the gloss seems to be offering more a contrastive than a parallel instance of the usage of "race" and for her helpful comments on an earlier draft of these pages.

12. David Theo Goldberg, *Racist Culture* (Oxford: Blackwell, 1993), 63. For Goldberg, the crucial transformation that "race" undergoes lies in the movement from lineage and pedigree to the concept of a population characterized by "invariant, hereditable characteristics" (64). I take the reproduction of Calibans under the determinate force of an indeterminate "it" to be moving the lines in *The Tempest* in this direction.

The continuing pertinence of such "class racism" is the subject of an essay by Etienne Balibar in Balibar and Immanuel Wallerstein, *Race, Nation, Class*, trans. Chris Turner (London: Verso, 1991), 204–16, esp. 207–8 for a history of race that is coincident with the beginning of modern racialized slavery and the transformation of an aristocratic genealogical formation as the basis of power relations into a nationalized and racialized one.

Emmanuel Chukwudi Eze, *Achieving Our Humanity* (New York: Routledge, 2001), 26, also affirms a connection between theories of lineage and modern racial formation.

13. As Kathleen Brown documents in "Native Americans and Early Modern Concepts of Race," in *Empire and Others*, ed. Martin Daunton and Rick Halpern (Philadelphia: University of Pennsylvania Press, 1999), esp. 82–83, skin color is by no means invariably registered in early modern designations of difference. A similar argument is offered at greater length in Roxann Wheeler, *The Complexion of Race* (Philadelphia: University of Pennsylvania Press, 2000).

14. Michel Foucault, *Il faut défendre la société* (Paris: Seuil/Gallimard, 1997). Two of these lectures, in which Foucault lays out a definition of power that does not depend upon the sovereign apparatus, have long been available in English as "Two Lectures," in Michel Foucault, *Power/Knowledge*, ed. Colin Gordon (New York: Pantheon, 1980), 78–108. The short summary of the course that Foucault submitted at its conclusion was translated as "Society Must Be Defended," in Michel Foucault, *Ethics*, ed. Paul Rabinow (New York: New Press, 1997), 59–65. In *Race and the Education of Desire* (Durham, NC: Duke University Press, 1995), Ann Laura Stoler has examined Foucault's concept of race in these lectures. The lectures are now available as *Society Must Be Defended*, trans. David Macey (New York: Picador, 2003). Robin Blackburn, *The Making of New World Slavery* (London: Verso, 1997), 13, has recourse to Foucault's theory in delineating the novelty of New World racism. Eze, *Achieving Our Humanity*, also supports the Foucauldian account: "The rise of Enlightenment race speech is an expansive transition from the racialization of the West to the racialization of the world" (33).

15. Paul Gilroy, *Against Race: Imagining Political Culture beyond the Color Line* (Cambridge, MA: Harvard University Press, 2000).

16. Sylvia Wynter, "The Ceremony Must Be Found: After Humanism," *boundary 2* 12, no. 3, and 13, no. 1 (Spring–Fall 1984): 19–70, at 43.

17. For the sexualization of printing metaphors, see, e.g., Wendy Wall, *The Imprint of Gender* (Ithaca, NY: Cornell University Press, 1993), and Margreta de Grazia, "Imprints: Shakespeare, Gutenberg, and Descartes," in *Alternative Shakespeares,* ed. Terence Hawkes, vol. 2 (London: Routledge, 1996), 63–94. For a congruent analysis of this moment in *The Tempest,* see Joan Pong Linton, *The Romance of the New World* (Cambridge: Cambridge University Press, 1998), 155. In rather disquieting ways, in John Edgar Wideman, *Philadelphia Fire* (New York: Vintage, 1990), a novel that avowedly offers itself as a rewriting of *The Tempest* (see, e.g., 132), Miranda's lines are analyzed as "the spurned woman speech" (139), and Caliban's attempted rape seems to be validated, both for its refusal of pedagogic colonization and as an answer to Miranda's desire: "Beastly ingratitude. She offered the word, Caliban desired flesh. She descended upon him like the New England schoolmarms with their McGuffey's Readers, the college kids with books and ballots. Caliban, witch's whelp that he was, had a better idea. Her need, his seed joined. An island full of Calibans. He didn't wish to be run through her copy machine. Her print of goodness stamping out his shape, his gabble translated out of existence. No thanks, ma'am" (140).

18. Roger Ascham, *The Schoolmaster,* ed. Lawrence V. Ryan (Ithaca, NY: Cornell University Press, 1967), 34.

19. Richard Halpern, *The Poetics of Primitive Accumulation* (Ithaca, NY: Cornell University Press, 1991), 94.

20. Richard Mulcaster, *The First Part of the Elementary* (Menston: Scolar, 1970), 30. I have considered these passages before in *Writing Matter: From the Hands of the English Renaissance* (Stanford: Stanford University Press, 1990), 32–33.

21. Frances Ferguson, *Solitude and the Sublime* (New York and London: Routledge, 1992), 30. Lower down on the same page, Ferguson remarks on the transcendentalism of Kant's sublime as "supremely egalitarian." Spivak, *A Critique of Postcolonial Reason,* devotes pages 1–37 to an analysis of Kant. I am indebted to Andrew Kitchen for assistance in grasping Spivak's argument.

22. Immanuel Kant, *The Critique of Judgement,* trans. James Creed Meredith (Oxford: Clarendon, 1952), 115. The "raw man" remains forever "checked" by the onslaught of the sublime (cf. 91). As Kant insists, the onrush of the sublime is initially a discomfiting experience (106, 108), one that, when overcome, serves to indicate "*the mere capacity of thinking which evidences a faculty of mind transcending every standard of sense*" (98), thereby demonstrating through this capacity the particular ability of the human to rise above nature (114). Kant connects this ability to innate moral sense (116). Spivak, pointing to the excluded figure of the "raw man," thereby points at a form of the not-quite-yet (and never-to-be) human, mired in nature, incapable of the reflexive turn that marks the disjunction between sensible onslaught and the beginning of sublime thought.

23. Kant, *The Critique of Teleological Judgement,* part 2 of his *Critique of Judgement,* 27. The choice of Fuegians in Kant resonates with *The Tempest,* suggesting how long-standing this prejudice is. As John Gillies notes in *Shakespeare and the Geography*

of Difference (Cambridge: Cambridge University Press, 1994), by serving Setebos, "the god which Antonio Pigafetta describes as being worshipped by the Patagonian Indians of the storm-beaten wilderness of Tierra del Fuego, Sycorax is identified with the most remote, God-forsaken and degenerate of sixteenth-century American types" (142). As Matthew Frye Jacobson indicates in *Barbarian Virtues* (New York: Hill and Wang, 2000), 144, the trope persists in Darwin's *Descent of Man,* where the Indians of Tierra del Fuego are invoked as the example of those whose development, although from a common human origin, nonetheless places them across an "unbridgeable" divide.

24. Immanuel Kant, *Observations on the Feeling of the Beautiful and Sublime,* trans. John T. Goldthwait (Berkeley: University of California Press, 1960), 113.

25. Robert Bernasconi, "Introduction" to the volume he edited, *Race* (Oxford: Blackwell, 2001), 1. Bernasconi pursues the point in his contribution to the volume, "Who Invented the Concept of Race?" 14–15, and in "Kant as an Unfamiliar Source of Racism," in *Philosophers on Race,* ed. Julie K. Ward and Tommy L. Lott (Oxford: Blackwell, 2002), 145–66.

26. Goldberg, *Racist Culture,* 32. As Goldberg generalizes from this example, "one way for Enlightenment philosophers committed to moral notions of equality and autonomy to avoid inconsistency on the question of racialized subordination was to deny the rational capacity of blacks, to deny the very condition of their humanity" (32). Goldberg's critique of Kant and Enlightenment racism, one aspect of his relentless critique of liberalism, is worth comparing to the hard-hitting arguments of Charles W. Mills, *The Racial Contract* (Ithaca, NY: Cornell University Press, 1997), 70–72 on Kant, or to Gilroy, *Against Race,* 58–65, which considers Kant (and Locke) and concludes "that enlightenment pretensions toward universality were punctured from the moment of their conception in the womb of the colonial space" (65). Leon Poliakov, in "Racism from the Enlightenment to the Age of Imperialism," in *Racism and Colonialism,* ed. Robert Ross (The Hague: Martinus Nijhoff, 1982), 55–64, comments on Kantians' resistance to his own arguments about Kant as the founder of modern notions of race (see 58–60). For an earlier essay that insists on the centrality of race in Enlightenment thought, see Richard Popkin, "The Philosophical Basis of Eighteenth-Century Racism," *Studies in Eighteenth-Century Culture* 3 (1973): 245–62.

Bernasconi, "Who Invented the Concept of Race?" has linked Kant's category of race to his concept of purposiveness, and Bernasconi includes Kant's 1788 essay "On the Use of Teleological Principles in Philosophy" in *Race,* 37–56, to support his point. Phillip R. Sloan, "Buffon, German Biology, and the Historical Interpretation of Biological Species," *British Journal for the History of Science* 12, no. 41 (1979): 109–53, argues that "race" in Kant is linked to the development of categories in the *Critique of Pure Reason* (see 128–29, 134–35). Sloan values Kant's concept for the ways it reconciles morphology and history, but he is utterly silent on the history of the use of the category he commends as properly scientific. Similarly marred is John H. Zammito, *The Genesis of Kant's Critique of Judgment* (Chicago: University of Chicago Press, 1992), 214–19, as well as his *Kant, Herder, and the Birth of Anthropology* (Chicago: University of Chicago Press, 2002), which devotes only five (302–7) of its more than five hundred pages to the concept of race, never discussing Kant's views except to note the value of the distinction in the 1788 essay and elsewhere between description and interpretation.

27. Ronald A. T. Judy, *(Dis)forming the American Canon* (Minneapolis: University

of Minnesota Press, 1993), 146, the conclusion of an exacting reading of Kant's "Negro problem" that forms the central object of inquiry and critique in chapter 4 of Judy's book, "Critique of Genealogical Deduction."

28. See Emmanuel Chukwudi Eze, "Introduction" to the anthology he edited, *Race and the Enlightenment* (London: Blackwell, 1997), 2–3, which includes the passage from Kant's *Observations on the Feeling of the Beautiful and Sublime* and excerpts from Kant's "On the Different Races of Man" and also offers translations from the lectures on physical geography that compose two volumes in the standard German edition of Kant's works. Eze considers these questions more fully in "The Color of Reason: The Idea of 'Race' in Kant's Anthropology," *Bucknell Review* (*Anthropology and the German Enlightenment: Perspectives on Humanity,* ed. Katherine M. Faull) 38, no. 2 (1995): 200–241. This essay offers full bibliographical information on the critical tradition of reading (for the most part ignoring) the question of "race" in Kant. Much of the essay is included in Eze, *Achieving Our Humanity,* 77–111.

29. Citations from Immanuel Kant, *Anthropology from a Pragmatic Point of View,* trans. Victor Lyle Dowdell (Carbondale: Southern Illinois University Press, 1978), 203.

30. Kant, "On the Different Races of Man," as excerpted in Eze, *Race and the Enlightenment,* 43. In "Color of Reason," Eze seizes upon Kant's recourse to the notion of the "germ," or talent, that differentiates white Europeans from everyone else to argue that this is a biological concept that makes Kant's beliefs fully congruent with modern racism. I think it is certainly a prerequisite for that, even if not quite yet a systematic biologism. For further uses of the "seed" or "germ" as an originary predisposition dividing races, see Kant, "On the Use of Teleological Principles," in Bernasconi, *Race,* 44.

31. See George Best, "A True Discourse," in *Voyages,* ed. Richard Hakluyt, 8 vols. (London: Dent, 1907), vol. 2, from which all citations are drawn.

32. For a study that seeks to demonstrate that the genealogy of blackness in Genesis is a Renaissance invention bolstered by the slave trade, and not univocally supported by earlier readings of the Bible, see Benjamin Braude, "The Sons of Noah and the Construction of Ethnic and Geographical Identities in the Medieval and Early Modern Periods," *William and Mary Quarterly* 64, no. 1 (January 1997): 103–42, an issue devoted to "Constructing Race: Differentiating Peoples in the Early Modern World." For a similar argument with wide-ranging examples, including Best's "True Discourse," see Werner Sollors, *Neither Black, nor White, yet Both* (Cambridge, MA: Harvard University Press, 1997), ch. 3, "The Curse of Ham, or From 'Generation' to 'Race.'"

33. Jean Baptiste Labat, *Voyages aux Iles Françaises de l'Amerique* (Paris: Lefebvre, 1831): "[I]l me répondait que le gouverneur n'en etait pas plus sage; qu'il croyait bien que les blancs avaient leur raisons, mais qu'ils avait aussi les leurs; et que si on voulait considérer combien les femmes blanches sont orgueilleuses et désobéissantes à leurs maris, on avouerait que les nègres qui les tiennent toujours dans le respect et la soumission, sont plus sages et plus expérimentés que les blancs sur cet article" (174–75).

34. All citations from Isabel V. Hull, *Sexuality, State, and Civil Society in Germany, 1700–1815* (Ithaca, NY: Cornell University Press, 1996).

35. All citations from Immanuel Kant, *Lectures on Ethics,* trans. Louis Infield (New York: Century, 1930).

36. See Robin Schott, *Cognition and Eros* (Boston: Beacon, 1988).

37. See Eric O. Clarke, *Virtuous Vice: Homoeroticism and the Public Sphere* (Durham, NC: Duke University Press, 2000), 101–25.

38. Anthony Pagden, *The Fall of Natural Man* (Cambridge: Cambridge University Press, 1982, 1986), 16. For analysis of the pertinence of Aristotle's natural slave to Miranda's lines, see Gillies, *Shakespeare and the Geography of Difference,* 150–53, and Gillies, "The Figure of the New World in *The Tempest,*" in *"The Tempest" and Its Travels,* ed. Peter Hulme and William H. Sherman (London: Reaktion, 2000), 180–200, esp. 196. Ian Smith, "When We Were Capital, or Lessons in Language: Finding Caliban's Roots," *Shakespeare Studies* 28 (2000): 252–56, argues for a double derivation of barbarian/Barbarian, the latter designating Sycorax's north-African origin and not etymologically related to the Greek *barbaros.* For further speculation on this etymology, see Paul Baepler, "Introduction," *White Slaves, African Masters* (Chicago: University of Chicago Press, 1999), 2.

39. Aristotle, *The Politics,* trans. T. A. Sinclair (New York: Penguin, 1962), 28. Julie K. Ward, "*Ethnos* in the *Politics:* Aristotle and Race," in *Philosophers on Race,* ed. Ward and Lott, 14–37, attempts to argue that because Aristotle is unsystematic in his treatment of "barbarians," he does not deploy a racial category.

40. Some of the points developed here depend upon the deployment of the thematic contrast of art and nature in Frank Kermode's introduction to his Arden edition of *The Tempest* (London: Methuen, 1954), and the similarly precritical essay by John E. Hankins, "Caliban the Bestial Man," *PMLA* 62 (1947): 793–801, which points to the importance of Aristotle's depiction of bestiality in the *Ethics.* I call this work "precritical" because its outlining of a thematic fails to ask questions about the historical pertinence of such contrasts and implicitly values the values of those who label others as beasts or natural slaves. For a critique of Kermode along these lines, see Malcolm Evans, *Signifying Nothing* (Athens: University of Georgia Press, 1986), 71–81.

41. Sylvia Wynter, "1492: A New World View," in *Race, Discourse, and the Origin of the Americas,* ed. Vera Lawrence Hyatt and Rex Nettleford (Washington, DC: Smithsonian Institution Press, 1995), 34.

42. Aimé Césaire, *Une Tempête* (Paris: Seuil, 1969), 25, and *A Tempest,* trans. Richard Miller (New York: Ubu, 1992), 11–12; Edouard Glissant, *Caribbean Discourse,* trans. J. Michael Dash (Charlottesville: University Press of Virginia, 1989), 140.

43. In *Liberty before Liberalism* (Cambridge: Cambridge University Press, 1998), Quentin Skinner outlines one aspect of this early-seventeenth-century republicanism with barely a pause over the fact that theorists decrying slavery *for Englishmen* had no qualms about enslaving Africans. Warren Montag, in *Bodies, Masses, Power: Spinoza and His Contemporaries* (London: Verso, 1999), links this notion of slavery and tyranny to Locke, arguing further (as I do later in the text) that "not only does he not call into question the enslavement of Africans, . . . he provides the foundation of right upon which a certain slavery can be established" (109). Montag alludes here to the arguments on just war in the second *Treatise,* correlating it with Locke's role in writing the Fundamental Constitution of Carolina; he also notes the Royal African Company's invocation of the notion of the just war in defending slavery (110) and Locke's justification of seizure of territory in the New World as "unowned" by Native Americans (111). James Tully also develops this last point in *An Approach to Political Philosophy: Locke in Contexts* (Cambridge: Cambridge University Press, 1993), 137–55, and Kathy

Squadrito disputes it in "Locke and the Dispossession of the American Indian," in *Philosophers on Race,* ed. Ward and Lott, 101–24. Peter Hulme, in "The Spontaneous Hand of Nature: Savagery, Colonialism, and the Enlightenment," in *The Enlightenment and Its Shadows,* ed. Peter Hulme and Ludmilla Jordanova (London: Routledge, 1990), notes that Locke offers a central division between those who merely collect food from nature's hand and those who labor; the former are the Native American inhabitants; the latter, the Europeans, are justified in their colonial activity since such acts of cultivation prove their rationality, their ability to own property, and therefore their humanness (30).

Similar arguments about Locke and Enlightenment thought that abhors slavery but never comments on the actual institution are offered by Susan Buck-Morss, "Hegel and Haiti," *Critical Inquiry* 26 (Summer 2000): 821–65, who seeks to argue that Hegel's master-slave dialectic is a response to the Haitian revolution. Buck-Morss is hard-pressed to explain how such responsiveness fits with his notorious opinions of Africa and endorsement of slavery in *The Philosophy of History,* to which I turn later in the text.

44. All citations from John Locke, *Two Treatises of Government,* ed. W. S. Carpenter (London: J. M. Dent, 1924).

There is an extensive literature on the question of slavery in Locke. Since Locke is often viewed as the most important theorist of modern liberal conceptions of liberty, many commentators wish to regard Locke's views on slavery as in no way contributing either to that institution or to modern practices of democracy. For some representative examples, see the essays by Bernard R. Boxill, "Radical Implications of Locke's Moral Theory" (29–48), and William Uzgalis, "'The Same Tyrannical Principle': Locke's Legacy on Slavery" (49–77), in *Subjugation and Bondage,* ed. Tommy L. Lott (Lanham, MD: Rowman and Littlefield, 1998), as well as Uzgalis, "'An Inconsistency Not to Be Excused': On Locke and Racism," in *Philosophers on Race,* ed. Ward and Lott, 81–100. What makes such arguments difficult to believe is not merely the logic of Locke's text— which assumes that those who instigate a just war are themselves not even in a state of nature and therefore have no rights; as Betty Wood puts it in *The Origins of American Slavery* (New York: Hill and Wang, 1997), "Locke was able to justify the institution of slavery by arguing that it lay outside the realm of the social contract" (63)—but also Locke's role in writing the Fundamental Constitution of Carolina, which declares that "[e]very freeman of Carolina shall have absolute power and authority over his negro slaves, of what opinion or religion whatsoever" (cited in Blackburn, *The Making of New World Slavery,* 275 n. 92). Moreover, modern democracy and slavery were not seen as contradictory for the first century of the history of the United States, a point underlying the argument of Theodore W. Allen in *The Invention of the White Race,* 2 vols. (London: Verso, 1994–97).

45. George Lamming, *The Pleasures of Exile* (Ann Arbor: University of Michigan Press, 1992 reprint of 1960 text), 110.

46. Cited in Eze, *Achieving Our Humanity,* 99. In "Perpetual Peace," Kant also develops a view of the threatening lawlessness of the state of nature fully in line with Locke on the justification of war against those who have no place in civil society; see *Achieving Our Humanity,* 79. Moreover, as Bernasconi notes in "Kant as an Unfamiliar Source," 152, Kant affirmed that Blacks were slaves by nature.

47. Lamming is citing G. W. F. Hegel, *The Philosophy of History,* trans. J. Sibree

(Buffalo, NY: Prometheus Books, 1991), 99. Lamming supplies the italics in his citation. I am pleased to recall here my indebtedness to S. Asad Raza for a discussion some years back of Lamming's relationship to Hegel. For a stunning reading of Hegel, which takes these remarks to mean that the European has not yet arrived at the understanding that the African possesses, precisely by not being tethered to an always ungraspable futurity and linear progression, see James A. Snead, "Repetition as a Figure of Black Culture," in *Black Literature and Literary Theory*, ed. Henry Louis Gates Jr. (New York: Methuen, 1984), 59–79, esp. 62–65. My thanks to Brent Hayes Edwards for drawing this extraordinary essay to my attention.

48. Lamming's point could be compared to the reading of the pedagogic scene offered by Denise Albanese in *New Science, New World* (Durham, NC: Duke University Press, 1996), 76–77. She distinguishes Shakespeare's Miranda's education of Caliban from Prospero's more indexical—and hierarchical—act of showing him the sun and moon and giving him names for them (1.2.335–36), arguing that Miranda's education gives Caliban access to his "purposes" (1.2.356). Therefore, according to Albanese, this is not to keep Caliban entirely in his place, and she finds it significant that such an education is Miranda's doing, thus an inscription of her potential for rebellion against her father. Thus, Albanese seeks to link female gender with racial difference. This potential distinction between father and daughter was also forcefully suggested to me by Paul Yachnin. Nonetheless, I remain convinced by Ania Loomba, who, in *Gender, Race, Renaissance Drama* (Manchester: Manchester University Press, 1989), stresses that "these lines underline Miranda's implication in the colonialist project. She has been taught to be revolted by Caliban ('abhorred slave'); to believe in his natural inferiority ('thy vile race') and inherent incapacity to be bettered ('which any print of goodness wilt not take'); to feel sorry for the inferior native ('I pitied thee') and to try and uplift him ('took pains to make thee speak'); and to concur totally in his 'deserv'd' confinement. Miranda thus conforms to the dual requirements of femininity within the master-culture: by taking on aspects of the white man's burden the white woman only confirmed her own subordination" (154–55).

49. Judith Shklar, "Self-Sufficient Man: Dominion and Bondage," in *Hegel's Dialectic of Desire and Recognition*, ed. John O'Neill (Albany: State University of New York Press, 1996), situates Hegel's master-slave dialectic within an Aristotelian framework. Hegel reiterates the naturalness of slavery to Africa in part III of the 1830 *Encyclopedia*, where he finds a strict correlation between the geographical situation of the interior of Africa, surrounded by mountains, he claims, and "universal slavery without resistance" (*Hegel's Philosophy of Subjective Spirit*, ed. and trans. M. J. Petry, 3 vols. [Boston: D. Reidel, 1978], 2:69).

50. See also *Hegel's Philosophy of Subjective Spirit*, 2:53–55, 63–65. The first of these passages is one that Buck-Morss seizes upon, since in it Hegel alludes specifically to the revolution in Haiti; however, he does so to indicate the derivativeness of the slave revolt, as if it depended upon "Christian principles" (2:55), making it a realization of European ideas. In part this is also Buck-Morss's claim, as if the only way slavery could be recognized as intolerable was by way of Enlightenment precepts. It is, in part, such suppositions that Ronald Judy challenges when he seeks to show that someone like Frederick Douglass did not need literacy or Western consciousness to know that slavery was wrong.

51. For the Kantian texts, see Christian M. Neugebauer, "The Racism of Hegel and Kant," in *Sage Philosophy,* ed. H. Odera Oruka (Leiden: E. J. Brill, 1990), 264.

52. On this question, see Leah Marcus, *Unediting the Renaissance* (London: Routledge, 1996); a discussion of the blue eyes as a crux appears in the introduction to the book, subtitled "The Blue-Eyed Witch" (5–17). Marcus fastens on the description of the "blue-eyed hag" (1.2.269) as an instance of a polysemy in *The Tempest* that cannot be reduced to its usual reading, that is, that the blue around the eyelids connotes pregnancy. As Marcus suggests, that reading gained ascendancy under the racializing thought of nineteenth-century editors who could not countenance an African with blue eyes. As Marcus also argues, however, blue eyes had yet to achieve in Shakespeare's era the modern association with blonde-haired white women. Marcus proposes her reading as a way of keeping Shakespeare unedited, as if the riches of his text belie later readings of Sycorax as racially other and sexually voracious. Obviously, much in *The Tempest* leads to that portrait and to a way of limiting the meaning of blue eyes, if not quite of fully determining them. It needs also to be added that "black" people in the New World can have blue eyes; that north Africans, who under some racial regimes are not thought to be black, also can be blue-eyed; that such people become "black" in a U.S. context but not necessarily in an African one. Marcus treats the blue-eyed witch as automatically a challenge to racial polarization, depending upon a black/white binary that has limited purchase historically and geographically.

53. Foucault, *Society Must Be Defended,* 254–55; *Il faut défendre:* "En effet, qu'est-ce que le racisme? C'est, d'abord, le moyen d'introduire, dans ce domaine de la vie que le pouvoir a pris en charge, une coupure: la coupure entre ce qui doit vivre et ce qui doit mourir. Dans le *continuum* biologique de l'espèce humaine, l'apparition des races, la distinction des races, la hiérarchie des races, la qualification de certaines races comme bonnes et d'autres, au contraire, comme inférieur, tout ceci va être une manière de fragmenter ce champs du biologique que le pouvoir a prise en charge" (227).

54. All citations from Giorgio Agamben, *Homo Sacer: Sovereign Power and Bare Life,* trans. Daniel Heller-Roazen (Stanford: Stanford University Press, 1998).

55. See Paul Brown, "'This thing of darkness I acknowledge mine': *The Tempest* and the Discourse of Colonialism," in *Political Shakespeare,* ed. Jonathan Dollimore and Alan Sinfield (Ithaca, NY: Cornell University Press, 1985), 48–71, esp. 64–66, which concludes with a stunning analysis of how Caliban's lines in 3.2 about the island music, rather than indicating that Shakespeare granted Caliban humanity in exalted poetry, show instead how fully Caliban is represented as having accommodated himself to colonial inanition, where he can only dream of dreaming; hence, too, his final lines about the wisdom of Prospero.

56. Frantz Fanon, *Black Skin, White Masks,* trans. Charles Lam Markmann (New York: Grove Press, 1967), 166.

57. Aimé Césaire, *Discourse on Colonialism,* trans. Joan Pinkham (New York: Monthly Review Press, 1972), 21, from which further citations are drawn.

58. Jamaica Kincaid, *A Small Place* (New York: Penguin, 1988), 34, 36. Kincaid ends her book also imagining a "human" solution to the problem: "[O]nce you cease to be a master . . . you are just a human being, and all the things that adds up to. So, too, with the slaves, once they are free, they are no longer noble and exalted; they are just human beings" (81).

59. David Scott, *Refashioning Futures: Criticism after Postcoloniality* (Princeton: Princeton University Press, 1999), 193.

60. Carolyn Cooper, *Noises in the Blood: Orality, Gender, and the "Vulgar" Body of Jamaican Popular Culture* (London: Macmillan, 1993), 142; cf. 149–50, 156, 162, as well as the discussion that opens Timothy S. Chin's essay "'Bullers' and 'Battymen': Contesting Homophobia in Black Popular Culture and Contemporary Caribbean Literature," *Callaloo* 20, no. 1 (1997): 127–41, which is situated in controversies about dance-hall lyrics advocating the murder of battymen. For a parallel, consider Velma Pollard, *Dread Talk: The Language of Rastafari* (Barbados: Canoe; Montreal: McGill-Queen's University Press, 2000), a celebration of the linguistic virtuosity of Rasta and its "universal" appeal against colonial suffering. Pollard notes the masculinism of Rasta, pointing out that in its lexicon "man" means a Rastafarian, while "men" means whites and homosexuals: "[T]he form 'men,' which in Dread Talk means 'homosexual,' must always be avoided in a movement that views homosexuality negatively within a Jamaica that is distinctly homophobic" (103), she records, with complete neutrality. But one must ask, it would seem to me, the limits of liberation that comes from such a vision. And, of course, this language also speaks to the musical practitioners that Gilroy and Scott value.

61. Page 55. My thanks to Caroline Levine for drawing this column to my attention. Bloom registers his antipathy in his editor's note and introduction to the collection he edited, *Caliban* (New York: Chelsea House, 1992), xv, 1, 4.

INDEX

Abeng (Cliff), 79–84, 117–18; female-
female relations in, and class, 80–81,
82; male-male desire in, 102–3; and
race, 80, 83; Clare Savage in, 71, 83;
and sexuality, 80, 82–84, 91, 103
Agamben, Giorgio, 138, 140, 144
AIDS, 105, 106, 107
Albanese, Denise, 185n. 48
Alexander, M. Jacqui, 48, 76, 78, 97, 105,
159n. 18, 174n. 126
Algiers, 160n. 25
Als, Hilton, 105, 109–10
anticolonialism, 5, 37, 46
Aristotle, 132, 133, 138
Arnold, A. James, 176n. 144
Ascham, Roger, 124

Barnes, Natasha, 164n. 57, 166n. 170
battyman, 102, 103, 104, 105. *See also*
Caribbean
Bejel, Emilio, 151n. 16
Berlant, Lauren, 84
Bernasconi, Robert, 127, 181n. 26
Best, George, 129
Blackburn, Robin, 150n. 12
black nationalism, 78, 93, 95, 109, 141
Blayney, Peter, 61
Bloom, Harold, 146
Bowen Barbara, 162n. 41
Brand, Dionne, 76, 77, 78, 79, 168n. 81
Brathwaite, Edward Kamau, 87,
172n. 112; and gendered representa-
tions, 88–91; relation to Cliff, 85, 88,
90–91; relation to Lamming, 86–87;
and representations of sexuality, 89,
104–5; uses of Caliban, 84, 85, 86,
88; uses of Sycorax, 87–88, 90
Bray, Alan, 48, 51–52
Brown, Bev E. L., 89, 171n. 107
Brown, Paul, 50, 139, 161n. 33, 186n. 55
Brown, Wendy, 149n. 7
Buck-Morss, Susan, 184n. 43

Burnett, Mark Thornton, 55
Butler, Judith, 177n. 1

Caliban: as (in)human, 41–42, 117,
132, 136–37 (*see also* human); and
language, 132–38; name, ix, 4, 6, 16,
122; race of, 4, 29, 120–24, 137 (*see
also* race); as would-be rapist, 20, 49,
51, 55, 62, 96, 137
"Caliban" (Fernández Retamar): Brathwaite in, 84; and Cuban revolution, 6,
7; and gender, 7, 11, 151n. 14; Lamming in, 12, 14; Martí in, 6, 10, 11;
mestizaje in, 6, 16, 18; and race, 12;
Rodó in, 8, 9; Sarduy in, 8, 12; and
sexuality, 8, 11; Shakespeare in, 9
"Caliban's Daughter" (Cliff), 70–79;
gender in, 73; in relation to Césaire,
91, 96–97; in relation to Lamming,
71, 72, 79; in relation to Fernández
Retamar, 71; sexuality in, 75, 76
cannibalism, 4, 48
Caribbean, ix, 4, 16, 142–44; feminism
in, 63; gender in, 77; sexuality in, 48,
53, 72–73, 104, 105. *See also* battyman; mati work; zami
Cartelli, Thomas, 176n. 146
Cervantes, 160n. 25
Césaire, Aimé, 92, 94; *Cahier d'un
Retour au Pays Natal,* 97, 98, 100,
118; *Discourse on Colonialism,* 140;
and negritude, 93, 98; in relation to
Cliff, 91, 96–97, 100–101, 118–19; in
relation to Lamming, 95; in relation
to Wynter, 92, 93, 95. *See also Une
Tempête*
Chancy, Myriam, 91, 99, 172n. 111,
173n. 113
Chin, Timothy, 79, 102, 107, 114,
177n. 149
Chow, Rey, 154n. 42
Clarke, Eric, 131

189